Changing Global Comparative Advantage: Evidence from Asia and the Pacific

Changing Global Comparative Advantage: Evidence from Asia and the Pacific

Ligang Song

Addison Wesley Longman
in association with
The Australia–Japanese Research Centre
The Australian National University

ADDISON-WESLEY

Addison Wesley Longman Australia Pty Limited
95 Coventry Street
Melbourne 3205 Australia

Offices in Sydney, Brisbane, Perth, and associated companies throughout the world.

First published 1996

Copy edited by Gary Anson and Beth Thomson
Index by Raylee Singh
Typeset by Minni Reis
Printed in Australia by The Australian Print Group

The publisher's policy is to use **paper manufactured from sustainable forests**

National Library of Australia
Cataloguing-in-Publication data

Song, Ligang.
Changing global comparative advantage: evidence from Asia and the Pacific

Bibliography.
Includes index.
ISBN 0 582 81084 1.

1. Comparative advantage (International trade).
2. International trade - Economic models. I. Australia-Japan Research Centre. II. Title.

382.1042

I wish to acknowledge a special debt to my former teacher and supervisor, Dr Saburo Okita, who died in 1993. His knowledge and enlightenment, his wisdom and kindness will always be remembered. This book is dedicated to his memory.

Foreword

This important book expands the frontier of empirical research on contemporary patterns of international trade. It provides a significant extension of the empirical hypothesis — first rigorously examined by Edward E. Leamer in his *Sources of International Comparative Advantage: Theory and Evidence* (1984) — that international trade is determined by resource endowments. Included are a careful discussion of relevant economic theory of the determinants of international trade, a substantial data preview and a variety of econometric analyses intended to deal with problems such as errors-in-variables and weakness in the data information.

The book makes a number of important contributions. One, using updated data, it demonstrates that cross-country differences in resource endowments still play an important role in determining patterns of trade. Two, the book identifies some structural changes taking place in the relationships between trade and resource endowments in the new sample period. Three, the volume updates the prior means for both GNP and net export equations in applying the Bayesian econometric techniques in the study. Four, the book carries out detailed factor content studies in a cross-country setting, shedding new light on the controversial Leontief Paradox. Finally, the book discusses the success of Asia and the Pacific economies in expanding exports against a background of changing global comparative advantage.

The study represents a considerable effort at collecting and analysing data on international trade and resource endowments. Comprehensive data displays constitute a convenient and up-to-date array of information about the international economy. This highly-specialised volume will prove an excellent reference tool for researchers, academics as well as for students in the field of international trade. I would also commend the book to other readers concerned with Asia and the Pacific economies.

Lawrence J. Lau
Professor of Economics
Stanford University

Contents

Tables

Acknowledgements

I wish to thank Professor Peter Drysdale, Professor Ross Garnaut and Mr Ben Smith for their guidance and supervision of this work. I am also grateful to Dr Rodney Falvey for helpful comments on the book's central argument. Professor Drysdale in particular deserves special thanks for his encouragement and constant support at various stages of my research at the Australian National University.

Professor Edward E. Leamer's encouragement was also very important in helping me to maintain the momentum to complete the research. I am grateful to him for providing me with the SEARCH program and manual, and in particular for his encouraging comments on the work. I also wish to thank Professor Lawrence J. Lau and Professor Kym Anderson, who made helpful and constructive comments and suggestions.

I would like to express my appreciation to Professors Wu Dakun, Guo Ding, Du Houwen and Huang Da for their early teaching and guidance during my time as an undergraduate student at Renmin University, Beijing, from the late 1970s to the early 1980s and later as a teacher at the university. I also wish to thank Professors Sadasumi Hara, Chung-Hsun Yu and Hiroshi Kitamura at the International University of Japan, where I undertook my master's degree in the period 1983–85.

I wish to thank the Australian National University for providing me with a publications subsidy for this book. I am grateful too for the ANU Scholarship given to me by the university.

My work at the university was made possible also by the support of the Ford Foundation. The assistance and encouragement rendered by its staff, especially Mr Peter Geithner, Mr Peter Harris and Dr Steve McGurk, is gratefully acknowledged.

The International Economic Databank at the Australian National University, from which the original trade data used in this study were obtained, provided me with a comprehensive source of trade and other economic statistics. Thanks go to Ms Prue Phillips and Ms Diana Elias of the Databank for their help and assistance with this aspect of my work. The resource data were assembled by me.

I am also grateful for the support and fellowship of the staff and my fellow students at the Australia–Japan Research Centre, for workshops, research facilities and an environment highly conducive to concentration and productivity.

I wish to thank Ms Beth Thomson for her excellent editing of the work. Thanks go also to Ms Denise Ryan for coordinating publication of this work, to Mr Gary Anson for editorial assistance and to Ms Minni Reis for desk-top production of this book.

Finally, I would like to thank my parents for their guiding influence over my life and for instilling in me the belief that the whole purpose of education is to serve society; and my wife, Hong, and daughter, Xiaofeng, for their love, encouragement and support, and who, more than anyone else, look forward to seeing this book brought into being.

Preface

In his influential work, *Sources of International Comparative Advantage: Theory and Evidence* (1984), Professor Edward E. Leamer used cross-country data to the mid-1970s to establish a link between trade and resource endowments and to identify sources of international comparative advantage and the changing roles they play in determining patterns of international trade. The main aim of this book is to examine to what extent the trends identified by Leamer in earlier data continued into the 1980s.

The book looks at the resource supplies that have determined comparative advantage and asks whether structural change has occurred in patterns of trade and resource endowments over time. It shows that 10 trade aggregates (two primary products, four crops and four manufactured goods) are, in general, well explained by 11 resource endowments (capital, three categories of labour, four categories of land, plus coal, oil and minerals). The results also suggest that structural change took place in the patterns of trade and resource endowments in the period 1965 to 1988, and consequently that shifts in sources of international comparative advantage occurred during this time. They also suggest that a substantial amount of trade in commodities, particularly manufactured commodities, may be explained by factors that go beyond the Heckscher–Ohlin framework.

A key factor sustaining the growth in the Asia–Pacific region has been trade, which is argued to be fundamentally determined by changing patterns of national factor endowments such as capital and labour. Throughout the book, strong evidence is provided of changing patterns of factor endowments in Asia and the Pacific, particularly East Asia, from the 1960s to the 1980s.

My hope is that the book's comprehensive new data on the global economy will make it a useful reference work for those who are interested in international trade.

Ligang Song
Canberra

1 Patterns of trade, resource endowments and comparative advantage

Objectives

Sources of International Comparative Advantage: Theory and Evidence, written by Edward Leamer in 1984, is widely regarded as a landmark in the empirical analysis of international trade. In this work Leamer establishes, through a rigorous methodology, the linkage between trade and resource endowments, using cross-country data up to the mid-1970s. This enables him to identify with accuracy the main sources of international comparative advantage and the changing roles that these play in determining patterns of international trade.

The principal objective of this book is to examine to what extent the trade and resource trends identified by Leamer for the 1950s and the 1970s continued into the 1980s and to identify changing patterns of international comparative advantage, using Bayesian econometric methods. A second objective is to present, in a clear and logical way, patterns of trade and resource supplies of 61 economies from the 1960s to the 1980s, extending Leamer's work in this area. A third objective is to seek empirical evidence for the relationship between net trade in factor services and the ranking of relative factor abundance, particularly in a cross-country setting, using the Heckscher–Ohlin–Vanek (HOV) theoretical model. Finally, the book discusses the implications for trade in Asia–Pacific economies of the determinants of trade specialisation.

A theme running through the entire book is that cross-country differences in factor endowments continue to play an important role in determining patterns of international trade. While the results reported in the book largely support this view, they also suggest that a substantial amount of trade in commodities, particularly manufactured commodities, may be explained by factors that go beyond the Heckscher–Ohlin framework.

The book is motivated by the following considerations. First, there is a need to update Leamer's work using his analytical framework. In Leamer's study, the model estimation was based on data collected in 1958 and in 1975. The period that has since elapsed has been long enough to allow for an examination of structural change in sources of international comparative advantage. One merit in applying Leamer's method is in being able to specify and compare two points in time: both the determinants of comparative advantage at one point in time, and changes in those determinants over time.

Table 1.1 provides evidence of a significant change in the structure of world trade during the period 1970–89. The table shows the share of total world exports and annual percentage change in exports of three broad commodity categories: agriculture, mining and manufacturing. Manufactured products as a share of total world exports increased steadily from 1970 to 1989, while the shares of both agriculture and mining declined. Annual growth rates of exports of manufactured products continued to be above those of all products, and above those of agriculture and mining in particular. The growing share of trade in manufactured products is also evident in changing import and export patterns of trade in manufactured goods, as presented in Tables 1.2 and 1.3.

Table 1.1 Share of agriculture, mining and manufacturing groups in total world exports and average annual changes (%)

	Share in world exports[a]			Average annual changes in exports		
	1970	1980	1989	1960–70	1970–80	1980–89
Agriculture	16.5	12.5	11	4	3.5	3.5
Mining	12	22	9.5	7	1.5	-4.5
Manufacturing	50	45.5	57	10.5	7	8
All products				8.5	5	4.5

Note: a Discrepancies between summation of these three groups and 100 are due to trade in commercial services; percentages based on monetary value of products.

Source: Modified table based on *International Trade 86-87* (1987), *International Trade 87-88*, Volume I (1988), and *International Trade 89-90*, Volume I (1990), General Agreement on Tariffs and Trade, Geneva.

Table 1.2 shows imports of manufactured products as a share of the total imports of developed countries. Table 1.3 shows exports of manufactured products as a share of the total exports of selected developing countries. There has been a steady rise in imports of manufactured products as a share of the total imports of developed countries; in some countries this increase has been dramatic.[1] This trend suggests that there has been a relocation of industry, particularly labour-intensive manufactured industries, from developed countries to developing countries, guided presumably by shifting comparative advantage. The data presented in Table 1.3 support this view.

Table 1.2 Imports of manufactured products into developed countries, 1965–90 (%)

Country	Share of total imports			
	1965	1970	1980	1990
Australia	77.21	82.40	75.98	86.40
Austria	65.41	69.84	69.03	81.51
Belgium–Luxembourg	55.81	59.41	60.49	74.17
Canada	74.01	79.56	73.20	83.19
Denmark	64.02	69.71	58.62	75.50
Finland	68.90	70.03	56.39	76.61
France	46.59	58.32	54.34	74.16
Germany, W.	48.32	54.82	54.98	73.99
Iceland	73.11	69.14	68.45	77.68
Ireland	63.92	69.97	68.48	78.74
Italy	35.98	46.28	45.64	66.76
Japan	19.64	25.32	19.30	45.27
Netherlands	61.53	64.07	54.67	71.77
New Zealand	76.59	76.28	65.86	81.60
Norway	70.21	70.95	67.16	74.98
Sweden	65.83	68.53	62.04	79.45
Switzerland	67.11	72.83	71.05	84.00
United Kingdom	33.97	45.09	61.91	76.74
United States	50.15	63.89	51.67	76.16

Source: United Nations trade data, International Economic Databank, the Australian National University.

Table 1.3 shows that the increase in selected developing countries' exports of manufactured products has indeed been substantial, especially in newly industrialised economies (NIEs). The data support the contention that many developing countries have become important sources of supply of manufactured products in the world market.

The data presented in Tables 1.2 and 1.3 encourage a search for the driving forces behind the changes that have taken place in world trade in the period 1965–88. This book explores this issue within the framework of the Heckscher–Ohlin theorem. Data samples are for 1965 and 1988, enabling comparison of changes over the time period as well as comparison between this study and Leamer's earlier work.

As stated earlier, an objective of this study is to update Leamer's trade dependence and resource abundance profiles, which constitute a convenient and important source of information about the international economy.[2] The trade dependence profiles illustrate the composition of net exports of 10 trade aggregates relative to GNP, while the resource abundance profiles depict the relative abundance of 11 different resources that are hypothesised to be sources of comparative advantage.

Table 1.3 Exports of manufactured products of selected developing countries, 1965–90[a] (%)

	Share of total exports			
Country	1965	1970	1980	1990
Argentina	5.66	13.90	23.20	29.18
Brazil	8.42	14.17	38.59	52.87
Burma	0.24	1.53	7.21	17.08
Chile	4.12	4.44	9.70	12.64
China	45.79	45.07	48.72	80.34
Colombia	6.46	8.07	20.37	25.79
Egypt	20.91	27.13	10.95	21.88
Ghana	0.94	0.57	0.96	15.57
Greece	13.29	34.57	47.48	54.06
Hong Kong	93.56	95.91	96.51	95.80
India	48.75	52.01	58.90	72.29
Indonesia	3.70	1.41	2.43	35.46
Israel	65.45	70.50	82.14	86.73
Korea	59.43	76.57	89.91	93.58
Malaysia	6.04	7.40	19.04	54.80
Mexico	16.42	32.53	28.08	44.12
Panama	1.93	3.56	8.93	62.25
Peru	0.71	1.52	16.94	17.50
Philippines	5.66	7.60	36.83	64.65
Portugal	61.63	63.86	71.76	80.73
Singapore	34.20	30.50	53.95	72.80
Spain	39.57	53.49	71.87	75.82
Taiwan	41.47	76.10	87.92	92.65
Thailand	3.05	8.01	28.08	64.27
Turkey	2.38	8.94	26.88	67.94
Yugoslavia	56.54	59.71	73.19	78.93

Note: a Country selection is based on general levels of development as well as regional distribution.

Source: United Nations trade data, International Economic Databank, the Australian National University.

These profiles are based on the Heckscher–Ohlin trade theorem. The central issue with regard to the profiles is whether countries with similar trade dependence profiles will have similar resource abundance profiles, as implied by the Heckscher–Ohlin theorem. Trade dependence and resource abundance profiles have been arranged in Appendix C in such a way that data for 1965 and 1988 for each country can conveniently be compared; in this way trends for both trade dependence and resource abundance can be observed visually.

A cross-country comparison of the productivity of key factor endowments (capital, labour and land) is also attempted in the book. This comparison provides another way of measuring factor abundance. The results are compared with those for the resource abundance profiles.

Numerous studies have tested the factor content of trade theorem. What sets this study apart from others is its use of a large and appropriately defined data set, particularly of resource data. Stern (1975, p. 5) points out that, 'lacking internationally comparable data, tests of the factor-endowments hypothesis have typically been concentrated on individual nations'. However, it is theoretically, methodologically and empirically feasible to carry out cross-country study of the factor content of trade theory, provided that internationally comparable data are available.

The data set originally designed and collected by Leamer and further developed in this study enables the researcher not only to obtain factor services embodied in net exports directly by applying the HOV model, but also to carry out study in a cross-country setting. Using a cross-country setting avoids the problem of bias associated with individual country studies.

Sign patterns of trade in factor services provide another criterion for measuring the relative abundance of a particular factor endowment, since a positive sign means that a country is a net exporter of a particular factor service, and therefore that it is relatively abundant in the factor. This argument is closely related to the controversial Leontief Paradox — a debate that has continued since 1954 when Leontief published his celebrated study 'Domestic Production and Foreign Trade: The American Capital Position Re-examined' (Leontief 1954). An attempt will be made to provide empirical evidence with respect to the main arguments put forward concerning this paradox, following the work of Leamer (1980), which marked a watershed in judging the Leontief Paradox.

Because of the importance of sign patterns of trade in factor services, one further step will be taken, based on Kohler (1991): to test the robustness of sign patterns of the HOV model in order to verify the accuracy of the data.

The Bayesian econometric techniques used in this study provide a formal procedure for introducing economic theories and judgement in the form of prior means into the data analysis. One motivation for applying the Bayesian method here is to deal with the problem of errors in variables. Data contracting measurement errors in all variables have significant effects on statistical inference (to be discussed in the next chapter). In this study, following the important work of Klepper and Leamer (1984) and Leamer (1984), the usefulness of applying the Bayesian method to the current data sets will be demonstrated. The Bayesian method requires that the researcher postulate the existence of prior information about relevant parameters. This information may come from different sources, an important one being previous empirical studies. This study can benefit greatly by utilising fully prior information provided by Leamer. Prior information about the parameters under study can also be extended further following Leamer's line of argument. This feature of the application of the Bayesian method reflects the process of the accumulation of human knowledge, since it involves a judgement about the role that human belief or opinion plays in model estimation.

The data requirements of an empirical study of this scale are demanding. Cross-country data sets of the net exports and resource supplies of 61 economies for both 1965 and 1988 have been assembled (and are available from the author upon request). These data sets not only lay the foundations for analysis in the book, but are in themselves valuable sources of information. For example, resource data are used for cross-country comparison of factor accumulation in per capita terms as well as over time for selected countries (41–5 out of 61 economies are selected in Chapters 3, 4 and 5 based on the relative importance of these economies in the world economy). This comparison of key factor endowments is used to reinforce a later argument regarding shifting comparative advantage between developed and developing countries. Again, net export data for manufactured commodities are used to form ladders of development; these ladders clearly reflect the process of structural change among the countries concerned, presumably driven by changing patterns of comparative advantage. Calculating the correlations between trade and resource data to provide evidence for the linkage between these two sets of data is a prerequisite for the statistical analysis that follows.

The main findings in the book may then be used to discuss trade development in selected Asia–Pacific economies, which number among the world's fastest growing economies. Why are these economies experiencing such phenomenal growth in foreign trade? The answer in part is that many of them are well endowed with natural resources and other factor endowments such as labour and, to a lesser extent, capital. The success of Asia–Pacific economies in expanding exports can be examined in a global context, against a background of changing patterns of international comparative advantage. This examination of overall patterns of comparative advantage and their changes over time may in turn shed light on the process of structural change and on the rapid development of trade in Asia–Pacific economies. In addition, various forms of data displays presented in the book provide convincing evidence that the success of Asia–Pacific economies in trade expansion can be partly explained by changing patterns of underlying resource endowments.

Structure

Chapter 2 first reviews major studies that have investigated empirically developments in factor content of trade theory. By focusing on Leamer's (1984, 1992) emphasis on a correct balance between issue, theory and data in empirical work, the chapter then introduces the theoretical framework, namely the HOV model, and the suitability of this model in analysing the relationship between factor endowments and patterns of trade in a multifactor, multicommodity and multicountry world. The Bayesian econometric method is also discussed here. The chapter thus provides both a theoretical and methodological foundation for subsequent analysis.

Chapter 3 presents and discusses trade and resource data. In the case of trade data, discussion focuses on the formation of trade aggregates, the behaviour of these aggregates and the ladder of development established by sorting the signs of net exports of the four manufactured aggregates. In the case of resource data, the aims are to introduce the definitions and the method of formation of the 11 resource variables; to describe the changing structure of resource supplies over time; and, most importantly, to present preliminary evidence of the linkage between trade and resource variables based on calculations of the correlations between trade/GNP and endowment/GNP and between trade per worker and endowments per worker. This evidence serves as the basis for econometric analysis in Chapter 6.

Chapter 4 goes one step further in describing the relationship between trade and resource endowments by presenting the results of the calculations upon which trade dependence profiles and resource abundance profiles are based. The central issue in this chapter is whether countries with similar trade dependence profiles will have similar resource abundance profiles, as implied by the Heckscher–Ohlin theorem. Consequently, the profiles have much to say about comparative advantage and its changing role over time. This chapter also attempts a cross-country comparison of the productivity of key factor endowments, which can provide another criterion for measuring the abundance ratio of a particular factor endowment. Thus the scope of this chapter goes beyond the simple presentation of data.

Chapter 5 focuses on the factor content of trade and factor abundance in a cross-country setting. The chapter looks first in detail at trade in factor services and factor abundance ranking in the United States in a three-factor setting. Capital, labour and land intensities of production, net exports and consumption for different years are calculated and compared. The effect of trade imbalance on factor abundance ranking is also assessed. The chapter then examines the relative abundance of capital and labour in a cross-country setting, using various criteria to measure relative factor abundance.

The chapter then extends this examination of factor abundance ranking in a cross-country setting to a multifactor case, so that the relative strengths of cross-factor and cross-country ranking of factor abundance can be compared. The chapter also carries out sign tests of the HOV model, from which the nonrobustness of the sign tests can be ascertained.

Chapter 6 carries out formal statistical analysis of the relationship between patterns of trade and factor endowments using various econometric methods, particularly the Bayesian econometric method. The chapter first points out some econometric problems associated with cross-section analysis and suggests solutions to these problems. Since prior information is needed to apply the Bayesian econometric method, the chapter discusses in detail how prior means are determined. A discussion of Bayes estimates follows. In addition, because prior information is used in this approach, a sensitivity analysis is carried out to determine the robustness of inferences.

Chapter 7, the concluding chapter, summarises the main findings of the book and sets out some general conclusions with respect to changing patterns of international comparative advantage. The theoretical and empirical implications of the findings are discussed. The chapter describes the main limitations of research undertaken as part of this book and indicates some directions for future research. Finally, the chapter discusses implications for Asia–Pacific economies of the findings of previous chapters, with the emphasis on shifting comparative advantage in the Asia–Pacific region.

Appendix A describes the data on which this study is based. Here will be found a country list with abbreviations; definitions of all variables and their sources; characteristics of the manufactured aggregates; and composition of skilled labour (LABOUR 1). Appendix B reports the results of sensitivity analysis of international comparisons of capital stock measures to different 'real' exchange rates. Appendix C consists of graphs illustrating the composition of trade and relative abundance of resources of each country studied in each of the two years under study.

This book represents a substantial effort to assemble up-to-date, cross-country data sets of trade and resource endowments for two points in time. In it, four land variables are defined and used for the first time. The new data sets enable structural changes in the relationship between trade and resource endowments over time to be identified and to be compared with Leamer's study. Empirical study of the accuracy of a weakened version of the HOV model proves that there is a general relationship between patterns of trade and patterns of resource endowments, thereby enriching our understanding of sources of international comparative advantage and changes in these over time.[3] The book provides comprehensive arrays of data to serve as a convenient and up-to-date source of information about the international economy. It also focuses on a relatively unexplored area, trade in factor services in a cross-country setting, with the results being used to measure the relative abundance of factor endowments as well as to address controversial issues raised by the Leontief Paradox. Finally, applying Bayesian econometric techniques, the book updates prior information provided by Leamer about key parameters for both GNP and net export equations, thus contributing to the process of accumulating human knowledge on the issues under study.

2 Analytical issues

Tremendous progress has been made in testing trade theories and predicting trade flows since 'the unveiling of Leontief's paradox in his test of the Heckscher–Ohlin factor endowments model for US trade' (Stern 1975, p. 11).[1] This chapter surveys those developments most closely related to the role of factor endowments in determining patterns of trade, a main concern of this book. The chapter is organised as follows. The first section reviews major works on factor content of trade theory, paving the way for further discussion in Chapter 5. The second section focuses on Leamer's (1984, 1992) emphasis on a correct balance between issue, theory and data in empirical work. The discussion here is intended to provide a framework for the analysis in Chapter 6. The third section surveys important developments in Bayesian econometric methods in general, and developments in applying these methods to trade studies in particular. The intention is to provide the methodological foundation for the analysis in Chapter 6.

Empirical studies of factor content of trade

In his article 'The Leontief Paradox, Reconsidered', Leamer (1980) began a new round of debate on the Leontief Paradox (Leontief 1954). The arguments presented in Leamer's article and those which followed by Brecher and Choudhri (1982a), Aw (1983), Sveikauskas (1983), Casas and Choi (1985), Maskus (1985), Bowen *et al.* (1987) and Kohler (1991) have substantially enhanced our understanding of the issues. The review in this section concentrates on these major works. However, it is useful first to mention briefly the Heckscher–Ohlin–Vanek (HOV) theorem, since it serves as the theoretical foundation for all the analysis in this book.

The HOV theorem (Vanek 1968) states that given the standard assumptions of international trade models,[2] there exists a set of positive scalars α_i, $i=1, ..., I$ such that the vector of net exports of country *i*, T_i, the vector of factor endowments of country i, E_i, and the $n \times n$ matrix of total factor requirements A bear the following relationship to each other:

$$AT_i = E_i - \alpha_i E_w \qquad (2.1)$$

where E_w is the world's endowment vector and $E_w = \Sigma E_i$, and α_i is the consumption share of country i which under the condition of balanced trade equals its share of world GNP. Equation (2.1), which says that net trade in factor services is theoretically equal to the excess supply of factors specifying an exact relationship between factor content and factor endowments, 'serves as a logically sound foundation for a study of trade-revealed factor abundance' (Leamer 1980, p. 497). Two equations that describe the relationship between capital and labour endowments and the implicit trade in capital and labour services can be given as follows:

$$K_T = K_i - \alpha_i K_w \qquad (2.1a)$$
$$L_T = L_i - \alpha_i L_w \qquad (2.1b)$$

where (K_T, L_T) are capital and labour embodied in net exports, (K_i, L_i) are the factor endowments of country i, and (K_w, L_w) are the world's factor endowments. Then the definition of factor abundance is, 'Capital in country i is said to be abundant in comparison with labour if and only if the share of the world's capital located in i exceeds the share of the world's labour force: $K_i/K_w > L_i/L_w$' (Leamer 1980, p. 497). Next, Leamer establishes the necessary and sufficient conditions for trade to reveal an abundance of capital; capital is revealed by trade to be abundant relative to labour if and only if:

$$K_i/(K_i - K_T) > L_i/(L_i - L_T) \qquad (2.2)$$

where $K_i - K_T$ by definition is equal to K_c, the amount of capital embodied in consumption; and similarly $L_i - L_T$ is equal to L_c, the amount of labour embodied in consumption (Leamer 1980, p. 498).

In analysing the case where the services of one factor are exported and the services of the other are imported, Leamer (1980, p. 499) gives the following two corollaries, which will be used in Chapter 5 when factor abundance rankings in a cross-country setting are discussed.

> Corollary 2
>
> If the net export of capital services and the net export of labour services are opposite in sign, then the factor with positive net exports is revealed to be the relatively abundant factor.

Corollary 3

Given that the net export of capital services and the net export of labour services are opposite in sign, then the capital per person embodied in exports (K_x/L_x) exceeds the capital per person embodied in imports (K_m/L_m) if and only if the country is relatively abundant in capital, $K_i/K_w > L_i/L_w$.

Leamer further proves that the comparison by Leontief of K_x/L_x with K_m/L_m is theoretically inappropriate, because 'if there are more than two commodities, the ordering of exports and imports by factor intensity, say $K_x/L_x > K_m/L_m$, is compatible with either order of factor abundance, $K_i/K_w < L_i/L_w$ or $K_i/K_w > L_i/L_w$' (Leamer 1980, p. 499).

However, Leamer claims that the Leontief criterion would hold in the many-commodity case only if the net export of capital services were positive and the net export of labour services were negative. As summarised by Maskus (1985), Leamer then develops three criteria for ranking factors according to their relative abundance. First, any factor exported net is more abundant than any factor imported net. Second, if two factors, such as capital (K) and labour (L), are both exported net, then $(K_x - K_m)/K_i > (L_x - L_m)/L_i$ or $K_T/K_i > L_T/L_i$ is sufficient to demonstrate capital abundance relative to labour. That is, the share of domestic capital exported must exceed the share of labour exported under capital abundance. Finally, if both factors are imported net, then the above inequality again suffices to reveal relative capital abundance, so that the share of capital imported is less than the share of labour imported. These conditions together imply that abundance ranking among factors may be established by ranking factors according to their total content in net exports relative to consumption; that is, $K_T/L_T > K_c/L_c$ for a country which is an exporter of both labour and capital services to be relatively capital abundant, and $K_T/L_T < K_c/L_c$ for a country which is an importer of both capital and labour services to be relatively capital abundant.

With regard to different sign patterns of factor services, Brecher and Choudhri (1982a, p. 820) argue that 'the fact that the United States exported labour services is in itself paradoxical'. This is because, according to equation (2.1), a country is a net exporter of labour services if and only if its aggregate expenditure per worker is less than that in the rest of the world. To see this point, let α_i represent country i's relative share in world expenditure, that is, $\alpha_i = C_i/C_w$, where C_i and C_w represent consumption (expenditure) in country i and the world. From the set of equations (2.1), trade in labour services can be written as:

$$L_T = L_i[1 - (\alpha_i L_w/L_i)] \qquad (2.3)$$

which implies $L_T > 0$ if and only if $C_w/L_w > C_i/L_i$, which is equivalent to $L_T > 0$ if and only if $L_i/L_w > Y_i/Y_w$. This condition means that country i is abundant in labour relative to all other factors when $L_T > 0$. Brecher and Choudhri then show that the evidence in the United States is inconsistent with this condition and conclude that the Leontief Paradox is still with us until the net export of labour services by the United States can be explained, possibly by departures from one or more of the restricted assumptions of the basic model. The significance of their argument is to point out the testable implications for the sign L_T in the HOV model.

Following this line of argument, Casas and Choi (1985) add another dimension to the issue by considering the situation under balanced trade. They demonstrate that 'it is not possible to uniquely link resource abundance or scarcity with the sign of the net export flow of factor services in the presence of a trade surplus or deficit' (p. 611). One solution they propose is to compute the factor services embodied in the net commodity exports that would have been observed under balanced trade conditions.[3] By computing the hypothetical balanced trade flows of factor services from existing trade data (compiled by Leontief and others), they find that the United States is a net importer of labour services under balanced trade. They then claim that under this condition the Leontief Paradox in terms of the indirect factor trade version of the HOV theory put forward by Brecher and Choudhri can be solved without resorting to relaxing some of its fundamental assumptions. The key point of their argument is that balanced trade conditions play an important role both in solving the problem raised by Brecher and Choudhri and in determining the ranking of factor abundance.

Addressing the issue in a slightly different way, Aw (1983, p. 734) argues that: '[I]t is not necessary to include both a third factor and require trade to be balanced in order to explain the net export of labour-intensive goods by a capital-rich country. A trade surplus may in some cases be a sufficient explanation'. He argues that 'when there is a "sufficiently large" trade surplus or deficit, the theoretically correct comparison must be between capital per man embodied in net exports and the nationally endowed capital per man' (p. 737). Thus, 'the Leontief factor–content ratio, defined as $(K_m/L_m)/(K_x/L_x)$, may be a misleading indicator of a country's relative factor endowments in the presence of "sufficiently large" trade surpluses' (p. 737). His argument in this sense provides a criterion for the cases of $K_T > 0, L_T > 0$ ('sufficiently large' trade surplus) and $K_T < 0, L_T < 0$ ('sufficiently large' trade deficit) to be examined. In the former case, $K_i/K_w < L_i/L_w$ if $K_T/L_T > K_i/L_i$. In the latter case, $K_i/K_w > L_i/L_w$ if $K_T/L_T < K_i/L_i$.

Stern and Maskus (1981), following Leamer's argument, calculated the relationship between capital per person embodied in net exports and capital per person in consumption based on factor content (direct plus indirect) of total US production, net exports and consumption for 1958 and 1972. Their results suggest that, while it holds for 1958, 'there is strong evidence of a reversal in the paradox' (p. 221): the Leontief Paradox evaporates by 1972. They claim that this reflects changes in the composition of trade. (Remember that Leamer, based on Leontief's findings, concluded that the Leontief Paradox did not hold for 1947, although the paradox could not be refuted for 1958.) Maskus (1985), however, using a different way of examining the same issue, reports that the scarce capital paradox did not evaporate by 1972. He concludes that 'the HOV assumptions are simply too restrictive for that version of the factor endowments theory to hold in an empirical context' (p. 211).

Bowen *et al.* (1987) use another version of the rank order hypothesis. They explicitly incorporate an adjustment term of trade balance in consumption share in equation (1): $\alpha_i = (Y_i - B_i)/Y_w$, where B_i is the trade balance. If trade is balanced, then α_i equals country i's share of world GNP. Now equation (2.1) can be written as:

$$AT_i = E_i - E_w(Y_i - B_i)/Y_w \qquad (2.4)$$

A typical kth element of (2.4) can be written as:

$$(F^A_{ki}/E_{kw})/(Y_i/Y_w) = [(E_{ki}/E_{kw})/(Y_i/Y_w)] - 1 \qquad (2.5)$$

where F_{ki} is the kth element of the factor content vector $F_i = AT_i$, and $F^A_{ki} = (F_{ki} - E_{kw}B_i/Y_w)$ is the factor content if trade were balanced. The quantity on the right-hand side of (2.5) is a measure of the relative abundance of resource k. Two qualitative implications of (2.5) can be seen: first, that trade reveals the abundance of resources compared with an average of all resources according to the sign of the net trade in factor services corrected for trade imbalance; and second, that trade reveals the relative abundance of resources when ranking the adjusted net exports of factor services across factors for an individual country and across countries for the same factors. It is important to note that the ranking of adjusted net factor exports (F^A_{ki}/E_{kw}) conforms to the ranking of factors by abundance for each country and factor.

Based on equation (2.5), formal tests of the conformity of the adjusted net factor export data (F^A_{ki}/E_{kw}) with the factor abundance data $[(E_{ki}/E_{kw})/(Y_i/Y_w)] - 1$ are carried out in Bowen *et al.* (1987). The proposition of conformity in sign between factor content and excess factor shares and the proposition of conformity between factor content and factor abundance rankings are tested, both factor by factor and country by country. In the case of the sign test, the proportion of countries for which the sign of the net trade in factor matches the sign of the corresponding factor abundance is reported; in the case of the rank test, both the Kendall rank correlation between the rankings and the proportion of correct orderings when the comparisons are made two at a time are reported.[4] The test results show that, using that particular data set,[5] these propositions receive relatively little support when tested for each factor as well as each country, though greater support is found for the rank proposition when pairwise comparisons are considered. This raises the question of whether the sign and rank tests are robust.

In demonstrating the conditions for sign and rank order tests of the HOV theorem, Kohler (1991) treats the contradictory test results obtained by Brecher and Choudhri (1982a) and Casas and Choi (1985) as an example of a 'nonrobust sign test'. His critical message is that 'different ways to perform a sign or a rank order test on the basis of the HOV model may lead to different outcomes, if the data do not strictly satisfy the HOV equations' (p. 159). Therefore, for any given data set, the question should first be asked as to whether the sign and rank order tests of the HOV theorem are robust. In line with this, Kohler establishes some conditions under which a given data set will support one (rank order or sign) hypothesis while at the same time failing to support another. This nonrobustness of both rank order and sign tests is very significant in the sense that it provides a measure for examining available data sets for credibility. However, for the current purpose, attention will be given only to the sign tests. This is simply because, as Kohler (1991, p. 159) points out, 'the apparent conflict between two recent re-examinations of the Leontief Paradox by Brecher and Choudhri (1982a) and Casas and Choi (1985) must be attributed to this non-robustness of sign tests of the HOV theorem'.

What Kohler defined as the four rank order hypotheses are, in fact, directly based on the HOV equations. The second hypothesis, called RH-II, is the *i*th row of equation (2.1). The first hypothesis, called RH-I, has the form , $AT_i/E_i = 1 - \alpha_i(E_w/E_i)$, which is directly derived from equation (2.1). As mentioned by Kohler, RH-I has been tested by Williams (1970), Harkness (1983), Maskus (1985) and, in a somewhat modified form (using the factor content of domestic consumption instead of domestic production in order to form the factor content ranking of factors), by Leamer (1980), Stern and Maskus (1981) and Sveikauskas (1983). The third hypothesis takes the form of equation (2.3), both with and without adjustment of trade balance. Finally, the fourth rank order hypothesis is equivalent to equation (2.5), namely the one used by Bowen *et al.* (1987).

After introducing the four hypotheses for rank order tests of the HOV theorem, Kohler claims that there is a corresponding sign test for each of the different rank order tests. These may be called SH-I, SH-II, SH-III and SH-IV. Furthermore, because the same equation may take different forms, the following is clear: 'SH-I and SH-II will always be simultaneously rejected or supported. The same holds true for SH-III and SH-IV. But choosing between SH-II and SH-III may be decisive for the outcome of the test' (Kohler 1991, p. 164). The sign tests will therefore be focused on a comparison of SH-II and SH-III. It is observed that the key factor between them is trade balance. In carrying out the sign tests between SH-II and SH-III, Kohler summarises the following inequalities, by which one hypothesis is supported and the other rejected:

$$0 < \frac{Y_i}{Y_w}E_w - E_i < \frac{B_i}{Y_w}E_w < AT_i \qquad (2.6)$$

According to equation (2.6), if B_i/Y_w and/or E_w are sufficiently large for $(B_i/Y_w)E_w$ to be greater than $(Y_i/Y_w)E_w - E_i$, while at the same time being less than AT_i, then SH-III will be rejected and SH-II will be supported. Therefore, equation (2.6) can be used as the basic criterion for the sign tests of the HOV model using the current data set.[6]

Several testable propositions emerge from the literature surveyed above. Is there a way of reconciling Leontief's results regarding the direction of US trade in labour services with Vanek's version of the Heckscher–Ohlin model without departing from the fundamental assumptions of the basic model? How do we view the linkage between resource abundance or scarcity and the sign of net export flow of factor services under the conditions of both balanced and imbalanced trade or in the context of both single and cross-country settings? If 'an important corollary of the HOV model of international trade is that under balanced trade a country will be a net exporter of the services of its abundant factors and a net importer of the services of its scarce factors' (Casas and Choi 1985, p. 610), can we rank factor abundance for the case of *n* factors, and is it relevant to have this corollary tested in a cross-country setting? Do cross-country data confirm Maskus' assertion that the Leontief Paradox is commonplace? What are the possible generalisations when the rankings of factor abundance are viewed and compared in the context of both single country and cross-country settings? For example, can we draw some conclusions regarding comparative advantage based on empirical studies and guided by factor content of trade theory? Are the sign tests of the HOV model robust? These questions will all be addressed in Chapter 5.

Issue, theory and data: essential elements in empirical work

A general but important consideration in carrying out empirical work is, as pointed out by Leamer (1992), to have a sensible balance between issue, theory and data.[7] Without this balance, the researcher can easily be led to 'the pursuit of theory for its own sake', without 'clear references to the issues and to the data' (Leamer 1992, p. 4). Conversely, the researcher may focus purely on the results without having a theoretical framework to back these up, an approach limited in value in that it cannot provide much insight into the issues. In the absence of a clear conceptual framework, substantial mistakes can also be made.[8] But how is one to achieve a balance between issue, theory and data? One piece of advice provided by Leamer (1992) is to 'take the theory just seriously enough' and to 'make a clear reference to the issues' (p. 49). The work carried out by Leamer in 1984 provides an excellent example of this.

The issue addressed in Leamer (1984) is what resource supplies determine comparative advantage. In other words, given the data about changes in composition of trade, where do the sources of international comparative advantage lie? Leamer's work is carried out against an appropriate theoretical framework, allowing the issue to be addressed properly.

Leamer's approach is theoretically based on the HOV model (equation 2.1). The model provides a solid foundation for running regressions of net exports on resource supplies. Leamer's selection of the HOV model to address his central concern is appropriate for the following reasons.

First, the HOV model lays the theoretical foundation for analysing trade patterns and resource endowments in a multifactor and multicommodity world; it therefore represents a very significant extension of the standard 2×2 Heckscher–Ohlin model. Leamer (1984) provides the following illustration of this. It has been argued that in some sense the Heckscher–Ohlin theorem is not altered by high dimensionality with the even model, $n = m > 2$, that is, an equal number of commodities and factors. This is because the factor price equalisation theorem holds in the even case regardless of the number of factors. However, the difficulty lies in the fact that the interpretation of the Heckscher–Ohlin equations in the 2×2 case depends on the properties of the inverse of a 2×2 positive matrix. In other words, the inverse of the factor intensity matrix A has one of two distinct sign patterns depending on the ordering of the capital intensities of the two goods. Things become much more complex at higher dimensions; in this case, it is in fact impossible to state the Heckscher–Ohlin theorem in a useful way analogous to its statement in a two-dimensional case. The solution is provided by the HOV model.

Second, since the issue of sources of international comparative advantage focuses on the linkage between trade and factor endowments, it can theoretically be explained in a linear way. The HOV model reflects the linear relationship between net exports and factor endowments. It serves as the working hypothesis for Leamer's empirical work, simply because only the linear form can be derived formally from a fully described general equilibrium model. However, the linearity assumption also constitutes a limitation of the approach. This is mainly because there is a great deal of evidence in the real world situation — the existing differences in factor returns across countries, for example — to imply that the relationship between patterns of trade and resource endowments can be explained better in a nonlinear fashion. Because of this, study of nonlinearities of the GNP equation may be required. Models that imply nonlinear GNP equations will also imply nonlinear trade equations. However, as pointed out by Leamer (1984, p. 157), 'this search for nonlinearities is clearly deficient on account of its lack of a firm foundation in economic theory, and it is offered only as an addendum to the main body of empirical work'.[9]

Third, the HOV model provides a flexible vehicle for model formulation. There are three concepts involved in HOV model formulation: factor intensity A; factor abundance $E_i - \alpha_i E_w$; and trade T. Most studies of trade have used measures of two of these sets of variables and have inferred the third. The main studies of this type are summarised here.[10] Leontief (1954) takes the measures of trade (T) and factor intensities (A) and from them infers the factor abundance vector ($E_i - \alpha_i E_w$). Works adopting this approach are regarded as factor content studies. Baldwin (1971) also uses measures of A and T to infer $E_i - \alpha_i E_w$, but by way of cross-section regression studies. Chenery (1960), Chenery and Taylor (1968), Leamer (1974), Chenery and Syrquin (1975), Bowen (1981) and Leamer (1984) use measures of trade T and endowments E and implicitly infer the inverse of the matrix of intensities A.[11] Hufbauer (1970) and Bowen, Leamer and Sveikauskus (1987) use measures of all three concepts and explicitly refer to the HOV equations. The current study will use Chenery's (1960) and Leamer's (1984) approach. With this approach, 'the HOV model is then judged to be accurate if the R^2 values of these regressions are high, though it needs to be understood that this is a weakened form of the model, which makes no reference to factor intensities' (Leamer 1984, p. 59).

In his work, Leamer (1984) made tremendous efforts to assemble large cross-country data sets of net exports and resource supplies for two points in time. These data sets are used in various ways to serve Leamer's research objectives and in referring to the issues raised throughout the study. For example, trade aggregates are formed with great care, ensuring that, as much as possible, they conform with underlying theory. Also, in order to 'provide vivid and memorable images of the international economy' (one of Leamer's main goals), 'four different media are used to construct these images — words, tables, graphs and econometric data summaries' (Leamer 1984, p. 84). Looked at from a number of perspectives, the data provide convincing evidence for the argument. For example, the clear presentation of trade dependence and resource abundance profiles not only provides a great deal of information about the international economy, it also suggests the hypothetical relationship of patterns of trade and patterns of resource endowments and indicates where the sources of international comparative advantage lie. These profiles will be treated independently in Chapter 4.

Leamer paid particular attention to the treatment of certain variables such as capital because: 'Gross national investment flows can be discounted and accumulated to form measurements of national capital stocks for cross-national comparisons of capital abundance. The formation of these capital stock figures can depend substantially on the method by which investment measured in different currencies is translated into real investment figures that are comparable across time and across countries' (Leamer 1988, p. 479). Leamer uses three methods to examine the sensitivity of international comparisons of capital stock measures to different 'real' exchange rates. The first method accumulates real investment in the local currency deflated by the home country price deflator for gross national investment and then translates it into US dollars using the base year (1980) exchange rate. The second method translates foreign currencies into US dollars in each year using the current exchange rate, then divides by the US deflator for gross investment to form a series on real investment. The third method substitutes the purchasing power parity rates of Summers and Heston (1984) for observed exchange rates. The results of applying these three methods to the current data set are set out in detail in Appendix B.

Most importantly, in Leamer's work data are treated seriously; the data are placed genuinely at risk to determine whether they are contaminated with measurement errors. Although serious measurement errors in variables can make entire data sets totally useless, most empirical studies assume that variables are free from measurement errors.[12] In this respect, Leamer's work represents a serious attempt to deal with the problems associated with data, in particular the problem of measurement errors in variables. The formal procedures for dealing with this issue will be discussed in the next section.

After the issue has been specified, theory formulated and data collected, a researcher may be tempted to 'test' the model; Leamer (1992) labelled this the 'testing' mentality (p. 3). This raises a fundamental concern regarding the role that a model plays in an empirical study and whether a model is testable or not. Leamer (1984) has pointed out that 'the general proposition that trade depends on resource endowments is not testable'[13] and that 'at best one demonstrates that the data can be organised so that there appears to be a relation between trade and some function of a set of measured resources' (p. xvi). Recently, Leamer (1992) again explicitly expressed this view as follows: 'A model is a powerful device for organising our thoughts; it is not literally true; indeed it derives its power from the very fact that it is *not* literally true. Thus there is no reason to test it. Instead of testing, we should be determining its accuracy and its usefulness' (p. 2). With regard to the various forms of theories or models of trade and sources of comparative advantage, he continues: 'These models are only tools, each of which is appropriate in some circumstances and inappropriate in others. Empirical enterprises should therefore not attempt to test the validity of the theories. Instead, empirical work might identify the circumstances under which each of the tools is most appropriate, or measure the "amount" of trade that is due to each of the sources' (p. 7).

Leamer's objective in his work is to measure the accuracy of a weakened version of the HOV model. This is mainly because, as Leamer says, his own work 'lacks a sensible and testable alternative hypothesis to the Heckscher–Ohlin model and in its absence this empirical study only measures the accuracy of the model and does not test it against a clear alternative. Nevertheless, this work can be influential if the Heckscher–Ohlin model is shown to be surprisingly accurate and if the data suggest surprising conclusions regarding the factor supplies that critically determine the direction of trade' (Leamer 1991b, p. 218). It is enough to say that Leamer demonstrates the usefulness of this approach in uncovering sources of international comparative advantage by indicating the extent to which the 'amount' of trade is determined by the availability of resource endowments.

According to Leamer (1984), the HOV equation can express trade in terms of endowment supplies or excess endowment supplies. For the econometric reasons pointed out by Leamer,[14] endowment supplies rather than excess endowment supplies is the form adopted. The 2-good 2-factor version of the HOV equation is as follows:

$$T_1 = \beta_{1L}(L - YL_w/Y_w) + \beta_{1K}(K - YK_w/Y_w), \tag{2.7}$$

$$T_2 = \beta_{2L}(L - YL_w/Y_w) + \beta_{2K}(K - YK_w/Y_w), \tag{2.8}$$

$$Y = w_L L + w_K K, \tag{2.9}$$

where T_1 and T_2 are net exports of the two commodities, Y is GNP, L is labour, K is capital, w_L and w_K are the factor returns, the w subscript indicates world totals and β_{ji} is a Rybczynski coefficient, namely the derivative of output j with respect to input i. In this form, trade is expressed in terms of the excess supplies of factors. The reduced form can be found by inserting (2.9) into (2.7) and (2.8):

$$T_1 = \theta_{1L}L + \theta_{1K}K, \quad (2.10)$$

$$T_2 = \theta_{2L}L + \theta_{1K}K, \quad (2.11)$$

$$Y = w_L L + w_K K, \quad (2.12)$$

where $\theta_{ji} = \beta_{ji} - Q_{jw}w_i/Y_w$, with Q_{jw} equal to world output of commodity j, $Q_{jw} = \beta_{jL}L_w + \beta_{jK}K_w$. Thus, regression of net exports on measured endowments would yield estimates θ_{ji} of the Rybczynski effects β_{ji} minus the product of the wage rate w_i times the consumption share Q_j/Y_w. Regression estimates of equations such as (2.10) can be used to recover the Rybczynski coefficients if we have other information on consumption shares and wage rates, the latter obtainable from a regression (2.12) of GNP on the observed factors.

However, for the present purpose, the coefficients of the reduced form of net export equations θ_{ji} are taken to be the indicators of sources of comparative advantage; that is, positive signs of the coefficients imply that resources contribute positively to the changes in trade aggregates under study, and therefore represent sources of comparative advantage, and negative signs represent sources of comparative disadvantage. As for the GNP equation, only positive signs are expected since, as mentioned above, the signs represent factor returns.

The question now is whether inferences based on those estimates are adequately robust or excessively fragile. The problem of measurement error is a main concern. The Bayesian econometric method is the formal way of dealing with this problem.

The Bayesian econometric method

As Zellner (1988, p. 27) points out, 'since the early 1960s there has been a considerable growth in the volume of Bayesian econometric research'. However, it was Leamer's work in 1984 that, for the first time, applied the method seriously to trade studies. The statement he made regarding his motive for applying Bayesian methods in that study represents the general argument in favour of using Bayesian methods: 'It is silly to act as if human judgment had no effect on data analyses. On the contrary, any sensible, convincing analysis of economic data has economics as a major input. A Bayesian analysis has a formal procedure by which economic judgment can be introduced into the data analysis. It treats opinion as equivalent to a previous hypothetical data set' (1984, p. xv). I will focus my discussion on how the procedure for Bayesian analysis can be accomplished in principle and the significance of doing so in practice. Thus the discussion lays the methodological foundation for the data analysis in Chapter 6.

The use of prior information about parameters, which 'may come from theoretical sources, from previous empirical studies, hunch, judgment, or what have you'

(Johnston 1984, p. 511), reflects the process of learning. This is in fact a very important aspect of applying Bayesian methods. As Zellner says, 'the learning model embedded in Bayes' Theorem is very useful in econometrics' (1988, p. 34). Leamer goes even further, claiming that Bayesian methodology is 'the only logical model of learning' (1991a, p. 225). This is mainly because, according to Bayesian methodology, 'the process of estimation is not one of deducing the values of fixed parameters, but rather of continually updating and sharpening our subjective beliefs about the state of the world' (Greene 1991, p. 199). It is, of course, a great advantage for this book to be able to utilise fully relevant knowledge and information obtained from the previous study. But, more importantly, this book itself constitutes a part of the process of learning.

One of the most important motivations for applying Bayesian methods in regression analysis is that it deals with the issue of errors in variables. This issue is extremely important, simply because it touches upon the very nature of inferences drawn from model estimation. Serious errors in variables can make inferences very fragile. Therefore, what is regarded as 'normal' or is taken for granted by researchers who follow classical principles has been challenged by Bayesians as 'deficient'. For a long time, however, this important issue was not discussed; the classical approach makes no compromise with Bayesian methods regarding the use of prior information.[15] Nevertheless, it has been repeatedly argued by Bayesians that Bayesian methods can do as well as the classical approach, or better.[16]

The first proper study of regression with all variables contaminated with measurement error was done by Klepper and Leamer (1984), who point out that: 'In most applications in economics, the possibility of measurement error in the regressors is ignored. This is not because it is generally believed that economic data are measured without error. Rather, it is a consequence of the fact that the procedures available to deal with measurement error in the regressors often require the use of prior information which in some sense is more heroic than the assumption of correctly measured regressors. Left to choose between the lesser of evils, the typical researcher generally opts for the simpler, more traditional approach' (p. 174).

In dealing with the problem of measurement errors in variables, Klepper and Leamer (1984) make an important contribution by presenting rigorously a complete k-variable generalisation of Frisch's results.[17] They begin with a computation of direct and reverse regressions.[18] The significance of their results is based on the following theorem: 'If b^D and all the b^i, $i = 1, 2, \ldots, K$, are in the same orthant, then the feasible set is the convex hull of the $K+1$ regressions b^D, b^1, b^2, ..., b^K. Otherwise, without additional information, the feasible set is unbounded, and each coefficient can take on any value given a suitable choice of the other coefficients' (Klepper 1988, p. 228).

Here, b^D denotes the vector of coefficients of the direct regression of y on x, and b^i denotes the vector of coefficients of the regression of x_i on y and the other x_j, $j \neq i$, after solving out the regression for y as the left-hand-side variable. If these $K+1$ regressions have sign changes, which is quite likely in most nonexperimental data sets, some prior information is needed to bound the feasible set. Klepper and Leamer consider two forms of prior restrictions: (a) the minimum squared correlation between the true variable and its measurement; and (b) the maximum value for the squared multiple correlation if the measurement errors in the explanatory variables are removed. Therefore, a restricted set of estimates will be bounded if one of the following restrictions is imposed.

1 The squared correlation between each true explanatory variable and its measurement exceeds $1-\lambda_1$, where λ_1 is the minimum eigenvalue of the correlation matrix of the measured explanatory variable.
2 The squared multiple correlation between the dependent variable and the true explanatory variable does not exceed:

$$R^2_m = R^2 + (1 - R^2)[\min_{i,j}((1 - b^j/b^D)^{-1})], \tag{2.13}$$

where R^2 is the squared multiple correlation based on the measured variables and b^j and b^D denote respectively the ith coefficient of b^j and b^D and the indices i, j select only those coefficients opposite in sign.

The other criterion is to report the proportion of the gap between R^2 and 1 that can be attributed to measurement errors without destroying the usefulness of the data:

$$g = (R^2_m - R^2)/(1 - R^2) = [\min_{i,j}((1 - b^j/b^D)^{-1})]. \tag{2.14}$$

Klepper and Leamer (1984) state that: 'The statistic g is a convenient summary statistic to indicate the sensitivity of conventional inferences to measurement error in the regressors. A value of g equal to one indicates that the $K + 1$ unadjusted regressions are in the same orthant ... a value of g equal to zero indicates that allowing even the smallest amount of measurement error in any of the regressors will cause the maximum likelihood region to be unbounded' (p. 178). Leamer (1984) also suggests the use of 'destructive diagnostics, which are sets of measurement error variances that would imply that the true explanatory variables are perfectly collinear' (p. 131). Evidence that the true data are perfectly collinear, detected by using destructive diagnostics, eventually leads to the same solution, namely resorting to prior information. This is because 'data sets with perfectly collinear explanatory variables cannot be used to estimate individual regression coefficients unless credible restrictions on the coefficients of some form are imposed' (Leamer 1984, p. 136).

To incorporate prior information formally into the model estimation, Leamer and Leonard (1983) formulated a method for pooling the prior sample with the data sample. The posterior estimates (Bayes estimates) for the parameters are then obtained. By hypothetically identifying a set of 'doubtful' variables, extreme values or 'bounds' of parameters can be calculated; this shows the ambiguity in the inferences about parameters induced by ambiguity in the choice of model. If the bound is wide, meaning that inferences based on model estimation are rather fragile, Leamer and

Leonard suggest that an effort should be made to narrow the family of models in order to sharpen the inferences. This idea leads to the use of prior information in the form of constraints on the parameters, which paves the way for using prior information on the parameters of both GNP and net export equations. After this prior information (means) for the coefficients of both GNP and net export equations is determined (equivalent to assuming that prior beliefs about the coefficient β can be summarised in a K-variate normal distribution with mean β_0 and variance matrix Ω_0), Leamer and Leonard are ready to pool the prior information with the information based on the sample in order to obtain the posterior density of coefficients (the Bayes estimates). This relationship can best be explained by the following posterior density function in which σ is assumed to be known (Greene 1991, p. 203):

$$E[\beta/y,X,\sigma] = \{\Omega_0^{-1} + [\sigma^2(X'X)^{-1}]^{-1}\}^{-1}\{\Omega_0^{-1}\beta_0 + [\sigma^2(X'X)^{-1}]^{-1}b\} \qquad (2.15)$$
$$= F\beta_0 + (I - F)b,$$

where

$$F = \{\Omega_0^{-1} + [\sigma^2(X'X)^{-1}]^{-1}\}^{-1}\Omega_0^{-1}$$

$$= \{Var[\beta_0]^{-1} + Var[b/y,X,\sigma]^{-1}\}^{-1}Var[\beta_0]^{-1}$$

and where β_0 is the prior mean, Ω_0 the prior variance matrix, and b the coefficient of least squares estimate. Greene (1991, p. 203) describes this as follows: 'This is a weighted average of the prior and the least squares estimates, where the weights are the inverses of the prior and the conditional covariance matrices. The smaller the variance of the estimator, the larger its weight, which makes sense'.

In selecting the weighting of two sources of information, namely prior information and sample information, Leamer and Leonard introduce the concept of *information contract curve*, which represents 'the 'Pareto efficient' set of estimates given two conflicting sources of information' (Leamer 1984, p. 139). Choosing specific points from a contract curve requires a comparison of the relative strengths of the two sources of information. In principle: '[I]f the sample information is relatively precise, it will be better to select points relatively close to the least-squares point. Conversely, if the prior information is relatively precise, we shall prefer points in the neighbourhood of the prior point' (p. 141). A formal way of comparing the strength of two information sources in practice is provided by Leamer (1984).

In pooling the prior sample with the sample based on fresh data, and using the partitioned inverse rule, Leamer proves in his work that the pooled estimates can be described as a function of the variance ratio σ_1^2/σ^2, namely the prior variance σ_1^2 over the sample variance σ^2. Therefore, according to Leamer, if the variance ratio is small the estimates will be close to the prior estimates, and if the variance ratio is large the estimates will be close to the least-squares estimates. The variance ratio varies from zero to infinity, and those points, in fact, form the locus of the *information contract curve*. By applying information regarding variance ratios, the specific point along the contract curve can be decided. The question now is how to obtain this information.

The variance σ^2, of course, can be estimated from the sample data, but obtaining the prior variance σ_1^2 poses greater difficulty. Because it is unlikely that a precise number for σ_1, the prior standard error, could ever be selected, Leamer suggests carrying out a sensitivity analysis in which several different values of σ_1 are selected. To be more specific, σ_1 might be constrained to an interval such as $0.5 \leq \sigma_1 \leq 2$. Thus: '[A]s σ_1 is varied in this interval, a subset of points on the contract curve is selected. Often this subset of points will be so narrow that the ambiguity that remains will be for practical purposes irrelevant' (Leamer 1984, p. 143). The interval of $0.5 \leq \sigma_1 \leq 2$ for constraining the prior variance will be applied in this book.

Based on the model formulation for GNP and net exports introduced earlier and on the analytical method described above, Leamer (1984) has provided full information about prior distribution and the way to choose prior information about parameters for GNP and net export equations. This is valuable for two reasons. First, by drawing from both theory and reality and incorporating the information thus obtained into the model estimation using Bayes' theorem, prior information can provide some insight into the inferences. Prior information can, therefore, contribute to a greater understanding of the links between theoretical implications and empirical results of the inferences, making them more meaningful. Second, prior information about parameters is valuable in the sense that it lays the foundation for later research. Based on the work done by Leamer, this book will update prior information about parameters when applying the new data set. This will be discussed further in Chapter 6.

Because of the difficulty of choosing prior variance when applying Bayesian methods, a sensitivity analysis is needed to examine whether or not the point estimates are sensitive to the choice of prior covariance matrix. This analysis can determine whether the data can be used to draw useful inferences about the parameters. Using the principal result, which states that restrictions on the prior covariance matrix imply restrictions on the pooled estimates, Leamer (1982) studied the effect of changing the prior variance-covariance matrix on the point estimates, applying the following procedure.

In order to show how estimates vary following changes in prior information, Leamer first selected a particular hypothetical prior covariance matrix Ω_0, which is multiplied by the prior standard error, σ_1 (a scalar). It is then assumed that the prior variance matrix Ω lies in an interval of matrices $\lambda_1\Omega_0 \leq \Omega \leq \lambda_2\Omega_0$, for some values of the scalars λ_1 and λ_2. Leamer (1982) proves that corresponding to this interval of prior covariance matrices is an ellipsoid of pooled (posterior) estimates. Next, from the ellipsoid of possible estimates, the extreme estimates of parameters of interest can be obtained. Finally, based on this information, the following outcomes regarding sensitivity of the choice of estimates to the choice of prior covariance matrix can be examined and adjusted: 'If this interval of estimates is small, it is reported that the choice of estimates is insensitive to choice of in the interval $\lambda_1\Omega_0 \leq \Omega \leq \lambda_2\Omega_0$. If the interval of estimates is too large to be useful, then a smaller interval of values is selected. If the interval is so small already that it cannot credibly be narrowed, then it is reported that the point estimates are so sensitive to the choice of prior covariance matrix that the data cannot be used to draw useful inferences about this parameter' (Leamer 1984, p. 144).

Following on from Leamer's work, Chapter 6 of this book will study the effect of changing the prior variance-covariance matrix on the point estimates, applying sensitivity analysis.[19]

3 Data

This chapter and the next aim to provide a clear picture of the patterns of trade and resource supplies of 61 economies from 1965 to 1988.[1] Also examined here are the relationships between trade data and resource data in the form of simple correlations. The next chapter, which contains a discussion of trade dependence and resource abundance profiles, will take this one step further. The first section of this chapter focuses on trade data, applying Leamer's method of forming trade aggregates, reporting the results and examining the behaviour of aggregates. Trade data on manufactures can be used to establish ladders of development by sorting the signs of net exports of the four manufactured aggregates. This offers a way of describing countries' stages of development. The second section defines and describes the formation of 11 resource variables and examines the changing structure of key resource supplies over time. The final section calculates correlations between trade aggregates and resource variables and discusses the implications of the correlation results for an understanding of the determinants of world trade structure. This can be regarded as a preliminary step for the econometric analysis in Chapter 6.

Net export data

Leamer (1984) grouped the 61 2-digit Standard International Trade Classification (SITC) commodity classes into 10 aggregates, using trade data from 61 economies. Of these, two are primary product aggregates (petroleum, raw materials), four are crops (forest products, tropical products, animal products, cereals) and four are manufactured aggregates (labour intensive manufactures, capital intensive manufactures, machinery, chemicals). These 10 aggregates will henceforth be abbreviated to PETRO (petroleum), MAT (raw materials), FOR (forest products), TROP (tropical products), ANL (animal products), CER (cereals), LAB (labour intensive manufactures), CAP (capital intensive manufactures), MACH (machinery), and CHEM (chemicals).

The correlations between the aggregates and their components are reported in Table 3.1. The results show that the correlations are in general high and the formation of aggregates successful. Several points are worth mentioning. First, of the 10 aggregates, the most successful formations are CAP, CER, FOR, TROP and ANL. Second, the formation of particular aggregates consisting of more diverse sources of commodities proves to be successful (CAP and MACH, for example). Third, some components with similar products in certain aggregates do not generate high correlations (such as mineral tar and crude chemicals from coal, petroleum and natural gas (SITC 52) in CHEM, and postal pack (SITC 91) and coin nongold, noncurrent (SITC 96) in LAB). Finally, while some correlations change dramatically across years — for example, coal, coke, briquettes (SITC 32) in MAT and special transactions (SITC 93) in LAB increase over time while gas (SITC 34) in MAT and fixed vegetable oils (SITC 42) in CER decrease over time — many remain constant. In addition, some changes take place over a long time interval (for example, hides, skins, furskins (SITC 21) in ANL and gas (SITC 34) in MAT) while others occur within a very short one (such as explosives (SITC 57) in CHEM).

The share of components in aggregates measured by the standard deviation is reported in Table 3.2. This is just another way of measuring the relationship between components and their aggregates, or the relative importance of the components in each of the aggregates. The standard deviation has the following characteristics.

First, in each of the 10 aggregates, a limited number of components dominate the share of that aggregate. Examples are nonferrous metals, metaliferous ores and metal scrap in MAT; paper and paperboard, wood, lumber and cork in FOR; fruit and vegetables, coffee, tea, cocoa, spices, etc. in TROP; meat and meat preparations, fish and fish preparations in ANL; cereals and cereal preparations, oil seeds, oil nuts and oil kernels in CER; clothing, miscellaneous manufactured articles in LAB; iron and steel, textile yarn and fabrics, etc., manufactures of metal in CAP; transport equipment, machinery, electrical machinery in MACH; and finally plastic materials, cellulose, etc., chemical elements and compounds in CHEM.

Second, some components are less important in their aggregates, such as: animal and vegetable oils, processed in ANL; miscellaneous food preparations, animal oils and fats in CER; postal pack not classified according to kind in LAB; leather and dressed furskins, sanitary, fixtures and fittings in CAP; firearms and ammunition in MACH; and mineral tar and crude chemicals from coal, petroleum and natural gas, explosives and pyrotechnic products in CHEM. In extreme cases, components play virtually no role in their aggregates; such as animal, n.e.s. in ANL and coins nongold, noncurrent in LAB.

Third, the shares of components within their aggregates also change over time. These changes imply the changing importance of particular components in their aggregates. For example, while gas, natural and manufactured in MAT, fish and fish preparations in ANL, clothing in LAB, manufactures of metal in CAP, electrical machinery, transport equipment in MACH and plastic materials, cellulose, etc. in CHEM increase their shares in the corresponding aggregates, meat and meat preparations, dairy products and eggs in ANL, textile, yarn, fabrics, etc. in CAP and machinery other than electrical in MACH diminish in importance in their aggregates over time.

Table 3.1 Cross-country correlations of components with aggregates (net export data), 1965–88

SITC	description	1965	1968	1971	1974	1977	1980	1983	1986	1988
	1. Petroleum (PETRO)									
33	Petroleum, petroleum products	1.0	1.0	1.0	1.0	1.0	1.0	1.0	1.0	1.0
	2. Raw materials[a] (MAT)									
27	Crude fertilizers, crude materials	.86	.82	.85	.80	.70	.77	.70	.78	.88
28	Metaliferous ores, metal scrap	.93	.95	.96	.95	.95	.92	.90	.89	.94
32	Coal, coke, briquettes	.07	.12	.40	.56	.50	.52	.55	.61	.68
34	Gas, natural and manufactured	.57	.52	.44	.28	.37	.29	.27	.23	.13
68	Nonferrous metals	.82	.83	.76	.62	.68	.74	.69	.61	.83
	3. Forest products (FOR)									
24	Wood, lumber, cork	.88	.82	.84	.85	.86	.86	.89	.86	.81
25	Pulp, waste paper	.97	.95	.94	.89	.91	.91	.89	.81	.83
63	Wood, cork manufactures	.66	.55	.55	.59	.61	.71	.66	.68	.69
64	Paper, paperboard	.92	.88	.87	.81	.82	.77	.85	.87	.78
	4. Tropical agriculture (TROP)									
5	Fruit, vegetables	.68	.66	.67	.56	.61	.60	.71	.77	.83
6	Sugar, sugar preparations, honey	.74	.83	.78	.81	.62	.64	.68	.71	.67
7	Coffee, tea, cocoa, spices, etc.	.87	.90	.87	.87	.90	.84	.86	.88	.85
11	Beverages	.45	.51	.54	.51	.37	.48	.58	.57	.71
23	Crude rubber	.38	.28	.32	.35	.38	.33	.34	.31	.47
	5. Animal products (ANL)									
0	Live animals	.64	.65	.59	.61	.63	.70	.64	.62	.63
1	Meat, meat preparations	.97	.98	.96	.96	.94	.93	.94	.94	.94
2	Dairy products, eggs	.83	.77	.74	.80	.71	.68	.73	.71	.51
3	Fish, fish preparations	.59	.64	.62	.60	.61	.65	.71	.76	.85
21	Hides, skins, furskins, undressed	.82	.76	.36	.42	.51	.52	.39	.36	.33
29	Crude animal, vegetable minerals	.76	.74	.71	.73	.59	.67	.68	.69	.70

Table 3.1 (continued)

SITC	description	1965	1968	1971	1974	1977	1980	1983	1986	1988
43	Animal, vegetable oils, processed	.13	.20	.15	.10	.14	.11	.21	.17	.16
94	Animal, n.e.s.	.51	.50	.66	.63	.38	.51	.69	.74	.68
	6. Cereals, etc. (CER)									
4	Cereals, cereal preparations	.94	.94	.94	.97	.96	.97	.96	.91	.98
8	Feeding stuff of animals	.78	.76	.82	.89	.81	.83	.79	.80	.91
9	Miscellaneous food preparations	.66	.67	.58	.63	.56	.46	.40	.19	.40
12	Tobacco, tobacco manufactures	.83	.86	.89	.90	.93	.89	.88	.81	.91
22	Oil seeds, oil nuts, oil kernels	.90	.92	.94	.95	.97	.96	.97	.94	.94
26	Textile fibers	.63	.67	.77	.78	.80	.86	.76	.65	.80
41	Animal oils, fats	.90	.91	.90	.92	.90	.93	.90	.82	.86
42	Fixed vegetable oils	.74	.23	.55	.38	.31	.32	.25	.18	.18
	7. Labour intensive[b] (LAB)									
66	Nonmetallic mineral manufactures	.61	.72	.61	.50	.66	.65	.69	.57	.25
82	Furniture	.17	.42	.33	.38	.63	.70	.64	.60	.25
83	Travel goods, handbags, etc.	.63	.91	.93	.90	.89	.86	.68	.65	.69
84	Clothing	.91	.87	.87	.73	.77	.80	.66	.70	.73
85	Footwear	.82	.77	.83	.80	.84	.88	.74	.77	.78
89	Miscellaneous manufactured articles, n.e.s.	.60	.84	.68	.59	.72	.62	.72	.64	.38
91	Postal pack. not classified according to kind	-.02	.01	.07	.08	.10	.07	.05	.03	-.07
93	Special trans. not classified according to kind	-.06	.22	.01	.05	.07	.06	.07	.16	.39
96	Coin nongold, noncurrent	-.44	-.29	-.66	.03	-.01	.36	.02	.08	.16
	8. Capital intensive (CAP)									
61	Leather, dressed furskins	.31	.28	.21	.05	.16	.11	.36	.38	.48
62	Rubber manufactures, n.e.s.	.64	.62	.77	.76	.86	.83	.92	.89	.85
65	Textile yarn, fabrics, etc.	.84	.87	.91	.79	.77	.64	.78	.76	.67
67	Iron and steel	.90	.91	.96	.98	.96	.95	.94	.91	.90

Table 3.1 (continued)

SITC	description	1965	1968	1971	1974	1977	1980	1983	1986	1988
69	Manufactures of metal	.66	.70	.79	.90	.85	.83	.89	.91	.90
81	Sanitary, fixtures, fittings	.42	.35	.36	.39	.32	.29	.45	.71	.72
	9. Machinery[c] (MACH)									
71	Machinery, other than electrical	.98	.96	.91	.92	.88	.87	.85	.91	.95
72	Electrical machinery	.97	.92	.92	.97	.97	.96	.96	.98	.96
73	Transport equipment	.95	.94	.87	.91	.93	.91	.93	.97	.97
86	Professional goods, instruments, watches	.75	.78	.80	.84	.86	.82	.89	.93	.94
95	Firearms, ammunition	.34	.25	.28	.11	.10	.10	-.06	-.08	-.13
	10. Chemicals (CHEM)									
51	Chemical elements, compounds	.93	.95	.88	.95	.95	.91	.86	.88	.89
52	Mineral tar and crude chemicals from coal, petroleum, natural gas	.31	.71	.33	.05	-.36	-.32	.04	.04	.00
53	Dyeing, tanning, colouring materials	.72	.75	.75	.82	.82	.75	.75	.79	.80
54	Medicinal, pharmaceutical products	.88	.85	.79	.73	.74	.72	.75	.72	.69
55	Essential oils, perfume materials	.66	.71	.66	.62	.62	.61	.65	.56	.65
56	Fertilizers, manufactured	.48	.55	.17	.58	.20	.53	.18	.27	.45
57	Explosives, pyrotechnic products	.73	.05	.37	.61	.56	.33	.21	.02	-.02
58	Plastic materials, cellulose, etc.	.94	.92	.90	.94	.89	.88	.82	.76	.81
59	Chemical materials, n.e.s.	.93	.94	.91	.91	.94	.94	.92	.92	.94

Notes:
a Numbers of observation are 60 due to missing data.
b Numbers of observation are 55 due to missing data.
c Numbers of observation are 61 due to missing data.

Table 3.2 Share of components in aggregates, 1965–88[a]

SITC	description	1965	1968	1971	1974	1977	1980	1983	1986	1988
	1. Petroleum (PETRO)									
33	Petroleum, petroleum products	1.0	1.0	1.0	1.0	1.0	1.0	1.0	1.0	1.0
	2. Raw materials (MAT)									
27	Crude fertilizers, crude materials	.07	.07	.06	.06	.05	.04	.04	.05	.04
28	Metaliferous ores, metal scrap	.37	.38	.40	.36	.29	.26	.21	.20	.25
32	Coal, coke, briquettes	.19	.16	.20	.23	.23	.19	.19	.20	.19
34	Gas, natural and manufactured	.03	.03	.07	.10	.23	.33	.36	.34	.23
68	Nonferrous metals	.34	.36	.26	.24	.19	.18	.19	.21	.28
	3. Forest products (FOR)									
24	Wood, lumber, cork	.32	.37	.38	.40	.41	.42	.35	.29	.31
25	Pulp, waste paper	.25	.22	.22	.24	.21	.20	.19	.18	.19
63	Wood, cork manufactures	.09	.10	.10	.08	.09	.09	.11	.12	.11
64	Paper, paperboard	.34	.30	.31	.29	.29	.29	.34	.41	.39
	4. Tropical agriculture (TROP)									
5	Fruit, vegetables	.32	.29	.31	.27	.27	.29	.32	.33	.40
6	Sugar, sugar preparations, honey	.12	.14	.15	.27	.11	.14	.10	.06	.05
7	Coffee, tea, cocoa, spices, etc.	.35	.34	.30	.24	.42	.32	.30	.35	.23
11	Beverages	.10	.13	.15	.11	.11	.14	.18	.19	.21
23	Crude rubber	.12	.10	.09	.11	.09	.11	.10	.07	.09
	5. Animal products (ANL)									
0	Live animals	.08	.09	.11	.10	.09	.11	.09	.08	.03
1	Meat, meat preparations	.38	.38	.35	.34	.30	.31	.28	.25	.25
2	Dairy products, eggs	.21	.18	.17	.19	.17	.17	.17	.14	.12
3	Fish, fish preparations	.15	.18	.15	.18	.22	.19	.27	.32	.38
21	Hides, skins, furskins, undressed	.08	.07	.11	.07	.09	.08	.07	.09	.07
29	Crude animal, vegetable minerals	.09	.09	.09	.11	.11	.11	.11	.11	.13
43	Animal, vegetable oils, processed	.01	.01	.01	.02	.01	.02	.01	.00	.01

Table 3.2 (continued)

	SITC description	1965	1968	1971	1974	1977	1980	1983	1986	1988
	6. Cereals, etc. (CER)									
4	Cereals, cereal preparations	.45	.42	.39	.50	.41	.48	.46	.36	.37
8	Feeding stuff of animals	.07	.07	.09	.06	.09	.09	.10	.12	.12
9	Miscellaneous food preparations	.02	.02	.02	.01	.02	.01	.02	.03	.03
12	Tobacco, tobacco manufactures	.07	.09	.08	.04	.06	.05	.06	.09	.12
22	Oil seeds, oil nuts, oil kernels	.12	.14	.19	.19	.22	.17	.19	.20	.18
26	Textile fibers	.20	.20	.16	.12	.13	.12	.10	.12	.13
41	Animal oils, fats	.03	.02	.03	.03	.02	.02	.02	.02	.02
42	Fixed vegetable oils	.04	.03	.05	.05	.06	.05	.06	.06	.04
	7. Labour intensive[b] (LAB)									
66	Nonmetallic mineral manufactures	.12	.11	.09	.10	.10	.10	.09	.07	.09
82	Furniture	.03	.05	.05	.06	.07	.08	.06	.07	.05
83	Travel goods, handbags, etc.	.01	.02	.02	.02	.02	.02	.02	.03	.04
84	Clothing	.21	.25	.29	.32	.32	.29	.26	.29	.30
85	Footwear	.08	.13	.15	.14	.14	.13	.12	.12	.09
89	Miscellaneous manufactured articles, n.e.s.	.21	.28	.24	.22	.23	.23	.33	.34	.23
91	Postal pack. not classified according to kind	.06	.04	.04	.03	.04	.03	.02	.02	.01
93	Special trans. not classified according to kind	.28	.11	.13	.11	.08	.08	.09	.07	.20
96	Coin nongold, noncurrent	.00	.01	.00	.00	.00	.03	.01	.00	.00
	8. Capital intensive (CAP)									
61	Leather, dressed furskins	.02	.02	.02	.01	.02	.02	.03	.03	.03
62	Rubber manufactures, n.e.s.	.05	.05	.05	.04	.06	.07	.07	.08	.08
65	Textile yarn, fabrics, etc.	.35	.31	.27	.15	.18	.18	.22	.24	.22
67	Iron and steel	.41	.44	.50	.65	.55	.54	.47	.42	.41
69	Manufactures of metal	.16	.16	.14	.13	.18	.18	.19	.21	.23
81	Sanitary, fixtures, fittings	.02	.02	.02	.01	.02	.02	.02	.02	.03

Table 3.2 (continued)

SITC	description	1965	1968	1971	1974	1977	1980	1983	1986	1988
	9. Machinery (MACH)									
71	Machinery, other than electrical	.44	.44	.42	.42	.36	.38	.30	.27	.30
72	Electrical machinery	.14	.15	.16	.15	.17	.17	.19	.21	.23
73	Transport equipment	.31	.31	.33	.35	.39	.37	.40	.44	.38
86	Professional goods, instruments, watches	.06	.07	.06	.06	.06	.06	.07	.07	.07
95	Firearms, ammunition	.05	.04	.03	.02	.02	.02	.03	.01	.01
	10. Chemicals (CHEM)									
51	Chemical elements, compounds	.26	.25	.24	.26	.26	.23	.23	.23	.24
52	Mineral tar and crude chemicals from coal, petroleum, natural gas	.01	.02	.01	.01	.02	.04	.02	.02	.02
53	Dyeing, tanning, colouring materials	.11	.10	.13	.11	.11	.09	.09	.11	.11
54	Medicinal, pharmaceutical products	.13	.13	.14	.11	.12	.11	.13	.13	.13
55	Essential oils, perfume materials	.05	.05	.05	.04	.06	.06	.06	.07	.05
56	Fertilizers, manufactured	.10	.10	.07	.10	.07	.10	.70	.07	.06
57	Explosives, pyrotechnic products	.01	.01	.01	.01	.01	.01	.01	.01	.01
58	Plastic materials, cellulose, etc.	.19	.19	.21	.24	.22	.22	.23	.22	.25
59	Chemical materials, n.e.s.	.13	.15	.14	.13	.14	.15	.16	.14	.14

Notes: a Share = $\sigma_i/\Sigma\sigma_i$; σ_i = standard deviation of component *i*.
b SITC 35 (electrical energy) is omitted due to missing data.

The behaviour of the aggregates also varies. The relative importance of the aggregates is summarised by the standard deviation in Table 3.3. While MAT, FOR and CHEM remain more or less the same over this period in terms of their aggregate shares, TROP, ANL, CER and CAP decrease and LAB and MACH increase during the same period. Not only that, the shares of LAB and MACH become dominant in world trade in 1988. They are followed by PETRO, whose share increased during the 1970s, peaked in 1980 and then undertaken a sharp decline in the 1980s. The changes of PETRO during the 1970s clearly reflect the impact of the two oil crises in that period on the composition of overall trade.

Table 3.3 **Aggregate share**[a]

AGG	1965	1968	1971	1974	1977	1980	1983	1986	1988
1. PETRO	.10	.10	.11	.22	.23	.28	.22	.11	.10
2. MAT	.07	.09	.09	.08	.07	.08	.08	.07	.07
3. FOR	.07	.07	.06	.05	.05	.04	.04	.04	.05
4. TROP	.08	.08	.07	.05	.05	.04	.04	.04	.04
5. ANL	.07	.06	.06	.04	.04	.03	.04	.04	.04
6. CER	.14	.11	.11	.12	.09	.10	.09	.05	.06
7. LAB	.06	.08	.08	.05	.07	.07	.11	.16	.13
8. CAP	.09	.09	.11	.10	.08	.07	.07	.07	.07
9. MACH	.27	.26	.26	.23	.27	.24	.27	.38	.40
10. CHEM	.05	.06	.05	.06	.04	.05	.04	.04	.05

Note: a Share = $\sigma_i/\Sigma\sigma_i$; σ_i = standard deviation of aggregate *i*.

Comparing these results with Leamer's, two points are worthy of note. The first is that machinery maintains over time approximately a 27 per cent share of world trade until 1983, as Leamer demonstrated (1984, p. 85). However, the share of machinery rises sharply from 27 per cent in 1983 to 40 per cent in 1988, indicating that trade in machinery accounted for 40 per cent of total world trade in the late 1980s. It is clear that this increase was offset by a reduction in the aggregate shares of tropical agriculture, animal products and cereals. The second point is that petroleum increases dramatically from 10 per cent in 1965 to 22 per cent in 1974 and to 28 per cent in 1980. However, it shows a sharp decline in the years 1980 to 1983 and again from 1983 to 1988, which reflects the absorption by the world economy in the late 1980s of oil shocks.

The cross-country correlations of the aggregates for 1965, 1971, 1980 and 1988 are reported in Tables 3.4 to 3.7. Because a positive correlation means that two aggregates tend to move in the same direction, a positive correlation can be interpreted as meaning that success in exporting one trade aggregate is associated with success in exporting the other. The economic meaning of this interpretation will become clearer after the correlations have been examined.

Table 3.4 **Aggregate correlation matrix (cross-country correlations, net export data), 1965**

AGG\AGG	1	2	3	4	5	6	7	8	9	10
1. PETRO	1.0									
2. MAT	.55	1.0								
3. FOR	.37	.73	1.0							
4. TROP	.56	.52	.45	1.0						
5. ANL	.41	.51	.52	.58	1.0					
6. CER	-.03	.31	.07	-.21	.19	1.0				
7. LAB	.03	-.33	-.10	.43	-.05	-.71	1.0			
8. CAP	-.43	-.74	-.40	-.24	-.41	-.62	.64	1.0		
9. MACH	-.62	-.70	-.67	-.87	-.68	.17	-.31	.33	1.0	
10. CHEM	-.56	-.57	-.60	-.87	-.57	.28	-.47	.20	.95	1.0

Table 3.5 **Aggregate correlation matrix (cross-country correlations, net export data), 1971**

AGG\AGG	1	2	3	4	5	6	7	8	9	10
1. PETRO	1.0									
2. MAT	.65	1.0								
3. FOR	.48	.70	1.0							
4. TROP	.59	.34	.35	1.0						
5. ANL	.50	.44	.41	.56	1.0					
6. CER	.04	.39	.12	-.34	.00	1.0				
7. LAB	.05	-.32	-.05	.59	.00	-.79	1.0			
8. CAP	-.46	-.77	-.38	-.05	-.21	-.73	.59	1.0		
9. MACH	-.75	-.71	-.59	-.79	-.66	-.14	-.15	.52	1.0	
10. CHEM	-.60	-.40	-.53	-.90	-.50	.21	-.57	.11	.83	1.0

Table 3.6 Aggregate correlation matrix (cross-country correlations, net export data), 1980

AGG\AGG	1	2	3	4	5	6	7	8	9	10
1. PETRO	1.0									
2. MAT	.60	1.0								
3. FOR	.38	.73	1.0							
4. TROP	.64	.35	.23	1.0						
5. ANL	.45	.62	.38	.39	1.0					
6. CER	-.47	.26	.21	-.41	.00	1.0				
7. LAB	.29	-.27	-.17	.53	-.24	-.71	1.0			
8. CAP	-.50	-.86	-.57	-.26	-.46	-.44	.33	1.0		
9. MACH	-.77	-.81	-.61	-.70	-.56	.01	-.16	.77	1.0	
10. CHEM	-.60	-.17	-.28	-.83	-.16	.50	-.74	.07	.58	1.0

Table 3.7 Aggregate correlation matrix (cross-country correlations, net export data), 1988

AGG\AGG	1	2	3	4	5	6	7	8	9	10
1. PETRO	1.0									
2. MAT	.64	1.0								
3. FOR	.43	.62	1.0							
4. TROP	.81	.52	.31	1.0						
5. ANL	.52	.78	.48	.47	1.0					
6. CER	-.46	.30	.07	-.31	.21	1.0				
7. LAB	.63	-.04	.00	.62	.07	-.79	1.0			
8. CAP	.11	-.51	-.16	.04	-.36	-.81	.62	1.0		
9. MACH	-.33	-.79	-.35	-.41	-.61	-.60	.23	.82	1.0	
10. CHEM	-.49	-.11	-.17	-.66	.01	.35	-.60	-.03	.20	1.0

These four tables show a clear pattern of behaviour for the 10 aggregates. In 1965, 1971, 1980 and 1988, the first five nonmanufactured aggregates (PETRO, MAT, FOR, TROP and ANL) are all positively correlated, CER being the exception. In 1965, 1971 and 1980, the four manufactured aggregates (LAB, CAP, MACH and CHEM) are positively correlated except for LAB with MACH and CHEM in 1965, 1971 and 1980. These results show that there is a clear distinction in patterns of exporting behaviour between nonmanufactured and manufactured aggregates. That is to say, on the whole, exports of nonmanufactured products are associated with exports of nonmanufactured products and exports of manufactured products are associated with exports of manufactured products.

One interesting phenomenon is that, apart from CER and the 1988 correlation between PETRO and CAP, LAB is the only aggregate to change its sign of correlation horizontally, suggesting that labour intensive products are on the edge of the distinction stated above between nonmanufactured and manufactured aggregates. In other words, although the association of exports of labour intensive products with both nonmanufactured and manufactured products varies, the pattern of the association remains basically the same over time.

However, some changes occur in the correlations between manufactured products in 1988: the correlation between LAB and MACH changes from negative in previous periods to positive. This shows a trend towards positive correlations between labour intensive aggregates and the three other manufactured aggregates. Whether this trend will continue remains to be seen, as more time is needed for a clear pattern to emerge. In addition, the pattern is further complicated by the changed sign of correlation between CAP and CHEM in 1988.

Another characteristic of these correlation matrices is that there are in general negative correlations between net exports of manufactured aggregates and net exports of nonmanufactured aggregates. This means that success in exporting manufactured products is accompanied by increased imports of nonmanufactured products. However, since these are cross-country correlations of net export data, the characteristics of different types of countries with regard to their patterns of exports still cannot be seen. Distinguishing different types of countries in terms of their performance in exporting manufactured products is achieved as follows.

A clear picture of the behaviour of manufactured aggregates along country lines is presented by sorting the signs of net exports of four manufactured aggregates. In so doing, a ladder of development can be formed showing how countries have upgraded themselves along the development path.[2] Tables 3.8, 3.9, 3.10 and 3.11 show the signs of aggregate net export data for 1965, 1971, 1980 and 1988 respectively. The manufactured aggregates are ordered to suggest a development process that begins with the export of aggregate 7 (LAB), which requires primarily unskilled workers. The next rung up the ladder of commodities is aggregate 8 (CAP), which requires capital. The more advanced countries, which are abundant in skills and capital, stand at the top along with export aggregates 9 and 10 (MACH and CHEM).

As Table 3.8 shows, in 1965 a long list of countries imported all four aggregates. Five countries or economies, Hong Kong, Israel, South Korea, Yugoslavia and Taiwan, exported aggregate 7 and imported the others. Another five, Austria, Belgium–Luxembourg, China, India and Portugal, exported aggregates 7 and 8 and imported aggregates 9 and 10. Sweden was placed on a special rung with exports of aggregate 9 only. France, Italy, Japan and the United Kingdom exported all four manufactured aggregates. While the former West Germany ranked high by exporting

Table 3.8 Ladder of development (signs of net exports of manufactured aggregates), 1965[a]

Aggregate				
7	8	9	10	Country
-	-	-	+	NETH
-	-	+	+	SWITZ, US
-	+	+	+	GER
+	+	+	+	FRA, ITLY, JAP, UK
-	-	+	-	SWE
+	+	-	-	AUST, BLUX, CHNA, INDA, PORT
+	-	-	-	HOKO, ISRL, KOR, YUG, TAIW
-	-	-	-	ARG, AUSL, BRAZ, BURM, CAN, CHLE, CLUM, CSTA, CYPR, DEN, DORE, ECUA, EGPT, LSAL, FIN, GANA, GRCE, HOND, ICE, INDO, IRE, LIBR, LIBY, MALY, MLTA, MAUR, MEX, NUZE, NIGR, NOR, PANM, PERU, PLIP, SRIL, SING, SPAN, THAI, TURK,, URGY, VELA
-	-	-	+	JAMC, PRGY

Note: a See Appendix A for country names and abbreviations.

aggregates 8, 9 and 10 and importing only aggregate 7, the most advanced countries were Switzerland, the United States and the Netherlands, which exported aggregates 9, 10 and 10 respectively. Although Jamaica and Paraguay both had chemical exports in 1965, they are not placed at the top of the ladder because their chemical exports (aluminium oxide in the case of Jamaica and extract of quebracho in the case of Paraguay) are better classified as raw materials.

There are several points to make regarding the position of particular categories of countries on this ladder in 1965. First, the markets for exporting aggregates 8, 9 and 10 were dominated by the advanced industrialised countries. Second, the newly industrialised economies (NIEs) had already shown signs of a 'take-off' by exporting aggregate 7, with the exception of Singapore, which was still on the bottom rung of the ladder at that time. Third, among those on the bottom rung of the ladder, there was a mixture of developed and developing countries. Finally, it is interesting to note that China, together with India and several other countries, ranked relatively high on the ladder by exporting aggregates 7 and 8.

By 1971, there had been noticeable changes in the ladder, as shown in Table 3.9. While the countries on the top rungs of the ladder remained more or less the same, a number of countries moved up the ladder by exporting both aggregates 7 and 8 and by exporting aggregate 7 only. For example, while Hong Kong and South Korea remained at their previous levels, Taiwan achieved remarkable progress by exporting capital intensive products within a short period of time. Similarly, Brazil and Turkey came out on the bottom rung of the ladder by exporting labour intensive products. This trend of upgrading continued throughout the 1970s.

Table 3.9 Ladder of development (signs of net exports of manufactured aggregates), 1971[a]

Aggregate 7	8	9	10	Country
-	-	-	+	NETH
-	-	+	+	SWITZ, US
-	+	+	+	GER
+	+	+	+	FRA, JAP, UK
+	+	-	+	BLUX*
-	+	+	-	SWE*
+	+	+	-	ITLY*
+	+	-	-	AUST, CHNA, INDA, PORT, SPAN*, EGPT*, TAIW*, URGY*
+	-	-	-	BRAZ*, DEN*, FIN*, HOKO, ISRL, KOR, TURK*, YUG
-	-	-	-	ARG, AUSL, BURM, CAN, CHLE, CLUM, CSTA, CYPR, DORE, ECUA, LSAL, GANA, GRCE, HOND, ICE, INDO, IRE, LIBR, LIBY, MALY, MLTA, MAUR, MEX, NUZE, NIGR, NOR, PANM, PRGY*, PERU, PLIP, SRIL, SING, THAI, VELA
-	-	-	+	JAMC

Note: a Asterisks indicate a change in the sign pattern since 1965.

As Table 3.10 shows, by 1980 the above trend had become even more obvious. First, among developed countries, while Japan remained at its previous level, France and the United Kingdom, previously in the same group as Japan, upgraded themselves by decreasing exports of labour intensive products and joined up with Germany. Canada was an extreme case, going from the bottom rung to the top. Second, China, Portugal and Uruguay stepped down the ladder over this period after losing exports of capital intensive products. Similarly, Egypt went down to the bottom after losing exports of both labour intensive and capital intensive products. Third, within a decade, Brazil and South Korea joined Taiwan, India and Spain by exporting both labour intensive and capital intensive products. Within the same period, Israel went even higher by exporting all manufactured products except machinery. Another exceptional case is Singapore, which moved several rungs up from the bottom of the ladder by exporting both labour intensive and chemical products. Finally, Colombia, Cyprus, El Salvador, Greece, Malta, Mauritius, Peru, the Philippines and Sri Lanka moved one rung up from the bottom of the ladder by exporting labour intensive products. Thus, by 1980, a group consisting of the NIEs and some other middle and low income countries had distinguished themselves from the low income countries by exporting labour intensive and some capital intensive products; they had also pushed most industrialised countries out of these markets.

Table 3.10 Ladder of development (signs of net exports of manufactured aggregates), 1980[a]

Aggregate				
7	8	9	10	Country
-	-	-	+	CAN*, NETH
-	-	+	+	SWITZ, US
-	+	+	+	FRA*, GER, UK*
+	+	+	+	JAP
-	+	+	-	SWE
-	+	-	+	BLUX*
+	+	+	-	ITLY
+	-	-	+	SING*
+	+	-	+	ISRL*
+	+	-	-	BRAZ*, INDA, KOR*, SPAN, TAIW
-	+	-	-	AUST*
+	-	-	-	CHNA*, CLUM*, CYPR*, DEN, LSAL*, FIN, GRCE*, HOKO, MLTA*, MAUR*, PERU*, PLIP*, PORT*, SRIL*, TURK, URGY*, YUG
-	-	-	-	ARG, AUSL, BURM, CHLE, CSTA, DORE, ECUA, EGPT*, GANA, HOND, ICE, INDO, IRE, LIBR, LIBY, MALY, MEX, NUZE, NIGR, NOR, PANM, PRGY, THAI, VELA
-	-	-	+	JAMC

Note: a Asterisks indicate a change in the sign pattern since 1971.

Table 3.11 shows the situation in 1988, the final year covered in this study. By 1988, things had changed considerably. A large number of countries had moved up the ladder of development by exporting labour and capital intensive products, pushing most industrialised countries even further out of these markets. A few economies, Taiwan and Israel for example, were even exporting machinery and chemicals.

Compared with the previous period under study — that is, 1980 — another three industrialised countries, Norway, the United Kingdom and the United States, had reached the top of the ladder by losing exports of aggregates 7, 8 and 9. They were followed by Switzerland, France, Germany and Sweden. One implication of the changes in pattern of exports in developed countries is that these changes have by no means been smooth. As Leamer says, 'it can be expected that the crowding of the markets of aggregates 7 and 8 causes serious adjustment problems for these most industrialised nations' (Leamer 1984, p. 88). Compared with other industrialised countries, Japan was in a unique position in that it was exporting all manufactured products except aggregate 10. This is perhaps one reason why Japan has had less serious adjustment problems than other industrialised countries; and there is still room for Japan to exploit further its trade opportunities without resorting to drastic structural adjustments.

Table 3.11 Ladder of development (signs of net exports of manufactured aggregates), 1988[a]

Aggregate				
7	8	9	10	Country
-	-	-	+	CAN, NETH, NOR*, UK*, US*
-	-	+	+	SWITZ
-	+	+	+	GER
-	+	-	+	FRA*
-	+	+	-	SWE
+	-	+	+	IRE*
+	+	+	-	JAP*, TAIW*
+	-	-	+	ISRL*
+	+	-	-	BLUX*, BRAZ, INDA, ITLY*, KOR, SPAN, TURK*, URGY*
-	+	-	-	ARG*, AUST
+	-	-	-	BURM*, CHNA, CLUM, CSTA*, DEN, DORE*, GRCE, INDO*, JAMC*, MALY*, MLTA, MAUR, MEX*, PERU, PLIP, PORT, SING*, SRIL, THAI*, YUG
-	-	-	-	AUSL, CHLE, CYPR*, ECUA, EGPT, LSAL*, FIN*, GANA, HOND, HOKO*, ICE, LIBR, LIBY, NUZE, NIGR, PANM, PRGY, VELA

Note: a Asterisks indicate a change in the sign pattern since 1980.

During the period 1980–88, the group of countries consisting of NIEs and a few other middle and low income countries continued to expand. With the upgrading of Indonesia, Malaysia and Thailand, all the ASEAN countries moved up the ladder of development and were exporting at least labour intensive products by 1988. This reflects the strong growth of export-oriented economies in East and Southeast Asia. In addition to these ASEAN countries, Burma, Costa Rica, the Dominican Republic, Jamaica and Mexico achieved notable progress as well. While Singapore stepped down the ladder to the second rung from the bottom, Taiwan again made remarkable progress by exporting three out of four manufactured aggregates (labour, capital intensive products and chemicals), and left Korea behind. Among those countries which upgraded themselves during this period, Turkey and Uruguay stand out. Apart from Brazil and Spain, they are the only countries which went from the bottom rung of the ladder to reach the level of exporting both labour and capital intensive products in the 1980s.

Several countries, for example Cyprus, El Salvador, Finland and Hong Kong, stepped down the ladder to the bottom during this period. The shifts in the export positions of Singapore and Hong Kong need further explanation, but this goes beyond the scope of the current study. Unlike China, India remained in the same position as in the 1960s. Finally, it is important to note that, contrary to other developed countries, Belgium–Luxembourg and Italy showed a downward movement throughout the entire period. This seems to indicate that there is a weak trend for some developed countries to re-emphasise low ranking manufactured industries, particularly labour intensive industries. In consideration of the difficulties surrounding structural change in those countries, it is not at all surprising that such a trend exists; if so, it would have significant implications for the process of development.

Resource data

This study selects 11 variables for resource endowments, following Leamer (1984). However, the definitions of four land variables have been changed in the present study; the justifications for this will be given later in the text. The 11 variables are defined as follows:

1. CAPITAL — Accumulated and discounted gross domestic investment flows since 1950, assuming an average life of 15 years with 13.3 per cent rate of depreciation according to the double declining balance method.
2. LABOUR 1 — Number of workers classified as professional or technical.
3. LABOUR 2 — Number of nonprofessional skilled workers.
4. LABOUR 3 — Number of unskilled workers.
5. LAND 1 — Arable land.
6. LAND 2 — Land under permanent crops.
7. LAND 3 — Permanent meadows and pastures.
8. LAND 4 — Forests and woodland.
9. COAL — Value of production of primary solid fuels (coal, lignite and brown coal).

10. MINERALS Value of production of minerals: bauxite, copper, fluorspar, iron ore, lead, manganese, nickel, potash, pyrite, salt, tin and zinc.
11. OIL Value of oil and gas production.

This list includes measures of land, capital and natural resources. Technological inputs are here measured only by LABOUR 1, the supply of professional/technical workers. More detailed definitions and sources of the 11 resource variables are provided in Appendix A.

As with the previous section, the key resource variables, namely capital and labour (LABOUR 1), are reported first. These variables are assumed to contribute to comparative advantage in manufactured commodities. Capital, different categories of labour and arable land are then used to calculate world resource shares over time.

Table 3.12 illustrates changing resource structure by showing the levels, ranks and annual rates of growth of capital stock. Table 3.13 shows changing resource supplies by presenting levels and average annual rates of growth of capital per worker. Table 3.14 gives numbers and average annual rates of growth in skilled labour for each country. Table 3.12 shows that the ten top ranking countries with regard to capital stock endowments in 1965 were: the United States, Germany, Japan, France, the United Kingdom, Italy, Canada, the Netherlands, Spain and Australia. Little change had taken place in 1974, except that China had joined the top ten. In 1988, India joined China and Japan as one of three Asian countries in this group. The United States remained dominant in capital stock endowments from the 1960s to the 1980s. While still behind in absolute terms, other Asian countries enjoyed relatively high growth rates in their capital stock endowments. Among these, China, Indonesia, Korea, Singapore and Taiwan enjoyed two-digit growth rates between 1965 and 1988. During the period, no other country in the sample matched these growth rates.

The average annual growth rates in capital stock for two subperiods are also reported in Table 3.12. During the period 1965–74, when almost all countries were enjoying high growth rates, the following countries were doing exceptionally well: China, Indonesia, Japan, Korea, Singapore, Thailand, Taiwan, Brazil and Greece. The figures for the period 1974–88 indicate that Asian and some Pacific countries were still maintaining exceptionally high growth rates, while the growth rates of countries in Oceania and all European countries except Yugoslavia had slowed.

Switzerland, Norway and Sweden dominated capital stock endowments per worker. Asian countries except Japan and some of the South American countries were ranked low, reflecting their large population bases and relatively high growth rates in their labour forces. Progress was made in these countries between 1965 and 1988, however, as seen in relatively high growth rates in capital per worker. Again, Japan is an exceptional case. Its ranking increased remarkably, from 20 in 1965 to four in 1988, reflecting its low population growth rate on the one hand and its rapid accumulation of capital on the other. Some of the other principal performers during this period included Korea, Singapore, Taiwan, Austria, Belgium–Luxembourg, France and Greece.

Table 3.12 Capital stock endowments in selected countries, 1965, 1974 and 1988

Country	Capita stock values (US$ million)						Annual growth rate (%)		
	1965	Rank	1974	Rank	1988	Rank	1965–74	1974–88	1965–88
Asia									
Burma	815	45	996	45	3 114	45	2.2	8.5	6.0
China	54 041	17	218 001	8	888 738	4	16.7	10.5	12.9
Hong Kong	8 754	36	18 084	38	59 447	28	8.4	8.9	8.7
India	84 778	13	137 203	15	274 769	10	5.5	5.1	5.2
Indonesia	13 194	31	33 788	27	159 524	19	11.0	11.7	11.4
Israel	11 112	33	24 326	33	30 456	38	9.1	1.6	4.5
Japan	440 142	3	1 305 263	2	2 278 775	2	12.8	4.1	7.4
Korea	8 722	34	38 518	26	167 346	17	17.9	11.1	13.7
Malaysia	7 024	38	15 609	39	48 269	30	9.3	8.4	8.7
Philippines	14 573	28	25 467	31	41 507	34	6.4	3.6	4.7
Singapore	2 108	42	11 781	40	36 668	36	21.1	8.4	13.2
Thailand	8 930	35	24 524	32	58 586	29	11.9	6.4	8.5
Turkey	18 274	25	39 405	25	83 729	25	8.9	5.5	6.8
Taiwan	6 728	39	27 086	30	77 746	27	16.7	7.8	11.2
North America									
Canada	130 113	7	208 727	9	394 572	8	5.4	4.7	4.9
Mexico	51 859	18	121 218	17	215 663	13	9.9	4.2	6.4
Panama	1 391	44	3 977	43	5 050	43	12.3	1.7	5.8
United States	1 384 608	1	2 017 665	1	2 913 986	1	4.3	2.7	3.3
South America									
Argentina	81 814	14	128 714	16	118 263	21	5.2	-0.6	1.6
Brazil	57 692	16	44 474	14	263 093	11	10.7	4.4	6.8
Chile	12 058	32	20 541	36	23 255	41	6.1	0.9	2.9
Colombia	10 006	30	21 689	34	38 626	35	5.1	4.2	4.6
Peru	18 977	24	20 939	35	26 754	40	1.1	1.8	1.5
Africa									
Egypt	6 711	40	9 998	41	41 942	33	4.5	10.8	8.3
Ghana	6 025	41	6 340	42	5 311	42	0.6	-1.2	-0.5
Europe									
Austria	47 187	20	85 767	20	116 969	22	6.9	2.2	4.0
Belg.–Lux.	60 914	15	116 177	18	143 354	20	7.4	1.5	3.8
Denmark	46 833	21	76 385	21	78 642	26	5.6	0.2	2.3
Finland	36 228	23	62 641	23	84 622	24	6.3	2.2	3.7
France	380 128	4	717 305	4	885 194	5	7.3	1.5	3.7
Germany, W.	579 844	2	900 945	3	1 032 054	3	5.0	1.0	2.5
Greece	16 327	26	41 201	24	45 937	31	10.8	0.8	4.6
Iceland	1 839	43	3 081	44	4 713	44	5.9	3.1	4.2
Ireland	9 288	34	19 031	37	28 691	39	8.3	2.9	5.0
Italy	331 021	6	519 115	6	659 636	6	5.1	1.7	3.0
Netherlands	120 269	8	192 798	10	204 026	14	5.4	0.4	2.3
Norway	42 893	22	67 255	22	105 148	23	5.1	3.2	3.9
Portugal	14 101	29	29 706	28	42 587	32	8.6	2.6	4.9
Spain	99 259	9	232 883	7	296 754	9	9.9	1.7	4.9
Sweden	93 899	11	148 550	12	171 421	16	5.2	1.0	2.6
Switzerland	91 555	12	145 864	13	178 008	13	5.3	1.4	2.9
United Kingdom	361 269	5	523 231	5	615 779	7	4.2	1.2	2.3
Yugoslavia	51 750	19	86 248	19	160 971	18	5.8	4.5	5.1
Oceania									
Australia	96 824	10	160 450	11	225 473	12	5.8	2.5	3.7
New Zealand	15 689	27	28 797	29	36 629	37	6.9	1.7	3.8

Table 3.13 **Capital per worker endowments in selected countries, 1965, 1974 and 1988**

Country	Capital per worker (US$) 1965	Rank	1974	Rank	1988	Rank	Annual growth rate (%) 1965–74	1974–88	1965–88
Asia									
Burma	82	45	77	45	179	45	-0.7	6.2	3.4
China	147	44	554	44	1 357	42	15.8	6.6	10.1
Hong Kong	6 020	25	9 660	25	20 234	22	5.4	5.4	5.4
India	449	42	571	43	883	44	2.7	3.2	3.0
Indonesia	361	43	718	42	2 332	39	7.9	8.8	8.4
Israel	14 776	16	19 665	19	18 096	23	3.2	-0.6	0.9
Japan	9 118	20	22 795	15	37 071	4	10.7	3.5	6.3
Korea	1 008	39	3 036	35	9 221	28	13.0	8.2	10.1
Malaysia	2 863	32	3 812	34	7 259	31	3.2	4.7	4.1
Philippines	1 268	38	1 622	39	1 938	41	2.8	1.3	1.9
Singapore	4 392	29	13 812	22	28 872	14	13.6	5.4	8.5
Thailand	645	41	1 278	40	2 062	40	7.9	3.5	5.2
Turkey	1 342	37	2 311	37	3 582	37	6.2	3.2	4.4
Taiwan	1 792	36	4 937	31	9 589	27	11.9	4.8	7.6
North America									
Canada	19 987	8	21 881	16	30 369	12	1.0	2.4	1.8
Mexico	4 576	27	7 101	28	7 351	30	5.0	0.2	2.1
Panama	4 127	30	7 014	29	6 107	32	6.1	-0.9	1.7
United States	19 815	10	21 318	17	24 068	18	0.8	0.9	0.8
South America									
Argentina	10 874	19	13 147	23	10 501	26	2.1	-1.6	-0.1
Brazil	2 547	34	4 174	33	4 983	34	5.6	1.3	3.0
Chile	5 049	26	6 301	30	5 187	33	2.5	-1.4	0.1
Colombia	2 689	33	2 825	36	3 896	36	0.5	2.3	1.6
Peru	6 074	24	4 681	32	3 964	35	-2.8	-1.2	-1.8
Africa									
Egypt	851	40	992	41	3 023	38	1.7	8.3	5.7
Ghana	2 231	35	1 709	38	1 013	43	-2.8	-3.7	-3.3
Europe									
Austria	14 002	18	26 333	12	32 555	11	7.3	1.5	3.7
Belg.–Lux.	16 721	13	29 743	9	33 842	8	6.6	0.9	3.1
Denmark	20 805	7	32 108	8	27 739	16	4.9	-1.0	1.2
Finland	17 820	12	28 217	10	33 540	10	5.2	1.2	2.8
France	19 170	11	32 114	7	35 138	6	5.9	0.6	2.7
Germany, W.	22 507	6	32 209	6	34 752	7	4.1	0.5	1.9
Greece	4 488	28	10 911	24	11 846	25	10.4	0.6	4.3
Iceland	27 044	5	35 011	5	35 707	5	2.9	0.1	1.2
Ireland	8 307	22	16 005	21	20 626	21	7.6	1.8	4.0
Italy	16 617	14	25 289	13	28 506	15	4.8	0.9	2.3
Netherlands	28 855	3	37 444	4	33 579	9	2.9	-0.8	0.7
Norway	35 307	2	44 305	2	50 310	2	4.2	0.9	2.2
Portugal	4 119	31	8 704	27	9 188	29	8.7	0.4	3.5
Spain	8 532	21	18 808	20	20 796	20	9.2	0.7	3.9
Sweden	27 217	4	40 466	3	39 598	3	4.5	-0.1	1.6
Switzerland	36 447	1	45 869	1	54 024	1	2.6	1.2	1.7
United Kingdom	14 534	17	20 083	18	21 814	19	3.7	0.6	1.8
Yugoslavia	6 205	23	8 819	26	15 120	24	4.0	3.9	3.9
Oceania									
Australia	19 939	9	27 223	11	29 067	13	3.5	0.5	1.7
New Zealand	15 291	15	23 898	14	24 617	17	5.1	0.2	2.1

Table 3.14 Skilled labour endowments in selected countries, 1965, 1974 and 1988

Country	Numbers of skilled labour (thousands) 1965	Rank	1974	Rank	1988	Rank	Annual growth rate (%) 1965–74	1974–88	1965–88
Asia									
Burma	218	25	515	23	418	35	10.0	-1.5	2.9
China	991	8	4 720	3	33 405	1	18.9	15.0	16.5
Hong Kong	74	41	99	42	217	39	3.3	5.7	4.8
India	3 206	2	6 487	2	8 398	3	8.1	1.9	4.3
Indonesia	804	9	1 034	12	1 984	12	2.8	4.8	4.0
Israel	86	40	234	34	384	36	12.0	3.6	6.7
Japan	2 655	3	4 466	4	6 331	4	6.0	2.5	3.8
Korea	225	24	406	25	1 143	17	6.8	7.7	7.3
Malaysia	118	33	184	36	505	30	5.1	7.5	6.5
Philippines	379	19	848	14	1 092	19	9.3	1.8	4.7
Singapore	23	43	87	43	141	43	16.2	3.5	8.3
Thailand	180	29	499	24	824	23	12.0	3.6	6.8
Turkey	299	21	682	19	1 099	18	9.6	3.5	5.8
Taiwan	172	30	269	32	555	28	5.1	5.3	5.2
North America									
Canada	690	11	1 307	10	2 157	10	7.3	3.6	5.1
Mexico	408	17	1 058	11	2 142	11	11.2	5.2	7.5
Panama	15	44	39	44	85	44	10.9	5.8	7.8
United States	7 547	1	13 156	1	18 524	2	6.4	2.5	4.0
South America									
Argentina	459	15	734	17	845	22	5.4	1.0	2.7
Brazil	702	10	1 661	8	3 643	7	10.0	5.8	7.4
Chile	117	34	182	37	318	37	5.1	4.1	4.4
Colombia	200	28	346	27	962	21	6.2	7.6	7.1
Peru	103	37	331	29	513	29	13.8	3.2	7.2
Africa									
Egypt	347	20	615	21	1 568	13	6.6	6.9	6.8
Ghana	60	42	137	39	210	40	9.6	3.1	5.6
Europe									
Austria	229	23	283	31	492	32	2.4	4.0	3.4
Belg.–Lux.	291	22	676	20	665	25	9.8	-0.1	3.7
Denmark	214	27	290	30	606	26	3.4	5.4	4.6
Finland	167	31	333	28	582	27	8.0	4.1	5.6
France	1 804	6	2 546	7	3 552	8	3.9	2.4	3.0
Germany, W.	1 958	5	2 741	6	4 187	6	3.8	3.1	3.4
Greece	124	32	215	35	454	33	6.3	5.5	5.8
Iceland	4	45	10	45	15	45	9.4	2.9	5.4
Ireland	87	39	110	41	199	42	2.7	4.3	3.7
Italy	1 056	7	1 498	9	2 661	9	3.9	4.2	4.1
Netherlands	384	18	685	18	1 306	14	6.6	4.7	5.5
Norway	112	35	247	33	445	34	9.1	4.3	6.2
Portugal	92	38	123	40	310	38	3.2	6.8	5.4
Spain	477	13	916	13	1 213	15	7.5	2.0	4.1
Sweden	521	12	811	15	1 182	16	5.0	2.7	3.6
Switzerland	216	26	385	26	498	31	6.6	1.8	3.7
United Kingdom	2 386	4	2 892	5	4 488	5	2.1	3.2	2.8
Yugoslavia	467	14	743	16	1 054	20	5.3	2.5	3.6
Oceania									
Australia	452	16	595	22	822	24	3.1	2.3	2.6
New Zealand	105	36	169	38	208	41	5.5	1.5	3.0

Table 3.15 **Skilled labour as percentage of total labour in selected countries, 1965, 1974 and 1988**

	Percentage						Annual growth rate (%)		
Country	1965	Rank	1974	Rank	1988	Rank	1965–74	1974–88	1965–88
Asia									
Burma	2.2	41	4.0	38	2.4	45	6.9	-3.6	0.4
China	0.3	45	1.2	45	5.1	39	18.0	10.9	13.6
Hong Kong	5.1	23	5.3	32	7.4	31	0.4	2.4	1.6
India	1.7	43	2.7	42	2.7	44	5.3	0.0	2.0
Indonesia	2.2	42	2.2	44	2.9	43	0.0	2.0	1.2
Israel	11.4	2	19.0	2	22.8	3	5.8	1.3	3.1
Japan	5.5	21	7.8	20	10.3	23	3.9	2.0	2.8
Korea	2.6	38	3.2	41	6.3	37	2.3	4.9	3.9
Malaysia	4.8	25	4.5	35	7.6	29	-0.7	3.8	2.0
Philippines	3.3	34	5.4	31	5.1	38	5.6	-0.4	1.9
Singapore	4.7	26	10.2	15	11.1	21	9.0	0.6	3.8
Thailand	1.3	44	2.6	43	2.9	42	8.0	0.8	3.5
Turkey	2.2	39	4.0	37	4.7	40	6.9	1.2	3.4
Taiwan	4.6	27	4.9	33	6.9	34	0.7	2.4	1.8
North America									
Canada	10.6	4	13.7	8	16.6	7	2.9	1.4	2.0
Mexico	3.6	32	6.2	27	7.3	32	6.2	1.2	3.1
Panama	4.5	28	6.8	26	10.3	24	4.7	3.0	3.7
United States	10.8	3	13.9	7	15.3	10	2.8	0.7	1.5
South America									
Argentina	6.1	19	7.5	22	7.5	30	2.3	0.0	0.9
Brazil	3.1	36	4.8	34	6.9	35	5.0	2.6	3.5
Chile	4.9	24	5.6	30	7.1	33	1.5	1.7	1.6
Colombia	3.9	31	4.5	36	9.7	26	1.6	7.1	4.9
Peru	3.3	35	7.4	24	7.6	28	9.4	0.2	3.7
Africa									
Egypt	4.4	29	6.1	28	11.3	19	3.7	4.5	4.2
Ghana	2.2	40	3.7	39	4.0	41	5.9	0.6	2.6
Europe									
Austria	6.8	17	8.7	19	13.7	16	2.8	3.3	3.1
Belg.–Lux.	8.0	13	17.3	3	15.7	9	8.9	-0.7	3.0
Denmark	9.5	7	12.2	10	21.4	5	2.8	4.1	3.6
Finland	8.2	12	15.0	5	23.1	2	6.9	3.1	4.6
France	9.1	10	11.4	12	14.1	13	2.5	1.5	1.9
Germany, W.	7.6	16	9.8	17	14.0	14	2.9	2.6	2.7
Greece	3.4	33	5.7	29	11.7	17	5.9	5.3	5.5
Iceland	6.4	18	11.1	14	11.1	20	6.3	0.0	2.4
Ireland	7.8	15	9.3	18	14.3	12	2.0	3.1	2.7
Italy	5.3	22	7.3	25	11.5	18	3.6	3.3	3.4
Netherlands	9.2	9	13.3	9	21.5	4	4.2	3.5	3.8
Norway	8.0	14	16.3	4	21.3	6	8.2	1.9	4.3
Portugal	2.7	37	3.6	40	6.7	36	3.2	4.4	4.0
Spain	4.1	30	7.4	23	8.5	27	6.8	1.0	3.2
Sweden	15.1	1	22.1	1	27.3	1	4.3	1.5	2.6
Switzerland	8.6	11	12.1	11	15.1	11	3.9	1.6	2.5
United Kingdom	9.6	6	11.1	13	15.9	8	1.6	2.6	2.2
Yugoslavia	5.6	20	7.6	21	9.9	25	3.4	1.9	2.5
Oceania									
Australia	9.3	8	10.1	16	10.6	22	0.9	0.3	0.6
New Zealand	10.2	5	14.1	6	14.0	15	3.7	-0.1	1.4

Table 3.16 World resource shares in selected countries, 1965 and 1988[a]

Country	Year	Resource share (%)				
		Capital	Skilled labour	Semiskilled labour	Unskilled labour	Arable land
Asia						
Burma	1965	0.02	0.7	1.05	0.91	1.27
	1988	0.02	0.36	1.09	1.01	1.11
China	1965	1.08	3.11	28.83	47.91	14.77
	1988	6.55	29.10	36.23	45.12	10.79
Hong Kong	1965	0.17	0.23	0.19	0.08	0.00
	1988	0.44	0.19	0.19	0.13	0.00
India	1965	1.69	10.06	9.05	31.18	19.76
	1988	2.03	7.32	10.85	36.77	19.34
Indonesia	1965	0.26	2.52	2.47	5.10	1.54
	1988	1.18	1.73	4.03	4.47	1.84
Israel	1965	0.22	0.27	0.10	0.03	0.04
	1988	0.22	0.33	0.11	0.03	0.04
Japan	1965	8.76	8.33	8.19	0.24	0.68
	1988	16.80	5.52	5.05	0.00	0.49
Korea	1965	0.17	0.71	1.08	0.58	0.26
	1988	1.23	1.00	1.35	0.45	0.23
Malaysia	1965	0.14	0.37	0.22	0.26	0.06
	1988	0.36	0.44	0.38	0.40	0.12
Philippines	1965	0.29	1.19	1.45	0.74	0.61
	1988	0.31	0.95	1.54	0.71	0.53
Singapore	1965	0.04	0.07	0.01	0.03	0.00
	1988	0.27	0.12	0.08	0.04	0.00
Thailand	1965	0.18	0.56	1.00	1.02	1.42
	1988	0.43	0.72	2.21	0.68	2.09
Turkey	1965	0.36	0.94	1.10	1.68	2.96
	1988	0.62	0.96	1.49	1.20	2.88
Taiwan	1965	0.13	0.54	0.50	0.20	0.10
	1988	0.57	0.51	0.66	0.07	0.09
North America						
Canada	1965	2.59	2.16	1.05	0.03	5.30
	1988	2.91	1.88	0.99	0.00	5.35
Mexico	1965	1.03	1.28	1.29	0.90	2.95
	1988	1.59	1.88	2.23	0.57	2.70
Panama	1965	0.03	0.05	0.04	0.02	0.05
	1988	0.04	0.07	0.06	0.02	0.05
United States	1965	27.57	23.67	11.33	0.16	22.43
	1988	21.48	16.15	9.34	0.12	21.90
South America						
Argentina	1965	1.63	1.44	1.18	0.15	2.46
	1988	0.87	0.74	0.89	0.14	3.03
Brazil	1965	1.15	2.20	2.41	2.02	2.82
	1988	1.94	3.18	3.43	2.34	7.75
Chile	1965	0.24	0.37	0.35	0.09	0.50
	1988	0.17	0.28	0.34	0.08	0.48
Colombia	1965	0.27	0.63	0.56	0.43	0.45
	1988	0.28	0.84	0.69	0.29	0.45
Peru	1965	0.38	0.32	0.33	0.28	0.27
	1988	0.20	0.45	0.46	0.24	0.40

Table 3.16 (continued)

Country	Year	Resource share (%) Capital	Skilled labour	Semiskilled labour	Unskilled labour	Arable land
Africa						
Egypt	1965	0.13	1.09	0.32	1.33	0.31
	1988	0.31	1.36	0.34	1.71	0.28
Ghana	1965	0.12	0.19	0.12	0.46	0.10
	1988	0.04	0.18	0.13	0.73	0.13
Europe						
Austria	1965	0.94	0.72	0.57	0.01	0.21
	1988	0.86	0.43	0.28	0.00	0.17
Belg.–Lux.	1965	1.21	0.91	0.61	0.01	0.12
	1988	1.06	0.58	0.33	0.00	0.09
Denmark	1965	0.93	0.67	0.37	0.01	0.35
	1988	0.58	0.53	0.20	0.00	0.30
Finland	1965	0.72	0.52	0.34	0.01	0.34
	1988	0.62	0.45	0.18	0.00	0.28
France	1965	7.57	5.66	3.28	0.04	2.42
	1988	6.52	3.10	1.98	0.00	2.13
Germany, W.	1965	11.54	6.14	4.33	0.06	0.98
	1988	7.61	3.65	2.34	0.00	0.85
Greece	1965	0.32	0.39	0.51	0.16	0.37
	1988	0.34	0.39	0.28	0.07	0.34
Iceland	1965	0.04	0.01	0.01	0.00	0.00
	1988	0.03	0.01	0.01	0.00	0.00
Ireland	1965	0.18	0.27	0.18	0.01	0.16
	1988	0.21	0.17	0.11	0.00	0.11
Italy	1965	6.59	3.31	3.13	0.42	1.60
	1988	4.86	2.32	1.81	0.14	1.06
Netherlands	1965	2.39	1.20	0.69	0.01	0.12
	1988	1.50	1.14	0.44	0.00	0.11
Norway	1965	0.85	0.35	0.23	0.00	0.10
	1988	0.78	0.39	0.15	0.00	0.10
Portugal	1965	0.28	0.29	0.38	0.29	0.47
	1988	0.31	0.27	0.33	0.15	0.24
Spain	1965	1.98	1.50	1.77	0.35	2.03
	1988	2.19	1.06	1.10	0.20	1.82
Sweden	1965	1.87	1.63	0.53	0.01	0.42
	1988	1.26	1.03	0.29	0.00	0.34
Switzerland	1965	1.82	0.68	0.42	0.01	0.05
	1988	1.31	0.43	0.26	0.00	0.05
United Kingdom	1965	7.19	7.48	3.99	0.17	0.92
	1988	4.54	3.91	2.17	0.00	0.81
Yugoslavia	1965	1.03	1.46	1.09	0.45	0.96
	1988	1.19	0.92	0.78	0.22	0.82
Oceania						
Australia	1965	1.93	1.42	0.80	0.01	4.21
	1988	1.66	0.72	0.64	0.00	5.46
New Zealand	1965	0.31	0.33	0.17	0.00	0.09
	1988	0.27	0.18	0.12	0.00	0.06

Note: a World here equals total of 61 economies.

The ranking of the United States fell from 10 in 1965 to 18 in 1988, reflecting that, relative to other countries, in the United States capital abundance actually declined. Although China ranked fourth on its capital stock endowment in absolute terms in 1988, its ranking for capital per worker remained low due to its large population and high labour participation rate. However, some progress was made in relative terms from 1974 to 1988 due to China's rapid accumulation of capital.

Table 3.14 shows skilled labour endowments (LABOUR 1) in absolute terms. On the whole, changes in ranking were less dramatic than those for changes in capital. The exceptions were China and Singapore. It can also be observed that those NIEs that enjoyed high growth rates in capital stock also experienced relatively high growth rates in skilled labour. Considering the vast differences in sizes of population across countries, it would make more sense to take skilled labour as a percentage of the total labour force as the criterion for examining changes in skilled labour endowments.

As Table 3.15 shows, percentages of skilled labour for developed countries were substantially higher than those for developing countries throughout the entire period. This implies that the former countries enjoyed a technological advantage over the latter, since this study measures technological inputs only by skilled labour. However, as shown in Table 3.14, developing countries did experience reasonably high growth in skilled labour, reflecting the effort they have put into education and training.

Bowen (1983, p. 403) points out that, 'in a multifactor context, resource abundance is appropriately determined by ranking a country's world shares of each resource'. Table 3.16 reports selected countries' world shares of five resources in 1965 and 1988 (world equalling 61 economies). In 1965 the United States was more abundant in capital than any other country. This was still the case in 1988, although the US share of capital declined from 27.57 per cent in 1965 to 21.48 per cent in 1988. Its share of skilled labour, arable land, semiskilled labour and unskilled labour, while still substantial, also declined over this period.

Japan increased its share of capital substantially, surpassing Germany to become second on the list by 1988, though its share of skilled and semiskilled labour declined during the period. Given this change, one would expect Japan's trade to have shifted towards more capital intensive sectors over this period. It should be noted, however, that the share of capital for all other developed countries except Canada declined, as did these countries' shares of skilled labour, semiskilled labour and arable land. (Canada and Australia, which increased their shares of arable land, were the exceptions here.)

In contrast to this, most developing countries, particularly NIEs, greatly increased their shares of capital and, to a lesser extent, semiskilled labour, but not in general their shares of skilled labour. In addition, there was a tendency for share of unskilled labour to decline in many developing countries. This evidence accords with *a priori* expectations that developing countries would participate increasingly in world production and trade of manufactures. By 1988, these developing countries were characterised by an abundance of semiskilled labour, followed by either capital and skilled labour (Korea, Taiwan and Argentina) or skilled labour and capital (India,

Thailand, Turkey, Mexico, Chile, Brazil and Colombia). Hong Kong and Singapore were most abundant in capital. China's share of capital, skilled labour and semiskilled labour increased dramatically, while its share of unskilled labour and arable land decreased.

Overall, the data indicate that patterns of international distribution of resources changed substantially between 1965 and 1988. In accordance with theory, these resource changes can be expected to have affected patterns of world trade. In the next section, evidence for this is provided by calculating cross-country correlations among trade and resource endowments.

Cross-country correlations

Correlations of trade with resource endowments are reported in Table 3.17; correlations of trade relative to GNP with endowments relative to GNP are reported in Table 3.18; and correlations of trade per worker with endowments per worker are reported in Table 3.19.

Tables 3.17 to 3.19 provide initial evidence that cross-sectional data could potentially be used to infer a relationship between changes in resource endowments and shifts in trade patterns. As Table 3.17 shows, there are high correlations between trade in machinery, chemicals and CAPITAL in 1965 and 1974, with fairly high correlations in 1988, and high correlations between trade in capital intensive products and CAPITAL in 1965 and 1974. Similarly, fairly high correlations can be seen between trade in these variables and LABOUR 1 and LABOUR 2 in 1965 and 1974, but not in 1988.

These results justify the substitution of the four land variables (this justification is reinforced by the results in Tables 3.18 and 3.19): exports of forest products have fairly high correlations with LAND 4 (forests and woodland); tropical agriculture exports have fairly high correlations with LAND 2 (land under permanent crops); exports of animal products have positive but rather low correlations with LAND 3 (permanent meadows and pastures); and exports of cereals are highly correlated with LAND 1 (arable land). COAL seems to play an important role in determining trade in machinery and chemical products, particularly in 1965 and 1974. Raw materials trade has fairly high correlations with MINERALS, and exports of labour intensive products have low but positive correlations with LABOUR 3 (unskilled labour). Petroleum trade has some puzzling correlations with OIL, which can be resolved by taking the following two measures into account in calculation of the correlations between trade and resource data.

In order to achieve a greater degree of accuracy in analysing the relationship between the two sets of data, the same calculations were conducted for both trade and resource data divided by GNP. The results are shown in Table 3.18, and indicate that petroleum trade is indeed highly correlated with OIL, and raw material trade is highly correlated with MINERALS and LAND 2. The results also confirm fairly large correlations of forest, tropical, animal and cereal trade with the corresponding four

Table 3.17 Correlations between trade and endowments[a]

	CAPITAL	LABOUR 1	LABOUR 2	LABOUR 3	LAND 1	LAND 2	LAND 3	LAND 4	COAL	MIINERALS	OIL
1965											
PETRO	**-.63**	-.60	-.27	.03	-.28	-.05	-.18	-.14	-.50	-.39	-.06
MAT	**-.58**	-.52	-.28	.02	-.09	-.06	.00	.20	-.42	.02	-.12
FOR	-.49	-.46	-.22	.00	-.17	-.09	-.18	.15	**-.49**	-.03	-.22
TROP	**-.83**	-.70	-.28	.09	-.34	.22	-.18	-.05	-.74	-.59	-.5
ANL	**-.49**	-.44	-.12	.09	-.09	.00	.09	.02	-.43	-.19	-.21
CER	.38	.39	.05	-.07	.50	.12	.56	.46	.39	.67	**.71**
LAB	-.38	-.33	.00	.08	-.38	.01	-.32	-.39	-.41	-.58	**-.60**
CAP	.26	.27	**.28**	.10	-.04	-.02	-.17	-.19	.14	-.11	-.20
MACH	**.87**	.76	.32	-.08	.35	-.01	.18	.12	.77	.50	.56
CHEM	**.88**	.75	.27	-.11	38	-.04	.18	.15	.75	.57	.62
1974											
PETRO	**-.90**	-.72	-.32	.05	-.39	-.05	-.19	-.19	-.53	-.38	-.35
MAT	**-.56**	-.32	-.22	.01	.03	-.08	.17	.18	-.09	.26	.04
FOR	**-.40**	-.24	-.16	.01	.02	-.04	-.06	.22	-.14	.27	.05
TROP	**-.80**	-.64	-.22	.12	-.33	.30	-.10	-.01	-.63	-.48	-.60
ANL	**-.56**	-.42	-.12	.12	-.16	-.06	.05	-.05	-.31	-.18	-.28
CER	.44	.59	.17	-.04	.63	.11	.49	.45	.60	.71	**.83**
LAB	-.41	-.48	-.09	.10	-.45	.08	-.35	-.35	-.53	-.64	**-.69**
CAP	**.42**	.14	.13	-.01	-.15	-.09	-.18	-.21	.00	-.21	-.23
MACH	**.78**	.53	.25	-.06	.17	.07	.01	-.04	.46	.13	.26
CHEM	**.69**	.51	.20	-.08	.22	-.22	.06	-.06	.57	.24	.40
1988											
PETRO	**-.85**	-.35	-.14	.09	-.44	.02	-.19	-.16	-.50	-.21	-.67
MAT	**-.57**	-.12	-.07	.06	.06	.07	.21	.22	-.02	.30	.00
FOR	**-.44**	-.20	-.14	-.03	-.05	.01	-.08	.27	-.17	.33	-.08
TROP	**-.70**	-.26	-.07	.10	-.27	.28	-.08	-.02	-.41	-.16	-.57
ANL	**-.57**	-.10	-.02	.11	-.01	.00	.11	.06	-.03	.09	-.11
CER	.41	.34	.15	-.02	.64	.17	.46	.40	.63	.46	**.86**
LAB	-.54	-.18	.05	.22	-.48	.04	-.23	-.34	-.46	-.43	**-.84**
CAP	-.06	-.18	-.06	.00	-.42	.03	-.27	-.17	-.45	-.28	**-.64**
MACH	**.30**	-.05	-.02	-.06	-.26	-.08	-.21	-.14	-.23	-.18	**-.31**
CHEM	**.43**	.13	-.02	-.14	.20	-.09	.06	.10	.28	.14	.41

Note: a Highest correlations are in boldface.

land variables. COAL is not only positively correlated with machinery and chemicals, but also with trade in capital intensive products, though the correlation declined between 1965 and 1988. Meanwhile, the correlations between trade in manufactures and capital changed from positive in 1965 and 1974 to negative in 1988, with the exception of trade in labour intensive products.

Table 3.18 Correlations between trade/GNP and endowments/GNP[a]

	CAPITAL	LABOUR 1	LABOUR 2	LABOUR 3	LAND 1	LAND 2	LAND 3	LAND 4	COAL	MIINERALS	OIL
1965											
PETRO	.33	-.14	-.12	-.04	.04	-.07	.05	-.04	-.06	-.07	**.99**
MAT	.03	-.02	-.08	.13	-.02	.59	-.03	.24	-.12	**.99**	-.02
FOR	.03	.02	.05	.01	.04	.06	.01	**.15**	-.07	-.03	-.04
TROP	-.29	.13	.09	.08	.01	**.59**	-.04	.16	-.21	.24	-.12
ANL	.05	-.07	-.10	.00	.09	-.15	**.30**	.04	.02	-.14	-.06
CER	-.03	.09	.27	.12	.29	.06	**.36**	.30	-.09	-.11	-.03
LAB	.14	-.28	.07	-.44	**-.45**	-.21	-.15	-.09	.14	-.19	-.10
CAP	.11	-.09	-.09	-.03	-.05	-.39	-.02	-.20	**.42**	-.31	-.11
MACH	.02	.01	.08	.03	.05	-.35	-.05	-.13	.39	**-.40**	-.19
CHEM	**.20**	-.18	-.09	.01	.02	-.20	.07	-.03	.17	-.07	.01
1974											
PETRO	-.06	-.05	-.01	.02	.00	.01	.01	.03	-.02	-.10	**.96**
MAT	-.11	.13	-.06	.16	.01	.40	.02	.26	-.06	**.97**	-.02
FOR	-.01	.03	.03	.06	.05	.22	.00	**.22**	-.03	.16	-.01
TROP	-.28	.14	.17	.07	.04	**.45**	-.01	.07	-.14	.15	-.07
ANL	.05	-.08	-.07	-.04	.02	-.11	**.13**	.03	-.02	-.12	-.07
CER	-.18	.09	.06	.14	**.31**	.05	.28	.32	.07	-.07	.01
LAB	.06	-.06	.04	-.09	-.12	**-.21**	-.11	-.16	.02	-.20	-.12
CAP	.04	-.06	.05	.01	.00	-.15	-.02	-.04	**.20**	-.13	-.02
MACH	.10	.01	.04	.08	.10	-.23	.08	-.11	**.23**	-.25	-.07
CHEM	.19	-.10	-.09	-.03	-.04	**-.25**	.00	-.06	.15	.03	.02
1988											
PETRO	.28	.13	.04	.07	.00	.08	.02	.13	.03	-.02	**.57**
MAT	.07	.23	.08	.33	.01	.51	.01	.35	.00	**.76**	.13
FOR	.03	-.08	.01	.06	.01	**.24**	-.02	.19	-.02	.16	.19
TROP	.09	.23	.17	.13	.04	**.49**	.02	.24	-.08	.27	-.08
ANL	-.07	-.15	-.06	**-.12**	-.05	-.04	.01	-.04	-.02	-.04	-.02
CER	-.07	-.22	-.04	-.15	.10	-.06	**.26**	.17	.09	-.09	.10
LAB	.18	.00	.16	-.22	-.04	-.22	-.09	-.29	.10	**-.28**	-.07
CAP	-.09	-.08	-.02	-.03	.01	-.04	.01	.08	**.13**	-.02	.02
MACH	-.02	-.18	.01	-.21	.05	-.32	.05	-.19	.08	**-.35**	.08
CHEM	-.15	**-.18**	-.04	-.05	.04	-.13	.05	.00	.07	-.03	.01

Note: a Highest correlations are in boldface.

Because of the possibility of measurement error in GNP, new correlations were obtained from the data divided by total labour force; these are reported in Table 3.19. The results indicate that GNP is highly associated with most resources, particularly CAPITAL, LABOUR 1 (skilled labour) and LABOUR 2 (semiskilled labour). The

Table 3.19 Correlations between trade per worker and endowments per worker[a]

	CAPITAL	LABOUR 1	LABOUR 2	LABOUR 3	LAND 1	LAND 2	LAND 3	LAND 4	COAL	MIINERALS	OIL
1965											
GNP	**.86**	.81	.59	-.64	.31	-.27	.22	.17	.50	.14	.12
PETRO	.15	-.15	-.32	.31	.45	.15	.10	.05	-.10	-.03	**.99**
MAT	-.18	-.17	-.25	.25	.30	.23	.05	.46	-.17	**.91**	.04
FOR	.14	.25	.09	-.11	.22	-.07	-.15	**.35**	-.13	.24	-.02
TROP	**-.54**	-.41	-.34	.34	-.11	**.43**	-.10	.01	-.26	.05	-.12
ANL	.34	.20	.27	-.27	-.02	-.15	**.34**	.00	.00	-.10	-.06
CER	.10	-.01	.10	-.08	**.33**	.05	.61	.33	.08	.07	-.05
LAB	**-.35**	-.18	.00	.02	-.32	-.04	-.25	-.23	.05	.18	-.27
CAP	-.23	-.12	-.03	.04	-.18	.02	.27	-.12	**.31**	-.07	-.22
MACH	-.26	-.18	.09	.11	-.26	.03	**-.34**	-.23	.24	-.15	-.27
CHEM	.04	-.12	-.02	.03	-.14	-.02	-.25	-.13	**.26**	-.02	-.12
1974											
GNP	**.94**	.78	.40	-.53	.33	-.19	.31	.14	.36	.14	.39
PETRO	.11	-.01	-.36	.33	.25	.31	.19	-.01	-.06	-.04	**.98**
MAT	-.02	-.06	-.10	.11	.41	.03	.41	.44	.20	**.76**	.08
FOR	.16	.32	.06	-.12	.12	-.08	-.16	**.35**	-.06	.24	-.11
TROP	**-.50**	-.41	-.11	.18	-.07	**.24**	.08	-.06	-.09	-.01	-.20
ANL	**.33**	.24	.24	-.26	-.04	-.17	**.29**	-.01	.00	-.06	-.11
CER	-.06	-.05	.07	-.06	**.52**	.09	.52	.53	.44	.27	-.25
LAB	-.38	-.26	.08	.01	-.28	-.11	-.29	-.16	-.09	-.13	**-.46**
CAP	-.13	-.12	.11	-.07	.12	-.05	-.21	-.06	.11	-.03	**-.38**
MACH	-.18	-.24	.06	.00	-.17	-.04	-.34	-.12	.09	-.08	**-.42**
CHEM	.04	-.01	.02	-.02	-.10	-.05	**-.23**	-.12	.10	.04	-.10
1988											
GNP	**.96**	.80	.41	-.56	.09	-.34	.09	.11	.25	.05	.30
PETRO	-.08	-.07	-.29	.28	.20	.24	.11	.12	-.01	.04	**.65**
MAT	.16	.08	.04	-.06	.45	-.02	.53	.43	.42	.46	**.54**
FOR	.14	.36	-.01	-.08	.16	-.03	-.09	**.45**	.02	.21	.04
TROP	**-.52**	-.30	-.08	.15	.05	**.38**	-.02	.02	-.04	.04	-.08
ANL	.23	.18	.17	-.19	-.04	-.14	**.27**	-.01	.00	-.02	.05
CER	.01	.01	.16	-.14	**.40**	.13	**.51**	.30	.33	.19	.12
LAB	**-.42**	-.23	.00	.06	-.17	.07	-.20	-.29	-.13	-.14	-.29
CAP	**-.14**	-.04	.03	-.02	.08	.13	-.03	.08	.04	.05	-.04
MACH	-.12	-.11	-.02	.05	-.04	.03	**-.21**	-.07	-.03	.00	-.18
CHEM	.13	**.14**	.01	-.04	.05	.00	-.09	-.02	.08	.04	.06

Note: a Highest correlations are in boldface.

results also confirm that petroleum trade and raw materials trade have high correlations with OIL and MINERALS respectively. Forest products trade is again highly correlated with LAND 4; trade in tropical products has fairly high correlations with LAND 2 and can also be explained in terms of capital scarcity (high negative correlations); trade in animal products is associated with LAND 3 as well as with CAPITAL; and trade in cereals is correlated highly with LAND 1, LAND 3 and LAND 4. With regard to the four manufactured aggregates, the results tend to confirm Leamer's conclusion that none is associated positively to any great degree with any resource except COAL, which has its greatest impact on capital intensive manufactures (Leamer 1984); but this impact also declined during the period under study. In addition, the results show that some manufactured aggregates are associated with scarcity of a particular resource. For example, trade in labour intensive products is closely associated with scarcity of capital and oil, and trade in machinery is associated with scarcity of LAND 3 and OIL, though some change took place in 1988.

In summary, the correlations between trade and resource endowments suggest that the commodity composition of trade in general can be understood in terms of 11 resource endowments. This is consistent with the interpretation of the Heckscher–Ohlin theorem. The evidence confirms the accuracy of the results obtained by Leamer in 1958 and 1975.[3] More specifically, the two primary product aggregates and the four crops seem likely to use one natural resource (such as oil, minerals or various lands) intensively, and trade in them can be expected to be explained by the abundance of associated resources. The four manufactured aggregates use capital, skilled labour and unskilled labour, and trade in them can be expected to be explained by combinations of resources as follows: LAB uses unskilled labour; CAP uses capital and unskilled labour; MACH uses skilled labour and a moderate amount of capital; and CHEM uses skilled labour and very large amounts of capital. Based on the evidence, the next step will be to add the corresponding resource data to the trade data. After this, the linkage between these two sets of data can be examined formally using econometric methods. This will lead to the exercise of measuring the accuracy of a weakened version of the Heckscher–Ohlin theory, which is the task of Chapter 6.[4]

4 Trade dependence and resource abundance profiles

This chapter contains a discussion of trade dependence profiles and resource abundance profiles, from which some tentative conclusions concerning the sources of comparative advantage can be drawn. The intent is to present trade and resource data clearly; and more importantly, to provide further evidence of the relationship between trade and resource endowments predicted by the Heckscher–Ohlin theory. In addition, these profiles, together with corresponding graphs in Appendix C, may serve as a useful reference in describing patterns of trade and resource supplies of 61 economies from the 1960s to the 1980s.

Theoretical background

It should be pointed out at the outset that the trade dependence and resource abundance profiles and corresponding graphs are theoretically based on the Heckscher–Ohlin–Vanek (HOV) equations. Following Leamer (1984), one of the HOV equations for the $m \times m$ model takes the form $T_j = \Sigma_i \beta_{ij} (E_i - \alpha_i E_{wi})$, where β_{ij} is an element of A^{-1}, the inverse of the matrix of factor intensities, and α_i is the GNP share Y_i/Y_w. This can be rewritten as:

$$T_j/Y_i = \Sigma_i \beta_{ij} ((E_i/Y_i) - (E_{wi}/Y_w))$$

$$= \Sigma_i \beta_{ij} (E_{wi}/Y_w)((E_i/Y_i)/(E_{wi}/Y_w) - 1) \qquad (4.1)$$

where T_j equals net exports of commodity j, Y_i equals GNP, E_i equals endowment of resource i, Y_w equals world GNP, and E_{wi} equals world endowment of resource i. In other words, the trade dependence ratio T_j/Y_i is a linear function of the resource abundance ratios $(E_i/Y_i)/(E_{wi}/Y_w) - 1$. Therefore, study of the relationship between trade patterns and resource supplies requires the calculation of both trade dependence and resource abundance ratios.

For trade and resource data in this study, it is expected that exports of natural resource products and crops will be explained by abundance in natural resources and land, and those of manufactured products by abundance in labour and capital. Because of the stringent assumption that GNP is a linear function of the factor endowments that underlies equation (4.1), any deviation from this assumption, such as nonlinearities between GNP and factor endowments (which may be anticipated in the case that scale economies are important), may affect the accuracy of predicting trade patterns using resource supplies. This applies also to the formal statistical examination of this relationship in Chapter 6. Other factors that may influence prediction include the mismeasurement of variables such as GNP and incomplete coverage of countries in the study. Even so, with regard to the comparison of resource and GNP shares, 'pairwise comparisons of the abundance ratios are nonetheless appropriate, since they will reveal the relative abundance of the two resources considered' (Leamer 1984, p. 104).

Trade dependence profiles

For convenience as well as consistency, Leamer's methods of forming trade dependence profiles and drawing the corresponding graphs have been used here. First, trade dependence ratios (net exports relative to GNP) of the 10 commodity aggregates, on which trade dependence profiles are based, are calculated. In order to put all the countries on the same scale, the data have been transformed logarithmically by the function $Z = \text{sign}(T/Y) \times \ln(1 + 100|T/Y|)$. The correspondence between the number Z in the graphs and trade as a percentage of GNP is reported in Appendix C.

The profiles have three basic features: they indicate the composition of trade; they reveal the general level of trade dependence relative to GNP (the shorter the bars in the profiles, the less trade dependent a country is); and they provide indicators of trade imbalance (countries in surplus will have bars primarily above the profile, and countries in deficit below). These three features of the trade dependence profiles raise several questions. Is it still the case that countries can be grouped according to the performance of the 10 trade aggregates, and in particular of the four manufactured aggregates? Do different groups of countries become more or less trade dependent from the 1960s to the 1980s? Are the trends of trade imbalance stable across countries over time or do they demonstrate dramatic changes? In this regard, is there a big difference between manufactured products and primary (resource) products, or between more diversified and more specialised exporters? The following discussion will refer to the relevant profiles in Appendix C; the development ladder discussed in the previous chapter is also used as background information.

After being transformed to put all countries on the same scale, the trade data still suggest that countries can be grouped according to the sign of net exports of manufactured products.

Country group 1: exporters of machinery or chemicals

While the exports of chemicals or machinery in 1965 were, in most cases, still limited to the most advanced countries — France, Germany, Italy, Japan, the Netherlands, Switzerland, the United Kingdom and the United States — a few more economies (again most of them are developed countries) had joined this category by 1988: Canada, Ireland, Israel, Norway, Sweden and Taiwan.[1] The export earnings of these economies (using data for 1988 as an example) vary. The earnings of some economies were concentrated solely in the manufactured commodities (Germany and Japan), earnings of others were based on a mixture of manufactured commodities and natural resource products (Canada, Israel, Norway, Switzerland, the United Kingdom), and the earnings of some economies were concentrated in a combination of manufactured commodities and crops (France, Ireland, the Netherlands, Sweden, the United States, Taiwan).[2] Viewed from the perspective of degree of trade dependence, the group of countries exporting machinery or chemicals in general became more trade dependent between 1965 and 1988, though countries varied in the types of commodities exported (due to changing patterns in their resource supplies). A brief discussion of the major trends for each country in this country group (in alphabetical order) follows.

France: France is one of the least trade dependent countries in this group. In 1965 France had positive net exports of all four manufactured products and net imports of all six nonmanufactured products. In 1988, while export dependence on both capital intensive manufactures and chemicals was less, France had become a net importer of both labour intensive manufactures and machinery. France's bill for petroleum as well as for materials dropped considerably over this period. Tropical products and cereals both switched from being modest import items to modest export items. In fact, during the entire period, sign changes in net exports of the four crop aggregates, particularly from negative to positive, are rarely seen. Cases such as this may suggest the continuity of 'an aggressive agricultural policy' (Leamer 1984, p. 97).

Germany: In 1965 Germany imported all nonmanufactured products plus labour intensive manufactures and exported the remaining three manufactured products with a heavy concentration in machinery. This pattern remained unchanged in 1988, with increases in net exports of all three manufactured products, particularly machinery. By 1988 the petroleum bill had increased slightly but that for materials had decreased. Net imports of all four crops had dropped substantially and there was a slight increase in net imports of labour intensive manufactures. Thus Germany became more trade dependent on manufactured products and less dependent on crops and materials during the period under study.

Italy: In 1965 Italy had net exports of all four manufactured products and net imports of all nonmanufactured products except tropical products. It had a higher degree of trade dependence than France. However, by 1988 both machinery and chemicals had switched from being export to import items. While capital intensive manufactures remained positive, their concentration had decreased substantially. By contrast, the concentration in labour intensive manufactures had increased greatly.

Thus trade dependence in manufactured products tended to increase in Italy during this period, while the country moved down the ladder of commodities. However, for materials and the four crops, trade dependence decreased remarkably. The other change of note is that Italy had emerged as a net exporter of petroleum by the end of the 1980s.

Japan: Japan, like Italy, had positive net exports of all four manufactured products in 1965, with higher concentrations in capital intensive manufactures and machinery and lower concentrations in labour intensive manufactures and chemicals. However, unlike Italy, Japan had only very small net exports of animal products, with rather high export dependence on capital intensive manufactures and machinery and relatively high import dependence on materials and cereals. By 1988 Japan had become increasingly dependent on exports of machinery and less dependent on exports of both labour and capital intensive manufactures. Japan switched from being a net exporter of chemicals in 1965 to a net importer of chemicals in 1988. Furthermore, contrary to common belief, the trade dependence profiles show that in Japan all nonmanufactured products except animal products were less trade dependent in 1988 than in 1965; overall trade dependence clearly demonstrates a similar pattern, reflecting Japan's declining trade dependence on labour and capital intensive manufactures during the period.

Netherlands: The Netherlands was unique in that it had net exports of chemicals and substantial animal product exports, with all other manufactures being imported in both 1965 and 1988. In addition to animal products, it also had net exports of tropical products in both years. From 1965 to 1988, dependence on chemical exports increased substantially. There was also a slight increase of dependence on exports of machinery, but import dependence on both labour and capital intensive manufactures fell. The Netherlands' trade dependence on all nonmanufactured products dropped considerably during the period.

Sweden: Sweden underwent dramatic changes in the composition of trade in manufactures. While in 1965 it exported only small amounts of machinery, in 1988 exports of machinery had increased greatly and Sweden's capital intensive manufactures had switched from being an import item to being an export item. Import dependence on labour intensive manufactures increased, while import dependence on chemicals dropped slightly during the period. Sweden had net imports of all other nonmanufactured products except forestry; it maintained a very high concentration of these throughout the period. Sweden imported less petroleum in 1988 than in 1965 but more materials.

Switzerland: Switzerland shows the most advanced pattern of trade among countries in this category, with net exports of only machinery and chemicals in both 1965 and 1988. In 1965 Switzerland had a heavy concentration in exports of machinery, but this had switched in 1988 to being a concentration in exports of chemicals. Also, as with Sweden, Switzerland witnessed increasing dependence on imports of labour intensive manufactures, a sign of further advancement in terms of upgrading the commodity composition of trade.

United Kingdom: The United Kingdom exported all four manufactured aggregates with a heavy concentration in machinery in 1965 and imported all other trade aggregates. In 1988 only chemicals remained as an export item, and with far less concentration than in 1965. However, the most dramatic change for the United Kingdom was the switch from being heavily dependent on exports of machinery in 1965 to being heavily dependent on imports of machinery in 1988. Like other countries in the category, the United Kingdom continued to lose its market for labour intensive manufactures. While both petroleum and materials changed from being import items in 1965 to export items in 1988, the United Kingdom substantially reduced its import dependence on all four crops during this period.

United States: With the exception of the export item of cereals, the United States ranks with Switzerland as one of the most advanced countries in terms of its patterns of trade. In 1965 it exported both machinery and chemicals, though with far less concentration than Switzerland in these items. In 1988, while the concentration in exports of chemicals remained basically the same, there was a marked swing towards imports of machinery. At the same time, the United States became increasingly dependent on imports of labour and capital intensive manufactures. Its export dependence on cereals was slightly lower in 1988 than in 1965; other nonmanufactured products showed a similar downward shift during this period, except for petroleum, whose import dependence increased greatly during the period.

Some more economies had joined this category by the end of the 1980s.

Canada: Canada was a unique case in that it imported all four manufactured aggregates with a heavy concentration in machinery in 1965. Its major export items in 1965 were materials, forest products and cereals. By 1988 Canada had made a big jump, exporting a marginal quantity of chemicals; the other three manufactured products were still being imported, though import dependence on capital intensive manufactures and machinery had lessened remarkably. Imports of labour intensive manufactures, meanwhile, had increased substantially. Canada's export dependence on cereals was also far lower in 1988 than in 1965, while export dependence on forest products, animals and materials remained more or less constant. The other notable change was Canada's switch from being a net importer to a net exporter of petroleum during this period.

Ireland: Within this category, perhaps the most dramatic changes in commodity composition of trade in manufactures took place in Ireland. In 1965 Ireland imported all four manufactures with a heavy concentration on machinery and, to a lesser extent, capital intensive manufactures and chemicals. However, by 1988 it had started to export all manufactured aggregates except capital intensive manufactures, and even import dependence on capital intensive manufactures had lessened greatly. Ireland's exports of animal products continued to be a major export item among nonmanufactured products. Cereals switched from being an import item in 1965 to an export item in 1988.

Israel: As a latecomer to the group, Israel exported only labour intensive manufactures and imported the other three manufactures, with a heavy concentration in machinery in 1965. In 1988 it was exporting some chemicals and had reduced its import dependence on both capital intensive manufactures and machinery. It had also substantially increased its export dependence on labour intensive manufactures, its major source of export earnings. During the period, the reduction of Israel's import dependence on cereals was also quite substantial, probably due to the adoption of new agricultural technology. For the same reason, animal products had changed from being a net import item to a net export item by 1988.

Norway: Norway was a net exporter of nonmanufactured products in 1965 and a net importer of manufactures, and remained so in 1988. It is included in this category because of its very small net exports of chemicals in 1988. Although its import dependence on capital intensive manufactures and machinery was very much reduced, in 1988 Norway relied on the major export items of petroleum and materials as its chief source of foreign earnings.

Taiwan: Taiwan exported only labour intensive manufactures in 1965; it relied on imports for all other manufactured products, particularly machinery. It also earned export earnings from forest products and tropical products. Tremendous progress has been made in Taiwan since then. By 1988 Taiwan was exporting all manufactured products except chemicals, with a heavy concentration still in labour intensive manufactures and, to a certain degree, in both capital intensive manufactures and machinery. This is evidence of a very substantial increase in industrialisation. By 1988 neither forest products nor tropical products were export items; instead, animal products had become a net export item. Taiwan's import dependence on petroleum and materials had also increased by 1988.

Country group 2: exporters of labour intensive and capital intensive manufactures

The period from the 1960s to the 1980s stands out in world economic history as the time when many developing countries, particularly in East Asia, were taking off in their pursuit of industrialisation. The evidence of this change is seen in the climb of increasing numbers of developing countries up the ladder of development by exporting labour intensive manufactures, which is on the lowest rung of the ladder (see Chapter 3). Some developing countries, particularly the NIEs, had progressed further, becoming suppliers of capital intensive manufactures. The group of exporters of labour intensive and capital intensive manufactures can be further subdivided into the following three categories, ordered by stage of development. First, Austria, Brazil, Belgium–Luxembourg, India, Korea, Portugal, Spain, Turkey and Uruguay were net exporters of capital intensive manufactures in 1965 and 1988. These countries are thought to be ahead of other countries in the same group in the development process and constitute subgroup 1. Second, a few countries exported labour intensive manufactures and imported all other manufactured aggregates in both 1965 and 1988:

China,[3] Yugoslavia and Israel (Israel can be placed here without taking into account its very small exports of chemicals in 1988). These three countries can also be regarded as a subgroup of country group 2. Third, some countries showed evidence of industrialisation by switching from importing to exporting the labour intensive manufactured aggregate: Burma, Sri Lanka, Colombia, Costa Rica, Denmark, the Dominican Republic, Greece, Indonesia, Jamaica, Malaysia, Malta, Mauritius, Mexico, Peru, the Philippines, Singapore and Thailand (subgroup 3). A brief discussion of the key features of each country's trade structure follows.

Subgroup 1

Austria: In 1965, Austria's exports were concentrated in labour intensive and capital intensive manufactures and forest products, and its imports in machinery, raw materials and cereals. By 1988 labour intensive manufactures had become an import item, evidence of movement up the ladder of development. However, upgrading was hindered greatly by the fact that exports of capital intensive manufactures relative to GNP fell substantially and import dependence on machinery increased, even though this was accompanied by slightly reduced dependence on imports of chemicals.

Brazil: Brazil depended in 1965 entirely on exports of nonmanufactured products, with a heavy concentration in exports of tropical products and, to a lesser extent, cereals. In 1988 both labour intensive and capital intensive manufactures were being exported. Brazil's dependence on imports of machinery and in particular chemicals had declined greatly, providing evidence of rapid industrialisation.

Belgium–Luxembourg: In 1965 Belgium–Luxembourg's exports were heavily concentrated in capital intensive manufactures. All nonmanufactures, particularly cereals and materials, were imported. By 1988 it was far less dependent on exports of labour intensive and capital intensive manufactures and at the same time more dependent on imports of machinery and chemicals. The other noteworthy change is Belgium–Luxembourg's switch from being a net importer to a net exporter of both petroleum and animal products.

India: In 1965 India was exporting both labour intensive and capital intensive manufactures with a high concentration in the latter. Other export items included tropical and animal products. However, by 1988 export dependence on labour intensive manufactures had increased greatly and export dependence on capital intensive manufactures had dropped substantially. This may indicate a movement away from the country's export-oriented development strategy during the period. India also had low export earnings from tropical products, animal products, petroleum and materials. The other notable change was India's lower import dependence on cereals in 1988 compared with 1965.

Korea: In 1965 Korea exported only labour intensive manufactures plus some animal products and materials, with heavy import dependence on chemicals, machinery and cereals. By 1988 it was exporting very large amounts of labour intensive manufactures, and capital intensive manufactures had changed from being a net import item to a large net export item. Korea's import dependence on machinery and chemicals also fell during this period. All this was evidence of very substantial progress in industrialisation.

Portugal: In 1965 Portugal had net exports of both labour intensive and capital intensive manufactures and of all crops except cereals; its import items were concentrated in machinery, chemicals, cereals and petroleum. By 1988 it had in fact moved a step backward by switching from exported capital intensive manufactures to imported capital intensive manufactures; import dependence on machinery and chemicals continued to rise. Portugal's main source of export earnings was exports of labour intensive manufactures.

Spain: In 1965 Spain imported all four manufactured aggregates and all nonmanufactured aggregates except tropical products, which was its only source of export earnings. By 1988 it had become substantially industrialised by exporting both labour intensive and capital intensive manufactures and had slightly reduced its dependence on exports of tropical products.

Turkey: Turkey provides another example of rapid industrialisation during the period. In 1965 it imported all four manufactured aggregates, and its export earnings were heavily dependent on cereals, tropical products and animal products. By 1988 the drive to industrialise made it possible to export both labour intensive and capital intensive manufactures. Cereals changed into an import item, and petroleum became another source of export earnings.

Uruguay: Uruguay shows a very similar pattern to that of Turkey. In 1965 Uruguay imported all manufactures and depended heavily on exports of animal products and cereals. By 1988 it had moved up the ladder of development by exporting both labour intensive and capital intensive manufactures; it had also substantially reduced its export dependence on animal products and cereals.

Subgroup 2

China: China was only marginally trade dependent in 1965, with modest exports of labour and capital intensive manufactures and animal products. It was most import dependent on cereals, with modest import dependence on machinery and chemicals. By 1988 it had increased its dependence on exports of labour intensive manufactures significantly and had become a net importer of capital intensive manufactures (a true reflection of its comparative disadvantage in this product category). The continuous process of modernisation and economic reform which started in the late 1970s led to China becoming more trade dependent. On the import side, China's dependence on machinery and chemicals increased tremendously. On the export side, in addition to exports of labour intensive manufactures — China's most important source of export earning — exports of petroleum, animal products, tropical products and materials had become important sources of earnings and were being used to finance large imports of machinery and chemicals. Also by 1988, China's import dependence on cereals had fallen substantially. This in itself is significant given the size of China's population and its relatively limited amount of arable land.

Yugoslavia: Yugoslavia's exports of labour intensive manufactures increased substantially from 1965 to 1988. All other manufactures continued to be imported, with heavy import dependence on machinery. By 1988 all nonmanufactures except cereals had become export items; of these, exports of forest products dominated.

Subgroup 3

Burma: Burma was a net exporter of cereals and forest products in 1965. By 1988, however, cereals had become a net import item (indicating the existence of errors in its agricultural policy). A small amount of exports of labour intensive manufactures gives Burma its place in this category.

Sri Lanka: In 1965 Sri Lanka had a single but substantial export item, tropical products. It was heavily dependent on imports of capital intensive manufactures, machinery and chemicals. By 1988, exports of labour intensive manufactures had surpassed exports of tropical products as Sri Lanka's most important source of export earnings. Its import dependence on capital intensive manufactures and machinery continued to rise.

Colombia: Colombia was basically a supplier of resources in 1965. Its export earnings were derived mainly from tropical products and petroleum. By 1988 it was exporting labour intensive manufactures and a greater quantity of petroleum, materials and animal products, along with its traditional export item of tropical products. As a result, its trade dependence increased greatly during the period.

Costa Rica: Costa Rica is similar to Sri Lanka. In 1965 it was very dependent on exports of tropical products and had some exports of animal products. By 1988 it was exporting labour intensive manufactures, and exports of tropical and animal products continued to rise. Its dependence on imports of other manufactures was lower in 1988 than in 1965.

Denmark: Denmark's single but substantial export item in 1965 was animal products. By 1988 it had moderate exports of labour intensive manufactures. Its dependence on exports of animal products and import dependence on all other manufactures decreased during the period. Also of note is that Denmark had become an exporter of cereals by 1988.

Dominican Republic: The Dominican Republic was a substantial exporter of tropical products in both 1965 and 1988. By 1988 it had become a substantial exporter of labour intensive manufactures. Dependence on imports of machinery and chemicals increased over this period. Dependence on imports of cereals also increased, to an even greater extent.

Greece: In 1965 Greece exported both tropical products and cereals. By 1988 it was exporting labour intensive manufactures, and its import dependence on other manufactures had also decreased. While petroleum switched from being a large import item to a moderate export item, cereals changed from being a fairly large export item to an import item during the period.

Indonesia: Indonesia was not very trade dependent in 1965, but trade dependence increased substantially during the period. In 1988 it was exporting labour intensive manufactures, although nonmanufactures, namely petroleum and materials, still played a key role in generating export earnings.

Jamaica: Jamaica was quite trade dependent in 1965, exporting tropical products and raw materials. By 1988 it was exporting large amounts of labour intensive manufactures, and its export dependence on tropical products had plummeted.

Malaysia: Malaysia was a substantial exporter of forest products, tropical products and materials in both 1965 and 1988. It became a substantial exporter of labour intensive manufactures in 1988. Petroleum and cereals switched from being import items in 1965 to export items in 1988. Malaysia's import dependence on the other three manufactures lessened over this period.

Malta: In 1965 Malta exported only very small quantities of raw materials and ran a large trade deficit. By 1988 it was exporting large amounts of labour intensive manufactures and its import dependence on both manufactures and nonmanufactures had fallen considerably. Petroleum switched from being a significant import item to a moderate export item over the period.

Mauritius: Mauritius was very dependent on imports of manufactures and crops in 1965; its single but very large export item was tropical products. By 1988, although its export dependence on tropical products had decreased, its import dependence on all nonmanufactures had also fallen; more significantly, labour intensive manufactures had become its main export item. Mauritius' import dependence on capital intensive manufactures and machinery continued to rise during the period.

Mexico: Mexico imported all manufactures and exported all nonmanufactures except forest products in 1965. By 1988 it was exporting some labour intensive manufactures. Although exports of petroleum were increasing rapidly throughout the period, cereals changed from being a rather large export item in 1965 to a fairly large import item in 1988. Mexico's import dependence on machinery and chemicals lessened over the period.

Peru: Peru exported only raw materials and tropical products in 1965. By 1988 labour intensive manufactures and petroleum had been added to its items of export. Peru's import dependence on other manufactures, particularly capital intensive manufactures, decreased over the period.

Philippines: The Philippines exported forest products, tropical products and cereals in 1965. By 1988 it was exporting large amounts of labour intensive manufactures. However, traditional export items, such as forest products and tropical products, had decreased substantially, and cereals in fact changed from being a large export item in 1965 to a fairly large import item in 1988.

Singapore: In 1965 Singapore was heavily dependent on imports of manufactures, particularly capital intensive manufactures, machinery and chemicals, as well as on imports of cereals. Its net exports were limited to petroleum and tropical products. By 1988 Singapore was exporting labour intensive manufactures, but it still had a heavy import dependence on capital intensive manufactures and, to a lesser extent, machinery. In addition to exports of tropical products, Singapore had small exports of forest products. Petroleum became a large import item.

Thailand: Thailand was a substantial net exporter of cereals and tropical products in 1965. By 1988 it had become a substantial exporter of labour intensive manufactures. Although export dependence on cereals was very much reduced during the period, Thailand was virtually exporting all nonmanufactures except petroleum in 1988. Dependence on imports of capital intensive manufactures decreased over the period, while dependence on imports of machinery and chemicals increased greatly.

Hong Kong: Hong Kong was highly trade dependent in 1965. Its net exports were completely concentrated in labour intensive manufactures. By 1988 it had become a net importer of virtually everything, with heavy import dependence on capital intensive manufactures, machinery and chemicals.

Country group 3: importers of manufactured commodities

The remaining countries in the sample had net imports of all four manufactured aggregates in both 1965 and 1988. Because this is a rather diverse group of countries in terms of commodity composition of trade, it is separated into two subgroups, diversified countries and specialised countries, the latter group having its export earnings concentrated in one or two commodity categories.

The first subgroup, diversified countries, consists of Australia, Chile, Cyprus, Ecuador, Ghana, Honduras, Iceland, Liberia, New Zealand, Nicaragua, Panama and Paraguay. Within this group, changes in trade patterns were also taking place from the 1960s to the 1980s: some countries changed from being more specialised to being more diversified, while just the opposite occurred in other countries. Some countries with diversified trade structures became even more diversified during the period. In addition, dramatic changes were taking place in some countries in their dependence on imports of various manufactured aggregates over time.

Subgroup 1

Australia: In 1965 Australia was exporting raw materials, tropical products, animal products and cereals with a heavy specialisation in the latter two. Its dependence on imports of manufactures was mainly concentrated in capital intensive manufactures and machinery, and to a lesser extent in labour intensive manufactures and chemicals. In 1988 it was more diversified in the sense that it had added petroleum to its list of export items, and its export concentration in traditional export items had also changed. For example, raw materials had replaced cereals as the main export item, and export dependence on tropical products, animal products and cereals had decreased greatly. Dependence on imports of all manufactures was also reduced, particularly capital intensive manufactures and chemicals.

Chile: In 1965 Chile was a specialised country in the sense that it only exported raw materials and forest products, with a heavy concentration in the former. However, by 1988 it had become much more diversified, exporting all nonmanufactures except petroleum. Dependence on imports of all four manufactures increased over the period.

Cyprus: In contrast to Chile, Cyprus was more diversified in 1965 than in 1988. It exported raw materials, forest products and tropical products in 1965. However, by 1988 it was a net exporter of only raw materials and tropical products and was far less trade dependent. Dependence on imports of manufactures except machinery lessened over the period.

Ecuador: In 1965 Ecuador was a net exporter only of tropical products and animal products with a heavy concentration in the former. In 1988 petroleum together with tropical products and animal products were its main export items.

Ghana: Ghana was quite diversified in 1965, exporting raw materials, forest products and tropical products, with a heavy concentration in the latter. By 1988 it had become even more diversified, adding animal products to its export items and with raw materials replacing tropical products as its main source of export earnings.

Honduras: Honduras was one of the most diversified countries in this group in 1965. It was a net exporter of all nonmanufactures except petroleum, with a heavy concentration in tropical products and substantial exports of cereals. In 1988 Honduras was still diversified, but the number of its net export items had shrunk, with only raw materials, tropical products and animal products being exported.

Iceland: In 1965 Iceland specialised in exporting animal products and cereals. By 1988 it had become more diversified, exporting raw materials as well. This was its second largest export item after animal products.

Liberia: In 1965 Liberia was a net exporter of raw materials and tropical products, with very heavy concentrations in both. By 1988 diversification had taken place, and Liberia was exporting petroleum and forest products as well. Liberia's increasing dependence on imports of labour intensive manufactures suggest that industrialisation had not yet started.

New Zealand: New Zealand's net export items were mainly animal products and cereals plus small amounts of forest products in 1965. By 1988 it was more diversified, having added raw materials and tropical products to its net export items. While its dependence on imports of labour intensive manufactures continued to rise, New Zealand's import dependence on capital intensive manufactures fell substantially during the period.

Nicaragua: Nicaragua was a net exporter of cereals, tropical products, animal products and materials in 1965, with a heavy concentration in the first two. By 1988 tropical products had replaced cereals as the most important export item and raw materials had become an import item. Dependence on imports of petroleum fell during the period.

Panama: In 1965 Panama was a net exporter only of tropical products and animal products. By 1988 export dependence on these two products had risen; at the same time, raw materials became a net export item. Panama's import dependence on labour intensive manufactures also rose continuously during the period.

Paraguay: In 1965 Paraguay was a net exporter of all four agricultural aggregates. It had a fairly high trade dependence on exports of quebracho extract, which is treated as a raw material. By 1988 Paraguay had become less export dependent on exports of agricultural products and more diversified, exporting some raw materials as well. Dependence on imports of labour intensive manufactures continued to rise.

The second subgroup of specialised countries consists of El Salvador, Egypt, Finland, Libya and Venezuela.

El Salvador: In 1965 El Salvador specialised in exporting tropical products and cereals, with rather high trade dependence. By 1988, while it still had large exports of tropical products, cereals had become an import item and El Salvador's specialisation had changed to exports of animal products. Dependence on imports of labour intensive manufactures fell substantially over the period.

Egypt: Egypt also demonstrates changing patterns of export specialisation over time. In 1965 its single export item was cereals; in 1988 it specialised in exporting large quantities of petroleum and some materials. Dependence on imports of all four manufactures increased substantially during the period.

Finland: Finland has a stable pattern of export specialisation over time. It exported forest products and animal products in 1965 and 1988, though export dependence was slightly lower in 1988 than in 1965. With the exception of labour intensive manufactures, Finland's import dependence on all three other manufactures decreased substantially during the period.

Libya: Libya in 1965 specialised in exporting very large quantities of petroleum. By 1988, while petroleum was still its main export item, Libya was also exporting small quantities of materials. Dependence on imports of all four manufactures fell rapidly throughout the period.

Venezuela: Venezuela also has stable patterns of export specialisation, exporting petroleum and raw materials in both 1965 and 1988. Import dependence on all manufactures except chemicals decreased during the period.

Resource abundance profiles

The focus in this section is on whether changes in resource supplies have played an important role in determining the trade patterns discussed in the previous section. More specifically, do countries with similar trade dependence profiles have similar resource abundance profiles, as implied by the Heckscher–Ohlin theorem? Answering the question requires the calculation of the resource abundance ratio $(E_i/E_{wi})/(Y_i/Y_w)$, the ratio of share of resource to GNP share. According to Leamer (1984, p. 103), '[i]f an endowment share E_i/E_{wi} exceeds the GNP share, the country is abundantly supplied in factor *i* compared with other resources on the average, and according to the Heckscher–Ohlin–Vanek theorem, the country's net exports will embody positive amounts of the resource'.

On the basis of these calculations, resource abundance profiles can be formed after the following data transformation has been adopted: if x represents a resource abundance ratio $(E_i/E_{wi})/(Y_i/Y_w)$, or the relative GNP $Y_i/\overline{Y}$, then what is graphed is $z = (5x - 5)/(x + 5)$. This function takes on the value -1 if $x = 0$ and 0 if $x = 1$, and it has an asymptotic value of 5 as x goes to infinity.[4] The correspondence between the numbers in the graphs and the resource ratios is given in Appendix C. In addition, according to Leamer (1984, p. 103): 'In the case of a resource, the graphed value is positive if the resource is abundant in the HOV sense, $E_i/E_{wi} > Y_i/Y_w$. In the case of the GNP variable, the graphed value of SIZE is positive if a country's GNP exceeds average GNP'. Resource abundance profiles accompany trade dependence profiles in Appendix C.[5]

Country group 1: exporters of machinery and chemicals

By definition, capital, which is used most intensively in production of machinery and chemicals, and a highly skilled labour force are the main contributors to exports of machinery and chemicals. In 1965 the countries in this category were generally abundant in CAPITAL and to a lesser extent in LABOUR 1. In many cases, they were relatively scarce in other resources. The CAPITAL abundant countries in 1965 were France, Germany, Italy, Japan, the Netherlands, Sweden, Switzerland and the United Kingdom. By 1988, a number of other countries had joined this group, exporting machinery and chemicals. The following countries were CAPITAL abundant in 1988: France, Germany, Ireland, the Netherlands, Norway, Sweden and Switzerland. Thus five countries — France, Germany, the Netherlands, Sweden and Switzerland — were CAPITAL abundant in both 1965 and 1988, exporting machinery and chemicals.

Land and natural resources were generally scarce in most countries in this group, with a few exceptions. For example, Canada was abundant in LAND 1 and LAND 4 in both years, Ireland was abundant in LAND 3 in both years, Italy was abundant in LAND 2 in 1965, and Sweden was abundant in LAND 4 in 1988. With regard to natural resources, Canada was abundant in MINERALS and OIL in both years, Germany in COAL in 1965, Norway in MINERALS in 1965 and in OIL in 1988, Sweden in MINERALS in both years, the United Kingdom in COAL in 1965, and the United States in COAL in 1988 and in OIL in both years. Scarcity of land and natural resources in these countries largely conforms with the trade patterns observed in the previous section; that is, those countries that have never exported agricultural products (Germany, Switzerland, the United Kingdom) or petroleum and raw materials (Japan, Taiwan) are among those found to be poorest in land and natural resources.

A clear pattern also emerged for the three categories of labour in these countries over time. LABOUR 3, the unskilled labour force, was scarce in all countries (except Taiwan in 1965) in both years. In 1965 some countries were abundant in both LABOUR 1, the highly skilled labour force, and LABOUR 2, the semiskilled labour force. Others were abundant only in LABOUR 1: France, Israel, the Netherlands, Sweden and the United Kingdom. It is surprising to observe that by 1988 all three categories of labour, and especially LABOUR 1 and LABOUR 2, were scarce in most developed countries (the exception being Israel, which was abundant in LABOUR 1 in 1988).[6] In this regard, it may be useful to compare productivity for LABOUR 1 in industrialised countries with that in developing countries; this will be discussed later on. As pointed out by Leamer (1984), a comparison of abundance ratios for the different labour groups within each country may also be meaningful. This is indeed the case: in both 1965 and 1988 all countries in this group were most abundant in highly skilled labour in the sense that LABOUR 1 > LABOUR 2 > LABOUR 3, the only exception being Taiwan, where LABOUR 2 > LABOUR 1 only in 1988. This provides some support for claiming that LABOUR 1, highly skilled labour, plays an important role in determining patterns of trade in machinery and chemicals.

Of the countries in this group that exported machinery and chemicals in 1965, France, Germany, Italy, Japan, the United Kingdom and the United States had larger than average GNP (see the SIZE bar); only the Netherlands, Sweden and Switzerland had a GNP smaller than the overall average. The situation remained the same in 1988; in other words, GNP in those countries that had joined this group by 1988 was still below the world average. Among countries with larger shares, only Italy and Japan increased the SIZE of GNP over the period. In the case of Japan, this increase was enormous.

It should be added that many countries in the other two groups also had a relative abundance of CAPITAL. These countries can be divided into two subgroups using the 1988 data. The first subgroup consists of those countries which exported one or more of the manufactured commodities: China, Costa Rica, the Dominican Republic, Hong Kong, Indonesia, Malaysia, Mauritius, Mexico, Singapore, Turkey, Egypt and Yugoslavia. The other subgroup consists of countries which did not export any of the four manufactured aggregates: Australia, Chile, Ecuador, Libya and Venezuela. A close look at the resource abundance profiles of these countries confirms Leamer's (1984) findings on the patterns of resource supplies in these countries: countries in the first subgroup were relatively abundant in some other resource compared with CAPITAL; and the CAPITAL abundant countries in the second subgroup with no exports of manufactures generally had a very great abundance of land and oil or minerals (for example, Australia, Libya and Chile).

Country group 2: exporters of labour intensive and capital intensive manufactures

The main characteristic that distinguishes countries exporting labour intensive and capital intensive manufactures from exporters of machinery and chemicals is that they are generally abundant in LABOUR. It is interesting and important too to notice that the skill ranking of the three categories of labour for this group of countries is markedly different from that of the last group. The following countries, a majority in this group, had a skill ranking of LABOUR 1 < LABOUR 2 > LABOUR 3 in 1965 and 1988: Brazil, Burma, Sri Lanka, Greece, Jamaica, Korea, Mauritius, Mexico, Peru, the Philippines, Portugal, Spain, Thailand, Turkey and Uruguay. This finding supports the view that different levels of skills in the labour force across countries constitute an important factor in determining their pattern of trade in manufactures; more specifically, LABOUR 2, semiskilled labour, plays the crucial role in determining trade patterns of labour intensive and capital intensive manufactures. This is even more significant if the issue is looked at from a dynamic perspective, namely that the countries involved are upgrading the skills of their labour forces through education and training and, by implication, their potential for exporting more sophisticated manufactured commodities along the path of industrialisation.

Several countries in this group still followed the skill ranking of the last group, namely LABOUR 1 > LABOUR 2 > LABOUR 3. These countries were Austria, Belgium–Luxembourg, Israel, Singapore and Yugoslavia. Among them, Austria was abundant in LABOUR 1 and LABOUR 2 in 1965 but not in 1988. Israel was abundant only in LABOUR 1 in both years. Singapore, like Austria and Yugoslavia, was abundant in LABOUR 1 and LABOUR 2 in both years. There were also a few countries that had just the opposite ranking, namely LABOUR 1 < LABOUR 2 < LABOUR 3. These were, not surprisingly, China, India, the Dominican Republic and Indonesia, the most densely populated countries in the world (apart from the Dominican Republic).

In general, the nonmanufactured products exported by countries in this group are well explained by their resource abundance. For example, Brazil exports cereals, tropical products and forest products because of its abundance of LAND 1, LAND 2 and LAND 4 respectively. China is able to export animal products because of its abundance of LAND 3. Colombia exports oil and raw materials as well as tropical and animal products because of its abundance of OIL, MINERALS, LAND 2 and LAND 3. Greece's exports of tropical products are very much related to its abundance of LAND 2. All nonmanufactured export items from Indonesia and Malaysia are nicely related to the corresponding resource abundance. Mexico exports oil and materials because of its rich endowment of oil and minerals. The Philippines and Thailand are good examples of countries exporting agricultural products based on their abundance of various lands. Sri Lanka exports tropical products because of its very abundant LAND 2. Portugal and Spain use LAND 2 to produce and export tropical products.

Country group 3: importers of manufactured commodities

The central issue for this group of countries is whether 'a shortage of CAPITAL is the explanation for importing all the manufactured commodities' (Leamer 1984, p. 107). In 1965 about half of the countries in this group did have a shortage of capital in the sense that their capital abundance ratios had negative values. However, by 1988 only four (out of 17) countries were scarce in capital, evidence that is hardly in conformity with the above explanation for importing all the manufactured commodities. Again, the issue was re-examined by comparing relative resource abundance, particularly between capital and other resource endowments. It is then found that almost all the countries are far more abundant in LAND than in CAPITAL, and about half of them are more abundant in either MINERALS or OIL than in CAPITAL. It could be that capital scarcity in relative terms may at least partly account for this group's dependence on imports of manufactured commodities.

However, for many countries in this group (Chile, Cyprus, Ecuador, El Salvador, Ghana, Honduras, New Zealand, Nicaragua, Panama, Paraguay, Egypt), CAPITAL abundance did increase over time. Consequently, a declining trend of dependence on imports of labour intensive manufactures was observed in about half of these countries from 1965 to 1988. A common feature in developing countries in this group is the rapid increase in abundance of LABOUR, particularly LABOUR 2 and LABOUR 3. However, the abundance in some of these countries of LABOUR 1 casts some doubt on the definition of this category of labour.[7]

Significantly, nonmanufactured products exported by countries in this group are well explained by these countries' resource abundance since these countries account for a large proportion of trade in nonmanufactured commodities. This and the similar findings mentioned above strongly support the validity of cross-country correlation between net exports of nonmanufactured aggregates and resource endowments, as hypothesised in the previous chapter.

Many countries in this group underwent various degrees of change in their resource profiles during the long time span covered by this study, 1965–88. For example, in Australia there was a declining trend in abundance in all three LABOUR categories as well as CAPITAL; abundance in the four LANDs remained basically the same, but Australia's abundance in COAL and MINERALS increased substantially and OIL in fact switched from being scarce to more abundant. There are many more examples of such changes; they can be seen clearly in Appendix C in the resource abundance profiles for countries in this group.

Cross-country comparison of productivity of key factor endowments

The other criterion for measuring the abundance ratio of a particular factor endowment is to compare its productivity with world average productivity, that is: 'world "productivity" divided by home "productivity" $(Y_w/E_{wi})/(Y_i/E_i)$. For example, if the resource is labour, the abundance ratio is world GNP per worker divided by home country GNP per worker. A country is therefore said to be abundantly supplied in labour if its labour productivity is less than the labour productivity of the world as a whole' (Leamer 1984, p. 103).[8] In other words, $(Y_w/E_{wi})/(Y_i/E_i) > 1$ implies that a country is abundant in *i* since its productivity is less than world productivity on average. If $(Y_w/E_{wi})/(Y_i/E_i) < 1$, then *i*'s productivity in the country concerned is higher than average world productivity, and therefore *i* is relatively scarce.

An international comparative study of the productivity of the most important factor endowments of land, labour and capital (CAPITAL, LABOUR 1, LABOUR 2 and LAND 1) will be carried out in order to see whether this approach can, from a different perspective, describe the relative abundance of these four factors across countries for a given year. Research of this type is of significance in that it provides another dimension for examining how efficiently each country utilises its basic factor endowments. It can only provide a broad picture of the productivity of the four categories of factor endowments, however, as the data are assembled at highly aggregated levels.

Table 4.1 reports the results of calculations of world productivity divided by home productivity of the four factor endowments for selected countries.[9] The first point to note is that productivity of CAPITAL underwent quite substantial changes from 1965 to 1988. The directions of these changes varied across different categories of countries, but a clear pattern or, more specifically, reversals in the trends of such changes can be observed. For example, in 1965 most developing countries in the table had ratios of less than one, indicating a high productivity of capital that reflected, according to the explanation given above, the relative scarcity of capital in developing countries at that time. By contrast, most developed countries, particularly in Western Europe, had ratios larger than one, suggesting just the opposite. Furthermore, from 1965 to 1988, the changes in ratios for these two country groups evolved in two general directions. The trend in most developing countries was for ratios to increase, mostly above one. This meant that declining productivity of capital was accompanied by increasing capital abundance in those countries, presumably as a result of rapid capital accumulation (see Table 3.13). Most developed countries, meanwhile, experienced declines in their ratios, though in most cases the ratios remained above one. It would seem that, compared with 1965, capital abundance in these countries had decreased, perhaps due to relatively slow accumulation of capital during the period (Table 3.13). There was a trend for productivity of capital to increase in developed countries, but this increase was not substantial: these countries' productivity of capital was still below the world average.

Second, without exception, the productivity of both LABOUR 1 and LABOUR 2 in developed countries increased from 1965 to 1988, reflecting a decline in abundance in these two labour categories during the period. However, the starting points of these two categories as well as their degree of decline differed. In 1965, for example, LABOUR 1 in developed countries was already relatively more abundant than LABOUR 2. Even with declines in both ratios, in 1988 the ratios for LABOUR 1 were in general higher than those for LABOUR 2: developed countries were still relatively more abundant in LABOUR 1 than in LABOUR 2 at the end of the 1980s.[10]

A similar trend was observed in other economies (Hong Kong, Brazil, Israel, Korea, Singapore, Taiwan, Thailand), indicating that they too were experiencing declining abundance in their labour forces. In Korea and Taiwan, these changes were substantial. In fact, the current labour shortages, particularly of professional and skilled labour, in some of these economies seem to confirm the trend of declining labour abundance. Some densely populated developing countries (Burma, China, Colombia, Egypt, Ghana, India, Indonesia, Mexico, Peru and, to a lesser extent, Argentina, Chile, Panama, the Philippines and Turkey), not surprisingly demonstrated different patterns with regard to changes in labour abundance over this period of time. The feature common to all these countries is that abundance in both categories of labour increased over time. For countries like Burma, China, India, Indonesia and Ghana, the increase was dramatic.

Third, as with capital and labour, changes in the productivity of LAND 1 (arable land) showed a mixed picture across countries from 1965 to 1988. In 1965 the ratio of productivity for LAND 1 in most European countries was already lower than one, indicating high productivity and lower abundance of arable land. By 1988, with the exception of a couple of countries, the ratio was even lower: these countries had become even less abundant in arable land. By contrast, the trend in countries in both North and South America (except Mexico) and in Africa was for abundance in arable land to increase. For countries like Argentina, Chile, Peru and Ghana, this increase was quite large. Abundance in arable land increased in some Asian countries (Burma, China, India, Indonesia, Malaysia, the Philippines and Turkey) and decreased in others. The reduction in abundance of arable land in Korea and Taiwan was quite substantial during this period. In Oceania, while Australia's abundance of arable land increased, New Zealand's decreased slightly over the same period.

In summary, some generalisations may be made from the discussion in this chapter. First, the principal findings are generally consistent with Leamer's. More specifically, trade dependence and resource abundance profiles for country groupings suggest that there is for the most part a close link between trade patterns, particularly in nonmanufactured goods, and resource endowments. In other words, countries with similar trade dependence profiles tend to have similar resource abundance profiles. A noticeable change is that, in comparison with Leamer's results, the number of countries in the group of exporters of labour intensive and capital intensive manufactures had become much larger by the end of the 1980s, indicating that comparative advantage was shifting with respect to labour and, to some extent, capital among different types of countries during this period. This, of course, also indicates that great progress was being made in the process of industrialisation and that an increasing share of world trade was dominated by trade in manufactured commodities.

Second, shifting comparative advantage was also taking place at a deeper level, namely with respect to capital and skilled labour. For example, with regard to net exports of manufactures, the trade dependence profiles show that most developed countries plus some NIEs are the main suppliers of the top three manufactured commodities, namely capital intensive manufactures, machinery and chemicals. The profiles also show that from 1965 to 1988 there was a general trend for net exports of manufactures from developed countries to decline. The exceptions were chemicals in the Netherlands and Switzerland, capital intensive manufactures and machinery in Sweden and machinery in Japan. On the other hand, some developing countries, particularly NIEs, became more dependent on exports of manufactures. These economies include Taiwan, Turkey, Korea, Brazil and Argentina. Not only that, a similar trend reflecting shifting comparative advantage can be identified in other developing countries; that is, there was a trend for import dependence on manufactures in some developing countries to decline. These countries include Ghana, Greece, Malaysia, Mexico, Peru, Singapore and Uruguay.

Table 4.1 Cross-country comparison of productivity of key factor endowments in selected countries, 1965 and 1988

	CAPITAL		LABOUR 1		LABOUR 2		LAND 1	
Country	1965	1988	1965	1988	1965	1988	1965	1988
Asia								
Burma	0.18	0.46	7.49	7.28	11.47	21.88	13.91	22.29
China	0.25	2.85	0.73	12.67	6.75	15.76	3.46	4.69
Hong Kong	1.60	1.30	2.14	0.56	1.71	0.56	0.02	0.00
India	0.59	1.24	3.51	4.47	3.16	6.62	6.90	11.80
Indonesia	0.05	2.57	0.49	3.78	0.48	8.83	0.30	4.03
Israel	1.10	0.84	1.33	1.24	0.50	0.40	0.20	0.15
Japan	1.70	0.95	1.61	0.31	1.59	0.29	0.13	0.03
Korea	1.01	1.18	4.10	0.96	6.28	1.30	1.50	0.22
Malaysia	0.84	1.76	2.23	2.18	1.31	1.87	0.38	0.60
Philippines	0.85	1.27	3.49	3.95	4.26	6.36	1.79	2.20
Singapore	0.75	1.76	1.26	0.80	1.01	0.55	0.01	0.00
Thailand	0.77	1.23	2.45	2.04	7.32	6.30	6.14	5.93
Turkey	0.75	1.46	1.94	2.26	2.26	3.52	6.10	6.81
Taiwan	0.84	0.75	3.39	0.63	3.14	0.86	0.65	0.11
North America								
Canada	0.89	0.99	0.75	0.64	0.36	0.34	1.83	1.83
Mexico	0.90	1.52	1.12	1.79	1.13	2.14	2.59	2.58
Panama	0.76	1.35	1.30	2.70	1.16	2.14	1.50	1.86
United States	0.70	0.71	0.60	0.54	0.29	0.31	0.57	0.73
South America								
Argentina	1.33	1.67	1.17	1.41	0.96	1.71	2.01	5.80
Brazil	0.88	0.92	1.68	1.50	1.84	1.62	2.15	3.67
Chile	0.70	1.37	1.07	2.21	1.01	2.75	1.47	3.82
Colombia	0.85	1.26	1.95	3.72	1.73	3.04	1.38	1.99
Peru	1.38	1.31	1.18	2.98	1.21	3.06	1.00	2.64
Africa								
Egypt	0.44	1.47	3.58	6.49	1.05	1.62	1.02	1.33
Ghana	1.04	1.24	1.63	5.81	1.08	4.00	0.90	4.26
Europe								
Austria	1.75	1.11	1.34	0.55	1.06	0.36	0.39	0.21
Belg.–Lux.	1.20	1.06	0.91	0.58	0.61	0.33	0.12	0.09
Denmark	1.61	0.91	1.16	0.83	0.64	0.32	0.60	0.47
Finland	1.56	0.98	1.13	0.80	0.73	0.28	0.74	0.45
France	1.35	1.12	1.01	0.53	0.58	0.34	0.43	0.36
Germany, W.	1.77	1.02	0.94	0.49	0.66	0.31	0.15	0.11
Greece	0.93	1.05	1.11	1.22	1.48	0.87	1.06	1.04
Iceland	1.30	0.97	0.48	0.36	0.41	0.30	0.00	0.03
Ireland	1.18	1.20	1.74	0.99	1.17	0.62	1.05	0.64
Italy	1.84	0.96	0.93	0.46	0.87	0.36	0.45	0.21
Netherlands	2.11	1.07	1.06	0.81	0.61	0.31	0.11	0.08
Norway	2.14	1.41	0.89	0.71	0.59	0.27	0.26	0.18
Portugal	1.28	1.24	1.32	1.07	1.73	1.30	2.14	0.94
Spain	1.49	1.05	1.13	0.51	1.34	0.53	1.53	0.87
Sweden	1.51	1.15	1.32	0.94	0.43	0.26	0.34	0.31
Switzerland	2.25	1.09	0.84	0.36	0.52	0.21	0.06	0.04
United Kingdom	1.26	0.89	1.31	0.76	0.70	0.42	0.16	0.16
Yugoslavia	1.50	3.86	2.14	2.99	1.59	2.53	1.41	2.67
Oceania								
Australia	1.47	1.14	1.08	0.49	0.61	0.44	3.22	3.74
New Zealand	0.99	1.14	1.04	0.77	0.53	0.50	0.29	0.24

Third, it is clear that the trade dependence profiles provide a good reference for examining the composition of trade, degree of trade dependence and trade imbalance of the 61 economies included in the study during the period 1965–88.

Fourth, developed countries, with the exception of a few resource-rich countries (Australia, Canada and, to a lesser extent, New Zealand), had quite similar resource abundance profiles. In other words, these countries had a scarcity of most resources including labour and were relatively abundant in capital, though this abundance in general tended to decline during the period. This may imply that capital (plus skilled labour, abundant in relative terms) was a major factor contributing to developed countries' comparative advantage in most sophisticated manufactured commodities; the trend towards a decline in capital abundance in developed countries is consistent with the shifting comparative advantage that took place throughout the period, as described above. Further evidence for this is that capital abundance in many developing countries, particularly relatively advanced ones, did increase during the period. As for developing countries, while their patterns of resource supplies varied, in general it would seem that the trade patterns of their resource commodities were well explained by their resource endowments.

Finally, cross-country comparison of productivity in key factor endowments provides another useful way of examining factor abundance. Several important findings have emerged regarding the productivity and abundance of CAPITAL. Cross-country abundance of capital is basically consistent with the results of the resource abundance profiles. The results are also largely consistent with the trends for capital accumulation, particularly in the form of capital/labour ratios as described in Chapter 3. The findings, although based on highly aggregated data, still verify the commonly accepted principle that the productivity of a particular factor tends to decline with a rapid increase in that factor. The results also reveal differences between developed and developing countries in terms of changing patterns of the productivity of CAPITAL during a significant period in world economic history.

The increase in abundance of LABOUR 1 and LABOUR 2 in many developing countries from 1965 to 1988 is consistent with the high growth rates for skilled labour in developing countries reported in Chapter 3. Clearly, in their pursuit of industrial growth, developing countries have made tremendous efforts to train and educate their populations during the period. A reduction in abundance of these two categories of labour coincides with labour shortages in densely populated areas such as the Asian NIEs. It can be anticipated that international migration will take place on a larger scale in areas experiencing rapid economic growth, driven by high demand for skilled labour.

Although the results in this chapter provide further evidence for a link between patterns of trade and factor endowments as implied by the Heckscher–Ohlin theorem, a full examination of the relationship requires multiple regression analysis. This will be taken up in Chapter 6. Chapter 5 will focus on trade in factor services and related issues from both a theoretical and empirical perspective, and have more to say about factor abundance, particularly in a cross-country setting.

5 Factor content of trade and factor abundance

An objective of this book is to provide empirical evidence for examining trade in factor services derived from the Heckscher–Ohlin–Vanek (HOV) model. The aims of analysis in this chapter are, first, to measure the relative abundance of factor endowments across factors and across countries,[1] and second, to discuss the implications of these measurements for trade in factor services. In addition, the discussion may shed light on controversial issues surrounding the Leontief Paradox. The chapter is organised as follows. Following on from Chapter 2, the first section presents empirical results for the United States using direct measures of factor endowments, factor endowments embodied in net exports and factor endowments embodied in consumption. The second section examines relative factor abundance in a cross-country setting and discusses implications for the 'Leontief type' argument. This section also carries out sign tests based on the HOV model.

Trade-revealed factor abundance in the United States

The issue addressed here is how to view the linkage between resource abundance or scarcity and the signs of net export flows of factor services (with the emphasis on capital and labour). For this purpose, the case of the United States will be examined in a three factor and multifactor context.[2] The factor content of trade theory as introduced in Chapter 2 suggests that the causes of international trade can be attributed primarily to differences in factor endowments between countries. The 11 resource variables used here are capital, three categories of labour, four categories of land, and minerals, coal and oil. (These variables were defined in Chapter 3.) The three factors used are capital, labour and land. The latter two are simply the summation of different categories of labour and land.

Following the three criteria introduced in Chapter 2 for ranking factors according to their relative abundance, Table 5.1 presents the results for capital, labour and land in production, net exports and consumption. The three years covered are 1965, 1974 and 1988. There are several ways of looking at the figures in this table. First, as mentioned in Chapter 2, abundance ranking among factors may be established by ranking factors according to their total content in net exports relative to consumption; that is, $K_T/L_T > K_c/L_c$ for a country which is an exporter of both labour and capital services to be relatively capital abundant, and $K_T/L_T < K_c/L_c$ for an importer of both capital and labour services to be relatively capital abundant. The figures show that the United States was an importer of both capital and labour services in all three years; therefore, if $K_T/L_T < K_c/L_c$, the United States would be relatively capital abundant compared with labour. This is indeed the case (see column B compared with column C for capital/labour in Table 5.1).

Table 5.1 Capital intensity (US$ thousand), labour intensity (thousands of people) and land intensity (thousands of hectares) of production, trade and consumption in the United States, 1965, 1974 and 1988

	Production $K_i\ L_i\ D_i$	Net exports $K_T\ L_T\ D_T$	Consumption $K_c\ L_c\ D_c$			
Factor	*A*	*B*	*C*	*A vs C*	*B vs C*	*B vs A*
1965						
Capital	1 384 608	-584 920	1 969 528	<	<	<
Labour	69 877	-327 101	397 008	<	<	<
Land	749 166	-1 097 154	1 846 320	<	<	<
Capital/labour	19.8	1.8	5.0	>	<	<
Land/labour	10.7	3.4	4.7	>	<	<
Capital/land	1.8	0.5	1.1	>	<	<
Labour/land	0.1	0.3	0.2	<	>	>
1974						
Capital	2 017 665	-940 278	2 957 943	<	<	<
Labour	94 645	-307 079	401 724	<	<	<
Land	720 800	-875 406	1 596 206	<	<	<
Capital/labour	21.3	3.1	7.4	>	<	<
Land/labour	7.6	2.9	4.0	>	<	<
Capital/land	2.8	1.1	1.9	>	<	<
Labour/land	0.1	0.4	0.3	<	>	>
1988						
Capital	2 913 986	-1 304 001	4 217 987	<	<	<
Labour	121 074	-409 768	530 842	<	<	<
Land	696 570	-799 877	1 496 447	<	<	<
Capital/labour	24.1	3.2	7.9	>	<	<
Land/labour	5.8	2.0	2.8	>	<	<
Capital/land	4.2	1.6	2.8	>	<	<
Labour/land	0.2	0.5	0.4	<	>	>

Similarly, capital is relatively more abundant than land and land is relatively more abundant than labour in the United States. Thus these three factor endowments in the United States can be ranked as capital > land > labour, a pattern that has remained unchanged throughout the entire period. (*A vs C* and *B vs A* basically reflect the cases of $K_i/L_i > K_c/L_c$ and $K_T/L_T > K_i/L_i$ respectively, essentially leading to the same results.) Therefore, no Leontief Paradox is evident in Table 5.1.

Second, Table 5.1 reveals the changing patterns of capital/labour, land/labour, capital/land and labour/land embodied in production, net exports and consumption over time. For example, capital/labour embodied in production, net exports and consumption tended to increase during the period under study. However, while the growth rate of capital/labour embodied in production accelerated during the two sub-periods 1965–74 and 1974–88, capital/labour embodied in net exports and consumption increased rapidly from 1965 to 1974 and at a slower rate than production from 1974 to 1988. In fact, capital/labour embodied in net exports and in consumption did not change greatly after 1974. Table 5.1 indicates that the trend for capital/labour embodied in net exports and consumption to increase was not matched by overall increases in capital/labour in the economy. This may mean that during this period the US export sector was left behind in terms of per capita capital input in comparison with the overall economy. This finding is important in that it suggests that using capital/labour embodied in net exports or trade as an indicator of the state of overall capital/labour in the economy may be inappropriate.

Further examination of various other ratios indicates that land/labour embodied in production, net exports and consumption declined over the period while capital/land increased substantially. This suggests that in general agricultural production in the United States became more capital intensive during the period.

Third, the fact that the United States remained an importer of labour services ($L_T < 0$) throughout the period suggests that the paradoxical result reported by Brecher and Choudhri (1982a) of the United States exporting labour services is a special case. It is not necessary, therefore, to conclude that one or more of the assumptions of the basic model should be relaxed.

Fourth, the abundance ordering of capital > land > labour referred to earlier conforms to the ordering of US shares of world capital, K_i/K_w (28, 23 and 21 per cent in 1965, 1974 and 1988 respectively) and world labour, L_i/L_w (7, 8 and 7 per cent in 1965, 1974 and 1988 respectively),[3] namely $K_i/K_w > L_i/L_w$. These results confirm the relative abundance of capital over labour in the United States according to the definition of factor abundance provided by Leamer (1980, p. 497): 'Capital in country *i* is said to be abundant in comparison with labour if and only if the share of the world's capital stock located in *i* exceeds the share of the world's labour force: $K_i/K_w > L_i/L_w$'. The results also lead to acceptance of the Heckscher–Ohlin theorem on the basis of these rankings. However, the US share of world income, Y_i/Y_w (39, 33 and 30 per cent in 1965, 1974 and 1988 respectively) exceeds its share of world capital, suggesting that there could be a scarcity of capital in the United States as measured by the right-hand side of equation (2.4) in Chapter 2.[4]

Finally, the fact that the United States remained an importer of both labour and capital services ($L_T < 0$ and $K_T < 0$) throughout the period can be regarded as a case of a 'sufficiently large' trade deficit, according to Aw (1983). It follows that $K_i/K_w > L_i/L_w$ if $K_T/L_T < K_i/L_i$. As Table 5.1 shows, that is also the case.

One factor which affects the above analysis is the issue of trade imbalance. As argued by Casas and Choi (1985), it is possible for a country with a trade deficit to import the services of an abundant resource, or conversely for a country with a trade surplus to export the services of a scarce factor. Therefore, it would seem appropriate to consider the effects of balanced and imbalanced trade on factor abundance ranking. A multifactor case for the United States in 1965 and 1988 is considered in order to provide a clearer picture of the ranking of factor abundance (Table 5.2).

Table 5.2 Total factor endowments, net exports[a] and factor abundance rankings in the United States, 1965 and 1988 (millions of US dollars/people/hectares)

Factor	E_i	E_{t^*}	E_t	E_{t^*}/E_i	Rank	E_t/E_i	Rank
1965							
Capital	1 384.61	-601.04	-584.92	-0.43	3	-0.42	3
Labour 1	7.55	-5.05	-4.95	-0.67	5	-0.66	5
Labour 2	61.63	-153.38	-151.64	-2.49	9	-2.46	9
Labour 3	0.70	-171.94	-170.54	-246.33	11	-244.33	11
Land 1	178.45	-136.10	-133.55	-0.76	6	-0.75	6
Land 2	1.88	-21.18	-20.99	-11.28	10	-11.18	10
Land 3	261.24	-355.37	-350.37	-1.36	7	-1.34	7
Land 4	307.60	-599.62	-592.25	-1.95	8	-1.93	8
Minerals	3 220.46	-1 605.60	-1 566.45	-0.50	4	-0.49	4
Coal	2 114.31	-433.85	-413.17	-0.21	2	-0.20	2
Oil	2 816.40	452.71	471.89	0.16	1	0.17	1
1988							
Capital	2 913.99	-1 173.92	-1 304.00	-0.40	4	-0.45	4
Labour 1	18.52	-16.04	-17.14	-0.87	5	-0.93	5
Labour 2	101.94	-227.06	-237.53	-2.23	9	-2.33	9
Labour 3	0.61	-150.30	-155.10	-248.43	11	-256.37	11
Land 1	187.88	-70.66	-78.89	-0.38	3	-0.42	3
Land 2	2.03	-19.81	-20.51	-9.74	10	-10.08	10
Land 3	241.47	-277.08	-293.58	-1.15	6	-1.22	6
Land 4	265.19	-386.18	-406.91	-1.46	8	-1.53	8
Minerals	6 637.17	-9 039.51	-9 538.40	-1.36	7	-1.44	7
Coal	29 799.95	4 177.51	3 362.19	0.14	2	0.11	2
Oil	69 840.37	27 840.30	26 503.84	0.40	1	0.38	1

Note: a E_{t^*} is net export of factor services based on $AT_i = E_i - \alpha_i E_w$ where α_i is country i's share of world income, namely Y_i/Y_w, and E_t is obtained from $AT_i = E_i - E_w(Y_i - B_i)/Y_w$, where B_i is overall trade balance.

Table 5.2 shows total factor endowments, net exports and factor abundance of 11 resource endowments in the United States in 1965 and 1988. The results show clearly that in 1965 oil, coal, capital, minerals, skilled labour and arable land are revealed by trade to be the most abundant factors in the United States according to Leamer's criterion that any factor exported net is more abundant than any factor imported net (Leamer 1980; see also Chapter 2). By 1988 the factor abundance ranking is as follows: oil, coal, arable land, capital and skilled labour. However, only oil in 1965 and coal and oil in 1988 are truly abundant, as shown by their positive signs.[5] Oil was revealed to be more abundant in both years.

It can also be seen that all factors except oil in 1965 and oil and coal in 1988, including capital and the different categories of labour, were net imported in both years. Ranking of factor abundance in terms of net exports of factor services under the condition that the country is an importer of most of its factor services is achieved by ranking the magnitude of net exports of these factor services. Hence capital in the United States was relatively more abundant than different categories of labour in both years. Although the ranking of different categories of labour did not change during the period, highly skilled labour had a clear lead over the other two categories of labour (semiskilled and unskilled workers). These two categories of labour and tropical land were at the bottom of the ranking in both years, suggesting the importance of human capital (education) in determining trade patterns in the United States.

The effect of trade imbalance on the ranking of factor abundance is examined simply by comparing the difference between net exports of factor services obtained first with and then without total trade imbalance adjustment, and then to see whether ranking is affected. As shown in Table 5.2, when relative factor abundance is ranked according to the ratio of factor services embodied in net exports over factor endowments (E_{t*}/E_i), adjustment for trade imbalance does not affect factor abundance ranking.

A cross-country setting for factor abundance ranking

It can be seen from the survey in Chapter 2 that most studies of factor abundance ranking in the framework of the Heckscher–Ohlin model focus on a single country, in most cases the United States. These single-country studies provide much insight into the issues under study. However, it may not be appropriate to apply their results to multicountry analysis. In order to obtain a more comprehensive picture of factor abundance ranking, it is worth trying to carry out a cross-country study using the same Heckscher–Ohlin framework, provided that direct measures of cross-country factor endowments are available. This section is directed to this purpose. It is hoped that the results obtained from using these measures and comparing changes over time will provide a wider spectrum for generalisations regarding cross-country comparison of factor abundance.

The Leontief-type argument concerning factor abundance can proceed with a larger number of countries and more factors. For discussion of the issue in a cross-country setting, 41 economies have been selected from the 61 sample countries. The case of two factors, capital and labour, will be discussed first.

Tables 5.3 and 5.4 show cross-country abundance of capital and labour in 1965 and 1988, based on information about capital/labour ratios and capital, labour and GNP shares, and a comparison of capital/labour embodied in net exports and capital/labour embodied in consumption.

The following four criteria will be used to examine the results reported in these two tables. First, factor abundance defined as $K_i/K_w > L_i/L_w$ is employed to compare a country's share of world capital and its share of world labour force. Second, $K_i/(K_i - K_T) > L_i/(L_i - L_T)$, the necessary and sufficient condition for trade to reveal an abundance of capital, is applied to the data. Third, either K_i/K_w (country i's world share of capital) or L_i/L_w (country i's world share of labour) is compared with Y_i/Y_w (country i's world share of GNP). Finally, K_T/L_T (capital/labour embodied in net exports) is compared with K_i/L_i (country i's capital/labour ratio).

The four criteria, subject to sign patterns of net exports of capital and labour services, are applied under the following four conditions, namely whether country i is a net exporter of both factor services (CASE 1), a net importer of both factor services (CASE 2), a net exporter of capital services and a net importer of labour services (CASE 3) or a net importer of capital services and a net exporter of labour services (CASE 4). The consistency of outcomes will be a focus of the following discussion.

As shown in Table 5.3, clear differences emerge between developed and developing countries with regard to the signs of net exports of capital and labour services in 1965. For example, of the 41 selected countries (19 developed countries and 22 developing economies), 14 developed countries are in CASE 3, namely net exporters of capital services and net importers of labour services, 11 developing economies are in CASE 4, namely net exporters of labour services and net importers of capital services, and another five developing economies are in CASE 2, namely net importers of both factor services. It would seem that developed countries are indeed more capital abundant in general than developing countries.[6] This can be verified by applying the above-mentioned four criteria.

Most countries are in CASE 3 or CASE 4, where net exports of capital services and net exports of labour services are opposite in sign. According to Corollary 3 in Leamer (1980) (see also Chapter 2), these two cases represent the situation under which the Leontief criterion (1954), namely capital per person embodied in exports K_x/L_x and capital per person embodied in imports K_m/L_m in country i, can be compared with country i's world share of capital K_i/K_w and with its world share of labour L_i/L_w. In this way, the Leontief-type argument can be applied in a cross-country setting, making it possible to judge from a wider perspective whether the Leontief Paradox has been resolved or is still with us.

Table 5.3 Relative abundance of capital and labour, 1965[a]

Country	K_T	L_T	$K_i/(K_i\text{-}K_T)$	$L_i/(L_i\text{-}L_T)$	K_T/L_T	K_i/L_i	K_i/K_w	L_i/L_w	Y_i/Y_w
Argentina	21 039	-4 727	1.346	0.614	-4.451	10.874	1.6	0.7	1.2
Australia	30 026	-8 609	1.450	0.361	-3.488	19.939	1.9	0.5	1.3
Austria	18 770	-2 358	1.661	0.588	-7.960	14.002	0.9	0.3	0.5
Belg.–Lux.	10 369	-6 546	1.205	0.358	-1.584	16.721	1.2	0.4	1.0
Brazil	-6 675	9 676	0.896	1.746	-0.690	2.547	1.1	2.2	1.3
Canada	-15 061	-22 753	0.896	0.222	0.662	19.987	2.6	0.6	2.9
China	-159 794	323 896	0.253	8.514	-0.493	0.147	1.1	36.3	4.3
Colombia	-2 142	1 919	0.866	1.597	-1.116	2.689	0.3	0.5	0.3
Denmark	16 204	-3 923	1.529	0.365	-4.130	20.805	0.9	0.2	0.6
Egypt	-9 493	4 615	0.414	2.413	-2.057	0.852	0.1	0.8	0.3
Finland	12 314	-2 787	1.515	0.422	-4.418	17.820	0.7	0.2	0.5
France	97 102	-37 222	1.343	0.348	-2.609	19.170	7.6	2.0	5.6
Germany, W	253 535	-40 013	1.777	0.392	-6.336	22.507	11.5	2.5	6.5
Greece	-3 456	-350	0.825	0.912	9.881	4.488	0.3	0.4	0.3
Hong Kong	1 321	-44	1.178	0.971	-29.920	6.020	0.2	0.1	0.1
Iceland	401	-222	1.279	0.235	-1.807	27.044	0.0	0.0	0.0
India	-62 191	158 946	0.577	6.365	-0.391	0.450	1.7	18.6	2.9
Indonesia	-243 174	-15 134	0.051	0.707	16.068	0.361	0.3	3.6	5.1
Ireland	178	-718	1.020	0.609	-0.248	8.308	0.2	0.1	0.2
Israel	-190	-1 526	0.983	0.330	0.124	14.777	0.2	0.1	0.2
Italy	150 955	-16 377	1.838	0.549	-9.218	16.618	6.6	2.0	3.6
Japan	181 598	-3 847	1.702	0.926	-47.205	9.119	8.8	4.8	5.2
Korea	-715	6 752	0.924	4.549	-0.106	1.008	0.2	0.9	0.2
Malaysia	-973	841	0.878	1.522	-1.157	2.863	0.1	0.2	0.2
Mexico	-7 044	-541	0.880	0.954	13.012	4.576	1.0	1.1	1.1
Netherlands	60 462	-7 888	2.011	0.346	-7.665	28.855	2.4	0.4	1.1
New Zealand	-329	-2 203	0.979	0.318	0.149	15.291	0.3	0.1	0.3
Norway	20 698	-3 068	1.933	0.314	-6.747	30.507	0.9	0.1	0.4
Peru	5 062	319	1.364	1.114	15.864	6.075	0.4	0.3	0.3
Philippines	-2 891	7 971	0.834	3.264	-0.363	1.268	0.3	1.1	0.3
Portugal	2 080	1 000	1.173	1.413	2.080	4.119	0.3	0.3	0.2
Singapore	-1484	-244	0.587	0.663	6.080	4.392	0.0	0.0	0.1
Spain	26 971	-2 938	1.373	0.798	-9.181	8.532	2.0	1.1	1.3
Sweden	30 689	-9 291	1.486	0.271	-3.303	27.217	1.9	0.3	1.2
Switzerland	48 801	-6 106	2.141	0.291	-7.992	36.447	1.8	0.2	0.8
Taiwan	-1 592	2 078	0.809	2.239	-0.766	1.792	0.1	0.4	0.2
Thailand	-3 124	11 407	0.741	5.695	-0.274	0.645	0.2	1.4	0.2
Turkey	-6 415	8 636	0.740	2.735	-0.743	1.342	0.4	1.3	0.5
United Kingdom	65 651	-34 733	1.222	0.417	-1.890	14.534	7.2	2.5	5.7
United States	-584 920	-327 131	0.703	0.176	1.788	19.815	27.6	6.9	39.5
Yugoslavia	16 799	1 295	1.481	1.184	12.974	6.205	1.0	0.8	0.7

Note: a K_T/L_T is capital/labour embodied in net exports; K_i/L_i is capital/labour embodied in production K_i/K_w is country *i*'s share of world capital stock and L_i/L_w is its share of world labour; Y_i/Y_w is share of world income. (K_i/K_w, L_i/L_w and Y_i/Y_w are expressed as a percentage.)

K_i/K_w can be compared with L_i/L_w simply by applying the first criterion above. It is found that $K_i/K_w > L_i/L_w$ is observed for all countries, the majority of them developed countries, in CASE 3. In addition, without exception $K_i/K_w < L_i/L_w$ is demonstrated for all countries in CASE 4, all of them developing economies. These findings are important because they suggest that capital per person embodied in exports K_x/L_x exceeds capital per person embodied in imports K_m/L_m for the former group of countries, and capital per person embodied in exports K_x/L_x is below capital per person embodied in imports K_m/L_m for the latter group. These findings support the view that no Leontief Paradox is evident in such a cross-country setting.

However, the argument used by Aw (1983), introduced in Chapter 2, complicates the above discussion a little. Aw argues that when there is a 'sufficiently large' trade surplus so that $K_T > 0$ and $L_T > 0$ (CASE 1) and when there is a 'sufficiently large' trade deficit so that $K_T < 0$ and $L_T < 0$ (CASE 2), $K_x/L_x > K_m/L_m$ does not imply $K_i/K_w > L_i/L_w$. The argument raises several issues with respect to relative factor abundance: First, as Aw's argument excludes CASE 3 and CASE 4, the above discussion is still relevant for these two cases. Second, the question of how to deal with CASE 1 and CASE 2 remains. The critical point here is that it is the link between $K_x/L_x > K_m/L_m$ and $K_i/K_w > L_i/L_w$ and not K_i/K_w and L_i/L_w which is of concern with CASE 1 and CASE 2. In this discussion, capital/labour embodied in net exports K_T/L_T will be compared with capital/labour embodied in production K_i/L_i, since Aw identifies this as the theoretically correct comparison when there is a 'sufficiently large' trade surplus or deficit (see also Chapter 2).

In 1965, although only a few countries are in CASE 1 and CASE 2, which are the cases that Aw's argument focuses on, conflicting results emerge. For example, of only three countries in CASE 1, $K_T/L_T > K_i/L_i$ for two and $K_T/L_T < K_i/L_i$ for one. Of eight countries in CASE 2, $K_T/L_T > K_i/L_i$ for four and $K_T/L_T < K_i/L_i$ for the other four. This shows that $K_T > 0$, $L_T > 0$ and $K_T < 0$, $L_T < 0$ are indeed compatible either with $K_i/K_w > L_i/L_w$ or $K_i/K_w < L_i/L_w$ as argued by Aw, and the Leontief-type measure, namely K_x/L_x and K_m/L_m, may not be used under such circumstances.

In principle, the first and second criteria are equivalent.[7] The latter is used here as an independent measure simply to examine its empirical validity since it involves separate measures such as $K_i - K_T$ and $L_i - L_T$. These are, respectively, equivalent to K_c, capital embodied in consumption, and L_c, labour embodied in consumption. Table 5.3 lists the results which, as expected, conform with those obtained using the first criterion; thus $K_i/(K_i - K_T) > L_i/(L_i - L_T)$ for all countries in CASE 3 and $K_i/(K_i - K_T) < L_i/(L_i - L_T)$ for all countries in CASE 4.

Application of the third criterion also leads to some significant findings. First, according to the right-hand side of equation (2.5) in Chapter 2, country *i* is relatively more abundant in factor *k* if its world share of *k* is larger than its world share of GNP, namely $E_{ki}/E_{kw} > Y_i/Y_w$. In applying this principle to the current two-factor case, it is observed that $K_i/K_w > Y_i/Y_w$ and $L_i/L_w < Y_i/Y_w$ for all countries in CASE 3, which reinforces the previous argument that developed countries are in general relatively more abundant in capital and less abundant in labour than developing countries. On the other hand, the opposite is the case for most countries in CASE 4, leading to a similar conclusion.

Second, in CASE 1 and CASE 4, where $L_T > 0$ is observed, L_i/L_w is always larger than or at least equal to Y_i/Y_w, providing empirical evidence to support Brecher and Choudhri's (1982a) formula (equation (2.3)); that is, $L_T > 0$ if and only if $L_i/L_w > Y_i/Y_w$. However, not one developed country is found in these two cases in 1965. In other words, all developed countries including the United States were net importers of labour services in 1965. Therefore, the paradoxical result that countries with greater capital abundance export labour services does not seem to occur.

Third, a few countries fall into CASE 2, as net importers of both capital and labour services. A common feature of these countries is that their world shares of both capital and labour are lower than or equal to (and certainly not larger than) their world shares of GNP. These results are natural, given that countries with net imports of capital and labour services can be expected to be relatively scarce in these factors.

Table 5.4 shows the results obtained for 1988 based on the same procedure.[8] In comparison with the situation in 1965, the following changes can be observed. First, while the number of developed countries in CASE 3 is about the same as in 1965, only two developing countries remain in CASE 4 by 1988. This, together with the fact that many developing countries fall into CASE 1, indicates that capital is in general more abundant in developing countries than previously, confirming the similar conclusions drawn in the last chapter.

Second, although it is still the case that $K_i/K_w > L_i/L_w$ for countries in CASE 3 and $K_i/K_w < L_i/L_w$ for countries in CASE 4, many developing countries are now in CASE 1, namely net exporters of both capital and labour services. Since countries in both CASE 1 and CASE 3 are net exporters of capital services, the question then is how to distinguish between developed and developing countries with regard to relative abundance in capital. The rank order of K_i/K_w and L_i/L_w provides a partial answer to this question. Unlike countries in CASE 3, for the majority of countries (all developing countries) in CASE 1, $K_i/K_w < L_i/L_w$, as shown in Table 5.4. Thus even though both developed and developing countries are net exporters of capital services, those countries with $K_i/K_w > L_i/L_w$ may be regarded as more capital abundant than those with $K_i/K_w < L_i/L_w$.[9]

Third, the results obtained by applying the second and third criteria to CASE 3 conform with those for 1965. In particular, it is still the case that L_i/L_w is always larger than or at least equal to Y_i/Y_w in CASE 1 and CASE 4, and there is still no developed country in either of these two cases in 1988. In addition, a few economies, namely Greece, Korea, Portugal, Singapore and Taiwan, have noticeably changed their ranking according to the second criterion during this period, providing convincing evidence of rapid accumulation of capital in these economies.

Finally, by 1988, more and more countries fall into CASE 1 and CASE 2. This again raises the problem of applying K_i/K_w and L_i/L_w together with K_x/L_x and K_m/L_m under such circumstances. Empirical results do justify the concerns raised about this. For example, although increasing numbers of countries are in CASE 1, countries are

Table 5.4 Relative abundance of capital and labour, 1988[a]

Country	K_T	L_T	$K_i/(K_i\text{-}K_T)$	$L_i/(L_i\text{-}L_T)$	K_T/L_T	K_i/L_i	K_i/K_w	L_i/L_w	Y_i/Y_w
Argentina	50 628	2 750	1.749	1.323	18.410	10.501	0.9	0.7	0.5
Australia	26 124	-17 331	1.131	0.309	-1.507	29.067	1.7	0.5	1.5
Austria	5 301	-10 461	1.047	0.256	-0.507	32.555	0.9	0.2	0.8
Belg.–Lux.	205	-13 780	1.001	0.235	-0.015	33.842	1.1	0.2	1.0
Brazil	-12 358	18 132	0.955	1.523	-0.682	4.983	1.9	3.1	2.1
Canada	6 687	-35 823	1.017	0.266	-0.187	30.368	2.9	0.8	2.9
China	583 566	616 594	2.912	17.054	0.946	1.357	6.6	38.4	2.3
Colombia	8 845	6 166	1.297	2.645	1.434	3.896	0.3	0.6	0.2
Denmark	-6 669	-7 902	0.922	0.264	0.844	27.740	0.6	0.2	0.6
Egypt	-1 351	8 427	0.969	2.547	-0.160	3.023	0.3	0.8	0.2
Finland	-1 191	-8 277	0.986	0.234	0.144	33.540	0.6	0.1	0.6
France	84 411	-75 588	1.105	0.250	-1.117	35.138	6.5	1.5	5.8
Germany, W.	83 927	-89 626	1.089	0.249	-0.936	34.752	7.6	1.7	7.4
Greece	-504	-1 967	0.989	0.664	0.256	11.846	0.3	0.2	0.3
Hong Kong	-16 362	-6 603	0.784	0.308	2.478	20.234	0.4	0.2	0.3
Iceland	-256	-493	0.949	0.211	0.518	35.708	0.0	0.0	0.0
India	50 927	282 874	1.228	11.041	0.180	0.883	2.0	18.2	1.6
Indonesia	104 806	61 523	2.915	9.934	1.704	2.332	1.2	4.0	0.5
Ireland	7 499	-1 276	1.354	0.522	-5.876	20.626	0.2	0.1	0.2
Israel	-6 300	-2 943	0.829	0.364	2.141	18.096	0.2	0.1	0.3
Italy	-28 813	-63 503	0.958	0.267	0.454	28.506	4.9	1.4	5.1
Japan	-49 081	-231 495	0.979	0.210	0.212	37.071	16.8	3.6	17.7
Korea	35 352	1 537	1.268	1.093	22.997	9.221	1.2	1.1	1.0
Malaysia	26 235	3 876	2.191	2.398	6.769	7.260	0.4	0.4	0.2
Mexico	76 256	11 792	1.547	1.672	6.467	7.351	1.6	1.7	1.0
Netherlands	16 879	-17 477	1.090	0.258	-0.966	33.579	1.5	0.4	1.4
New Zealand	5 568	-2 421	1.179	0.381	-2.300	24.617	0.3	0.1	0.2
Norway	29 060	-7 486	1.382	0.218	-3.882	50.310	0.8	0.1	0.5
Peru	6 415	4 189	1.315	2.637	1.531	3.964	0.2	0.4	0.2
Philippines	7 328	17 116	1.214	4.979	0.428	1.938	0.3	1.3	0.2
Portugal	6 442	86	1.178	1.019	74.855	9.188	0.3	0.3	0.3
Singapore	12 070	-1 826	1.491	0.410	-6.611	28.872	0.3	0.1	0.2
Spain	-1 941	-23 321	0.994	0.380	0.083	20.796	2.2	0.8	2.1
Sweden	25 804	-13 997	1.177	0.236	-1.844	39.598	1.3	0.3	1.1
Switzerland	10 061	-17 841	1.060	0.156	-0.564	54.024	1.3	0.2	1.2
Taiwan	-13 220	-3 340	0.855	0.708	3.958	9.589	0.6	0.5	0.8
Thailand	9 704	22 258	1.199	4.618	0.436	2.062	0.4	1.7	0.4
Turkey	25 358	16 031	1.434	3.182	1.582	3.582	0.6	1.4	0.4
United Kingdom	-103 416	-62 283	0.856	0.312	1.660	21.814	4.5	1.7	5.1
United States	-1 304 001	-409 768	0.691	0.228	3.182	24.068	21.5	7.1	30.1
Yugoslavia	119 528	5 430	3.884	2.041	22.011	15.120	1.2	0.6	0.3

Note: a K_T/L_T is capital/labour embodied in net exports; K_i/L_i is capital/labour embodied in production; K_i/K_w is country *i*'s share of world capital stock and L_i/L_w is its share of world labour; Y_i/Y_w is share of world income. (K_i/K_w, L_i/L_w and Y_i/Y_w are expressed as a percentage.)

still divided in terms of their patterns of K_T/L_T and K_i/L_i; $K_T/L_T < K_i/L_i$ for a majority of countries and $K_T/L_T > K_i/L_i$ for a few countries. It may, therefore, be inappropriate to link K_i/K_w and L_i/L_w with K_x/L_x and K_m/L_m, as argued earlier.

However, Table 5.4 shows that $K_T/L_T < K_i/L_i$ for all countries (including both developed and developing countries) in CASE 2. This raises the question of other underlying factors which determine changes in sign patterns with respect to capital and labour services embodied in net exports. Three possible solutions are given, as follows.[10]

The first possible solution is that other factor endowments which are not included in this two-factor world may play a role in determining the sign patterns of factor services embodied in net exports. For example, in the case of the United States, negative signs for both capital and labour services may have been influenced by a positive sign for oil in both years and for coal in 1988 (Table 5.2).

The second possible solution lies in the large differences in consumption share or country share of world GNP (last columns of Tables 5.3 and 5.4), which indicate that deviation from the basic Heckscher–Ohlin model's basic assumption of equal consumption share among countries exists.[11] Such deviation could be important for two reasons: first, there is a negative relationship between trade in factor services and consumption share; and second, there is a clear-cut difference in consumption share between developed and developing countries, the former generally having higher consumption shares than the latter.

It is important to address this negative relationship, as the magnitude of the consumption share of a particular type of country may affect both the sign and magnitude of its trade in factor services. Tables 5.3 and 5.4 show that net trade in capital services in many developed countries and some NIEs switched from positive in 1965 to negative in 1988 (CASE 2), and net trade in capital services in many developing countries switched from negative to positive during the same period (CASE 1).

Tables 5.3 and 5.4 also reveal the following important fact: the consumption shares of most developed countries, including the majority of NIEs, increased from 1965 to 1988, while those of developing countries dropped. In other words, the gap in consumption shares between developed and developing countries widened during the period. Thus cross-country differences in consumption shares may be said to constitute a factor in explaining the puzzling results with respect to sign patterns of capital services in 1988 revealed in Table 5.4.

The third solution, which is closely related to changes in consumption share, is that if the assumption of factor price equalisation is violated,[12] country i's income, Y_i (and as a consequence world total income, Y_w), can deviate from the value which would presumably be obtained if the assumption held. Countries with higher factor returns in general tend to have higher value of incomes.[13] Since developed countries are likely to have higher factor returns than developing countries, there is a tendency for cross-country differences in factor returns, other things being equal, to increase the consumption shares of developed countries and reduce the consumption shares of developing countries. This supports the argument of the second solution, as described above.

Factor abundance ranking in a cross-country setting can also be extended to a multifactor case. When a multifactor case is considered, the factor abundance ranking of a two-factor case, both in a cross-country setting and in relative terms for individual countries, may change.[14] This point is illustrated in Tables 5.5 and 5.6, which are based on equation (2.5).[15] According to equation (2.5), the relative abundance of resources, both across countries and across factors, can be revealed. Two points in time are selected in order to see changes in cross-country and cross-factor rankings over time.

Table 5.5 reports results for cross-country and cross-factor rankings of factor abundance for 1965. The following observations can be made regarding the cross-country ranking of factor abundance (see Table 5.6, columns). First, countries most abundant in capital in 1965 are, in general, developed countries (Switzerland, Norway, the Netherlands, Italy, Germany, Austria, Japan and Denmark); countries least abundant in capital are, in most cases, developing countries (with Indonesia, China and Egypt at the bottom of the list). The results are consistent both with Tables 3.12 and 3.13 (Chapter 3) and with Chapter 4's findings regarding exports of machinery and chemicals (see Chapter 4's discussion of resource abundance profiles).

Second, the results presented in Table 5.5 further confirm that the definitions of LABOUR 2 and LABOUR 3 are appropriate in the context of cross-country factor abundance. The following economies are among those most abundant in LABOUR 2 (semiskilled labour): Thailand, China, Korea, the Philippines, India, Taiwan, Turkey, Brazil, Portugal, Colombia and Hong Kong. With regard to LABOUR 3 (unskilled labour), China, India, Thailand, Egypt and Turkey rank at the top. However, the results again cast doubt on the definition of LABOUR 1 (highly skilled labour).[16]

Third, the relative abundance rankings of the four land variables, judged from a cross-country perspective, are consistent with observations regarding the distribution of LAND among countries, providing further support for the validity of using these variables. Thailand, Turkey, India, China and Australia are relatively more abundant in LAND 1 (arable land); Malaysia, Argentina, Brazil, Thailand, the Philippines, Colombia, Turkey and Spain are more abundant in LAND 2 (land producing tropical products); Australia, Argentina, Peru, Brazil, Iceland, Mexico, Turkey, Colombia and China are well endowed with LAND 3 (land producing animal products); and Brazil, Peru, Colombia, Canada, Australia, Thailand, Malaysia and Mexico are abundant in LAND 4 (forest land).

Finally, the three natural resource variables, MINERALS, COAL and OIL, provide the following results: Malaysia, Peru, Canada, Australia, Thailand, Sweden and Yugoslavia are relatively abundant in minerals; China, Korea, the United Kingdom, Taiwan, Australia and India are abundant in coal; and Colombia, Canada, Mexico, Egypt, Argentina, Peru and the United States are abundant in oil. These results are consistent with those of the resource abundance profiles reported in Chapter 4.

Table 5.5 Cross-country ranking and cross-factor ranking of factors by abundance, 1965[a]

Country	CAPITAL	LABOUR 1	LABOUR 2	LABOUR 3	LAND 1	LAND 2	LAND 3	LAND 4	MINERALS	COAL	OIL
Argentina	0.33	0.17	-0.04	-0.88	1.01	10.88	6.65	1.13	-0.83	-0.98	0.58
Australia	0.47	0.08	-0.39	-0.99	2.22	-0.77	20.85	3.59	2.33	0.95	-0.97
Austria	0.75	0.34	0.06	-0.99	-0.61	-0.79	-0.73	-0.74	-0.36	-0.64	-0.10
Belg.–Lux.	0.20	-0.09	-0.39	-0.99	-0.88	-0.91	-0.95	-0.97	-0.51	0.35	-0.98
Brazil	-0.12	0.68	0.84	0.54	1.15	9.28	5.45	16.52	0.22	-0.89	-0.62
Canada	-0.11	-0.25	-0.64	-0.99	0.83	-0.95	-0.54	3.85	4.05	-0.78	1.96
China	-0.75	-0.27	5.75	10.21	2.46	-0.78	2.06	0.09	0.49	3.82	-0.72
Colombia	-0.15	0.95	0.73	0.35	0.38	7.01	2.32	9.43	-0.77	-0.40	2.75
Denmark	0.61	0.16	-0.36	-0.99	-0.40	-0.96	-0.96	-0.97	-1.00	-0.92	-1.00
Egypt	-0.56	2.58	0.05	3.37	0.02	-0.56	-1.00	-1.00	-1.00	-1.00	1.35
Finland	0.56	0.13	-0.27	-0.99	-0.26	-1.00	-0.98	1.05	0.44	-1.00	-1.00
France	0.35	0.01	-0.42	-0.99	-0.57	-0.46	-0.85	-0.91	0.03	-0.35	-0.84
Germany, W.	0.77	-0.06	-0.34	-0.99	-0.85	-0.84	-0.94	-0.95	-0.65	0.77	-0.82
Greece	-0.07	0.11	0.48	-0.53	0.06	3.23	-0.06	-0.68	-0.43	-0.67	-1.00
Hong Kong	0.60	1.14	0.71	-0.22	-0.98	-0.98	-1.00	-1.00	-0.91	-1.00	-1.00
Iceland	0.30	-0.52	-0.59	-0.99	-1.00	-1.00	4.18	-0.82	-1.00	-1.00	-1.00
India	-0.41	2.51	2.16	9.89	5.90	1.88	-0.68	-0.11	-0.38	0.63	-0.88
Indonesia	-0.95	-0.51	-0.52	0.00	-0.70	0.51	-0.86	0.06	-0.88	-1.00	-0.43
Ireland	0.18	0.74	0.17	-0.95	0.05	-0.96	0.35	-0.95	-0.77	-0.14	-1.00
Israel	0.10	0.33	-0.50	-0.87	-0.80	-0.28	-0.76	-0.98	-0.05	-1.00	-0.85
Italy	0.84	-0.07	-0.13	-0.88	-0.55	0.32	-0.91	-0.93	-0.74	-0.99	-0.71
Japan	0.70	0.61	0.59	-0.95	-0.87	-0.85	-1.00	-0.78	-0.51	-0.34	-0.95
Korea	0.01	3.10	5.28	2.38	0.50	-0.26	-1.00	0.69	-0.11	3.10	-0.97
Malaysia	-0.16	1.23	0.31	0.60	-0.62	21.07	-0.99	2.89	15.47	-1.00	-1.00
Mexico	-0.10	0.12	0.13	-0.21	1.59	1.14	3.15	2.08	1.13	-0.88	1.38
Netherlands	1.11	0.06	-0.39	-0.99	-0.89	-0.94	-0.93	-0.99	-0.92	-0.30	-0.61
New Zealand	-0.01	0.04	-0.47	-0.99	-0.71	-0.94	1.61	0.02	-0.99	-0.56	-1.00
Norway	1.14	-0.11	-0.41	-0.99	-0.74	-0.94	-0.97	-0.25	0.16	-0.92	-1.00
Peru	0.38	0.18	0.21	0.02	0.00	0.13	5.55	10.73	11.97	-0.97	0.43
Philippines	-0.15	2.49	3.26	1.17	0.79	8.91	-0.85	0.88	1.37	-0.98	-1.00
Portugal	0.28	0.32	0.73	0.32	1.14	3.69	-0.85	-0.37	-0.25	-0.85	-1.00
Singapore	-0.25	0.26	0.01	-0.39	-0.99	-0.69	-1.00	-1.00	-1.00	-1.00	-1.00
Spain	0.49	0.13	0.34	-0.73	0.53	4.94	-0.40	-0.57	-0.01	-0.30	-0.99
Sweden	0.51	0.32	-0.57	-0.99	-0.66	-0.94	-0.97	-0.08	1.36	-1.00	-0.99
Switzerland	1.25	-0.16	-0.48	-0.99	-0.94	-0.97	-0.86	-0.95	-0.97	-1.00	-1.00
Taiwan	-0.16	2.39	2.14	0.23	-0.35	-0.33	-1.00	-0.30	-0.67	1.18	-0.95
Thailand	-0.23	1.45	6.32	3.44	5.14	9.11	-0.91	3.55	2.13	-0.99	-1.00
Turkey	-0.25	0.94	1.26	2.47	5.10	6.90	2.76	0.81	0.08	-0.26	-0.65
United Kingdom	0.26	0.31	-0.30	-0.97	-0.84	-0.97	-0.86	-0.99	-0.71	1.30	-0.99
United States	-0.30	-0.40	-0.71	-1.00	-0.43	-0.92	-0.58	-0.66	-0.33	-0.17	0.19
Yugoslavia	0.50	1.14	0.59	-0.34	0.41	0.74	-0.39	-0.44	1.36	0.52	-0.62

Note: a Columns show cross-country ranking; horizontal rows show cross-factor ranking; abundance is calculated according to equation (2.5).

Table 5.6 Cross-country ranking and cross-factor ranking of factors by abundance, 1988[a]

Country	CAPITAL	LABOUR 1	LABOUR 2	LABOUR 3	LAND 1	LAND 2	LAND 3	LAND 4	MINERALS	COAL	OIL
Argentina	0.67	0.41	0.71	-0.74	4.80	24.76	14.85	4.26	-0.75	-0.96	3.50
Australia	0.14	-0.51	-0.56	-1.00	2.74	-0.84	15.94	2.36	6.08	3.05	0.29
Austria	0.11	-0.45	-0.64	-1.00	-0.79	-0.87	-0.85	-0.81	-0.85	-0.95	-0.80
Belg.–Lux.	0.06	-0.42	-0.67	-1.00	-0.91	-0.98	-0.96	-0.97	-1.00	-0.89	-1.00
Brazil	-0.08	0.50	0.62	0.11	2.67	6.87	3.65	11.17	2.34	-0.88	-0.80
Canada	-0.01	-0.36	-0.66	-1.00	0.83	-0.96	-0.35	4.63	5.47	-0.09	2.87
China	1.85	11.67	14.76	18.63	3.69	0.90	7.06	1.31	3.07	13.16	-0.11
Colombia	0.26	2.72	2.04	0.30	0.99	8.15	9.35	9.44	1.12	2.00	1.51
Denmark	-0.09	-0.17	-0.68	-1.00	-0.53	-0.99	-0.98	-0.96	-0.97	-1.00	-0.57
Egypt	0.47	5.49	0.62	7.13	0.33	0.13	-1.00	-0.99	-0.57	-1.00	2.28
Finland	-0.02	-0.20	-0.72	-1.00	-0.55	-1.00	-0.99	0.69	0.01	-0.89	-1.00
France	0.12	-0.47	-0.66	-1.00	-0.64	-0.70	-0.88	-0.88	-0.81	-0.88	-0.94
Germany, W.	0.02	-0.51	-0.69	-1.00	-0.89	-0.96	-0.97	-0.95	-0.80	-0.32	-0.80
Greece	0.05	0.22	-0.13	-0.77	0.04	3.48	-0.05	-0.62	0.68	0.34	-0.94
Hong Kong	0.30	-0.44	-0.44	-0.60	-1.00	-1.00	-1.00	-1.00	-1.00	-1.00	-1.00
Iceland	-0.03	-0.64	-0.70	-1.00	-0.97	-1.00	2.71	-0.84	-1.00	-1.00	-1.00
India	0.24	3.47	5.62	21.43	10.80	1.94	-0.57	0.88	0.54	3.69	-0.48
Indonesia	1.57	2.78	7.83	8.77	3.03	15.36	0.50	10.48	5.25	-0.71	7.91
Ireland	0.20	-0.01	-0.38	-1.00	-0.36	-0.98	0.55	-0.91	2.09	-0.53	0.26
Israel	-0.16	0.24	-0.60	-0.90	-0.85	-0.54	-0.97	-0.98	0.58	-1.00	-0.98
Italy	-0.04	-0.54	-0.64	-0.97	-0.79	-0.17	-0.94	-0.94	-0.92	-1.00	-0.67
Japan	-0.05	-0.69	-0.71	-1.00	-0.97	-0.96	-1.00	-0.93	-0.96	-0.97	-0.99
Korea	0.18	-0.04	0.30	-0.57	-0.78	-0.81	-1.00	0.71	-0.88	-0.26	-1.00
Malaysia	0.76	1.18	0.87	1.00	-0.40	25.20	-0.99	3.43	2.51	-0.99	6.93
Mexico	0.52	0.79	1.14	-0.46	1.58	1.06	3.15	0.93	2.32	-0.63	2.24
Netherlands	0.07	-0.19	-0.69	-1.00	-0.92	-0.97	-0.96	-0.99	-1.00	-1.00	-0.52
New Zealand	0.14	-0.23	-0.50	-1.00	-0.76	-0.87	2.38	0.43	-0.75	-0.63	1.12
Norway	0.41	-0.29	-0.73	-1.00	-0.82	-1.00	-0.99	-0.30	-0.48	-0.98	5.75
Peru	0.31	1.98	2.06	0.62	1.64	1.98	9.49	20.22	23.79	-0.96	-0.38
Philippines	0.27	2.95	5.36	1.96	1.20	18.56	-0.71	1.06	6.64	-0.82	-1.00
Portugal	0.24	0.07	0.30	-0.41	-0.06	2.88	-0.88	-0.33	-0.75	-0.97	-1.00
Singapore	0.76	-0.20	-0.45	-0.72	-1.00	-1.00	-1.00	-1.00	-1.00	-1.00	-1.00
Spain	0.05	-0.49	-0.47	-0.90	-0.13	2.19	-0.71	-0.65	-0.22	-0.68	-0.95
Sweden	0.15	-0.06	-0.74	-1.00	-0.69	-1.00	-0.97	0.18	0.66	-1.00	-1.00
Switzerland	0.09	-0.64	-0.79	-1.00	-0.96	-0.98	-0.92	-0.96	-0.99	-1.00	-1.00
Taiwan	-0.25	-0.37	-0.14	-0.91	-0.89	-0.75	-1.00	-0.85	-0.99	-0.92	-0.49
Thailand	0.23	1.04	5.30	0.94	4.93	7.83	-0.87	0.86	0.56	-0.63	0.65
Turkey	0.46	1.26	2.52	1.84	5.81	8.71	0.18	1.21	0.24	0.74	-0.96
United Kingdom	-0.11	-0.24	-0.58	-1.00	-0.84	-0.98	-0.87	-0.98	-0.89	-0.22	0.08
United States	-0.29	-0.46	-0.69	-1.00	-0.27	-0.91	-0.53	-0.59	-0.58	0.16	0.66
Yugoslavia	2.86	1.99	1.53	-0.28	1.67	2.24	0.20	0.41	3.92	2.54	-0.13

Note: a Columns show cross-country ranking; horizontal rows show cross-factor ranking; abundance is calculated according to equation (2.5).

The following observations can be made about cross-factor ranking of factor abundance (Table 5.6, horizontal rows). First, without considering the various land and resource variables, it is still the case that developed countries are, in general, relatively more capital than labour abundant, while developing countries are more labour than capital abundant. This is in accordance with the results reported in Chapter 4 regarding cross-factor ranking of factor abundance.

Second, the inclusion of the various land and resource variables is observed to affect the cross-factor ranking of individual countries. For example, OIL and COAL are relatively more abundant in the United States than other factors including CAPITAL, and COAL is more abundant than any other factor in the United Kingdom, though a positive sign is observed for CAPITAL. The inclusion of land and resource variables provides a more comprehensive representation of relative factor abundance in individual countries.[17]

Third, cross-factor ranking captures information missing from cross-country ranking. For example, a cross-country comparison indicates that the United States is less abundant in all four categories of land; however, cross-factor ranking indicates that LAND 1 (arable land) is indeed more abundant than the other three categories of land, and that LABOUR 1 (highly skilled labour) is the most abundant category of labour in the United States.

Tables 5.5 and 5.6 also shed light on changes over time in factor rankings in both a cross-country and cross-factor setting and give some idea of how this way of measuring factor abundance performs at different points in time.

In comparison with 1965, several changes are observed when equation (2.5) is applied to the 1988 data. With regard to cross-country ranking, it is no longer the case that only developed countries are capital abundant. Many developing countries — for example, Yugoslavia, China, Indonesia, Singapore, Malaysia, Argentina, Mexico, Egypt and Turkey — are increasingly capital abundant.[18]

Comparison of cross-country factor rankings over time provides a convenient way of examining changes in relative factor abundance. To be more specific, by comparing corresponding columns in Tables 5.5 and 5.6, changes in ranking for each country over the period can be seen. For example, Australia is more capital abundant than Argentina in 1965, but less so in 1988. Again, among the Asian developing economies, China, Indonesia, Korea, Malaysia, Singapore and Thailand increase their relative abundance in CAPITAL remarkably during the period.

Comparison of cross-factor ranking over time provides an alternative way of examining changes in relative factor abundance. Specifically, by comparing corresponding rows in Tables 5.5 and 5.6, changes in the ranking of each factor can be seen. For example, while in the United States CAPITAL abundance ranking remains virtually unchanged from 1965 to 1988, relative abundance in OIL and COAL increases substantially. Again, while Australia's relative abundance in CAPITAL, three categories of labour and four categories of land (except LAND 1) decreases, its abundance in MINERALS, COAL and OIL increases sharply.

However, the credibility of the model on which these discussions are based, and in particular the robustness of sign changes when applying the HOV model, has still to be determined.

Sign tests of the HOV model can be carried out on the basis of equation (2.6) which, as stated in Chapter 2, represents cases where one sign hypothesis (SH-III) is rejected and the other (SH-II) is supported. Because the only difference between the two hypotheses lies in trade balance, the decisive role of trade balance can be observed by undertaking the tests. Furthermore, given that empirical data do not strictly satisfy the HOV model (equation (2.1)), sign tests can determine the extent to which the current data sets satisfy the HOV model, and a degree of confidence in the data sets can thus be established.

The total number (as a percentage) of changes in sign test results between hypotheses SH-II and SH-III is 43 per cent in 1965, 40 per cent in 1974 and 46 per cent in 1988.[19] As these figures show, the proportion of sign changes is large when trade balance is used for adjustment. In other words, choosing between hypotheses II and III may, to a certain degree, produce different test results. This point should be kept in mind when the results in Tables 5.5 and 5.6 are examined.

In summary, empirical study in this chapter of the factor content of trade in a cross-country setting reveals that the sign patterns of trade in factor services can provide another criterion for measuring the relative abundance of resource endowments. The results show that analysis of the factor content of trade in a cross-country setting is of benefit in uncovering factor abundance ranking, which is often less evident when data from only a single country are under scrutiny.

The relative abundance of skilled labour in comparison with the other two categories of labour in the United States suggests that human capital (education) plays an important role in determining trade patterns in the United States.

The results in this chapter also show that there is a discrepancy between capital/labour embodied in net exports and capital/labour in the economy, suggesting that it may be inappropriate to use capital/labour embodied in net exports or trade as an indicator of the state of overall capital/labour in the economy.

The United States remained an importer of labour services ($L_T < 0$) throughout the period under study; the empirical results in a cross-country setting show that this is the case for all developed countries. This suggests that what Brecher and Choudhri (1982a) describe as a paradoxical result is simply a special case, and it is therefore not necessary to conclude that one or more of the assumptions of the basic model should be relaxed.

The results in Table 5.2 show that adjusting factors for trade imbalance does not alter factor rankings in the case of the United States. Furthermore, the United States remains an importer of both capital and labour services ($K_T < 0$ and $L_T < 0$) throughout the period under study, being a case of a 'sufficiently large' trade deficit as described by Aw (1983). However, the results in Table 5.1 show that capital is still relatively more abundant than labour in the United States throughout the period, because when $K_T < 0$ and $L_T < 0$, $K_i/K_w > L_i/L_w$ if $K_T/L_T < K_i/L_i$.

A cross-country examination of factor abundance ranking in a two-factor (capital and labour) world shows that most developed countries are characterised by $K_i/K_w > L_i/L_w$, while the reverse is the case in all developing countries. These results indicate that in general no 'Leontief Paradox' exists; the results do not, therefore, support Maskus' assertion that the Leontief Paradox is commonplace.

It is of note that when US rankings of factor abundance are compared in the context of both a three-factor and a multifactor world, rankings of the basic factors (capital, labour and land) are in general consistent, though changes in ranking take place when factors such as labour and land are decomposed into categories.

Viewed from a cross-country setting, there is weak evidence that the linkage between $K_x/L_x > K_m/L_m$ and $K_i/K_w > L_i/L_w$ may break when there is a 'sufficiently large' trade surplus so that $K_T > 0$ and $L_T > 0$ and when there is a 'sufficiently large' trade deficit so that $K_T < 0$ and $L_T < 0$.

In the case of *n* factors, factor abundance ranking across countries and across factors generally produces results that are basically consistent with those reported in the previous two chapters. This further supports the corollary of the HOV model which says that under balanced trade a country will be a net exporter of the services of its abundant factors and a net importer of the services of its scarce factors (Casas and Choi 1985). Furthermore, the results suggest that cross-factor ranking of factor abundance may be more useful than cross-country ranking of factor abundance when equation (2.5) is applied.

6 Estimates of the trade dependence model

This chapter analyses data based on the linear Heckscher–Ohlin–Vanek (HOV) trade model. The first section sets out reasons for undertaking this empirical analysis. The second section discusses some econometric issues and possible solutions. The third section presents and discusses the results of Bayesian model estimation.

Objectives of the empirical analysis

Model estimation and analysis here are based on the maintained hypothesis that trade and GNP are linear functions of resource endowments. Because of the complexity of applying the general trade theory, and in the absence of fully articulated alternative models, 'the best we can do is to measure the accuracy of the maintained hypothesis' (Leamer 1984, p. 154). Nevertheless, several questions asked by Leamer concerning the general objectives of this kind of empirical study are relevant here. How well do the 11 measured resources explain trade? Do the coefficients take on unexpected values? Since the expected values of the coefficients are the prior means, major differences between estimates and these prior means need to be noted. Has the structural relationship between trade and endowments changed much over time? As the data in Chapter 3 demonstrated, an increasing number of countries are climbing the ladder of development to export manufactured products; has this shift been accompanied by a demonstrable shift in sources of comparative advantage, and what are the implications for adjustment issues? Analysis in this chapter has two additional objectives: to examine whether the four new land variables fit the model according to statistical criteria; and to demonstrate how trends identified by Leamer (1984) continued into the 1980s.[1]

Econometric issues and some solutions

Three critical problems arise in analysis of a cross-section data set of this type: heteroscedasticity, gross errors and chronic measurement errors. This section will focus on these issues and suggest some solutions, a necessary step preceding discussion of model estimation in the next section.

The most obvious problem confronting econometric study of a cross-section of countries is heteroscedasticity: variances of residuals may vary across countries. There is reason to believe that error terms associated with a very large country like the United States will have greater variance than those associated with small countries like the Philippines and Panama. Therefore, individual observations can influence the estimates to an unusually large extent.

The data set is likely to exhibit systematic heteroscedasticity, 'since the error term is hypothesised to represent unmeasured resource endowments and since countries with relatively large GNPs are likely to have relatively large stocks of the unmeasured resources' (Leamer 1984, p. 121). The solution to this problem is found in the traditional form of heteroscedasticity, which is systematically related to other variables. For example, the variance of residual i may be modelled as:

$$\sigma^2 = \alpha x^{\theta}, \tag{6.1}$$

where x is an observable and α and θ are unknown parameters. In the next section, this model will be used with an explanatory variable x_i to represent GNP. The three-step approach proposed by Harvey (1976) will then be used for the model estimation. First, the squared residuals are obtained by running an unweighted regression of the trade equations. Second, the logarithms of the squared residuals from an unweighted regression of the trade equations are regressed against the logarithm of GNP to estimate the coefficients α and θ in equation (6.1). Third, the predicted values of σ^2 from this auxiliary regression are used as weights for re-estimating the trade equation. Harvey demonstrates that the estimate of θ is consistent and that the corresponding weighted least-squares estimator is consistent and efficient.

The problem of gross errors (outliers) is not uncommon, but the method adopted here for dealing with it is unique. The method proposed by Belsley, Kuh and Welsch (1980) reports the consequences of one-at-a-time deletions of observations from the data set. The method is unique in that it makes use of a rather peculiar set of weights, with no weight put on one observation and equal weights put on all others. 'This informal approach does detect outliers and uncovers some sensitivities of the estimates, but it clearly cannot deal with extremes more than one at a time; nor does it properly yield estimates and standard errors that account for the fact that the data have been inspected for outliers' (Leamer 1984, p. 122). A list of countries is given in the next section that critically influence the estimates in that they often generate an extreme estimate if omitted.

Table 6.1 Direct and reverse regressions, CEREALS equation, 1988[a]

	CER	CAPITAL	LABOUR 1	LABOUR 2	LABOUR 3	LAND 1	LAND 2	LAND 3	LAND 4	COAL	MINERALS	OIL
CAPITAL	-2.54	-26.32	38.45	4.93	-13.83	-3.10	5.10	1.62	-11.33	1.44	0.47	3.17
LABOUR 1	-346.22	5 236.27	-19 681.36	4 069.96	582.43	-269.68	-1 651.25	-3 306.10	3 153.16	-2 984.39	-1 346.61	-1 290.82
LABOUR 2	-55.86	108.40	656.66	-927.76	263.83	-49.09	-276.86	11.87	-150.51	27.83	17.96	-118.77
LABOUR 3	-66.11	-359.57	111.22	315.79	-617.98	-325.31	166.07	-378.73	-473.77	39.57	-63.92	225.28
LAND 1	103.53	126.37	80.64	90.97	509.42	463.51	-65.45	425.11	620.20	-118.74	188.76	-37.42
LAND 2	283.38	-568.42	1 351.52	1 404.47	-711.83	-179.15	2 338.23	1 223.21	1 035.38	1 128.69	-960.55	159.83
LAND 3	-5.43	3.46	-51.84	1.15	-31.10	-22.29	-23.44	-130.04	-16.52	-29.63	31.73	39.70
LAND 4	-4.07	-18.15	37.08	-10.97	-29.18	-24.39	-14.88	-12.39	-136.10	17.27	41.57	-1.69
COAL	0.64	-0.37	5.55	-0.32	-0.39	-0.74	2.56	3.51	-2.73	4.38	-0.96	-2.09
MINERALS	-0.22	0.04	-0.87	0.07	-0.22	-0.41	0.76	1.30	2.28	0.33	-4.19	-1.17
OIL	0.15	-0.19	0.56	0.32	-0.51	-0.05	0.08	-1.10	0.06	-0.49	0.79	1.75

Note: a Each column contains a set of estimates formed by minimisation of the residuals in the direction indicated.

Table 6.2 Direct and reverse regressions, MACHINERY equation, 1988[a]

	MACH	CAPITAL	LABOUR 1	LABOUR 2	LABOUR 3	LAND 1	LAND 2	LAND 3	LAND 4	COAL	MINERALS	OIL
CAPITAL	107.35	173.78	187.33	25.00	204.30	114.64	539.25	181.56	138.57	146.24	306.77	51.58
LABOUR 1	-20 931.00	-36 526.00	-58 655.00	-69 577.00	-28 910.00	-21 926.00	-94 688.00	-73 725.00	-33 362.00	-46 668.00	-87 099.00	-11 711.00
LABOUR 2	598.16	139.28	1 988.30	10 202.00	-2 174.30	510.17	-11 892.00	1 806.20	934.38	1 414.50	5 480.60	1 212.20
LABOUR 3	907.64	1 727.40	1 253.60	-3 299.20	5 643.10	4 274.70	14 030.00	-4 668.50	2 355.70	1 938.60	1 052.80	-1 936.50
LAND 1	-940.05	-1 003.90	-984.70	-801.77	-4 427.30	-5 616.20	-10 490.00	4 795.90	-2 775.30	-3 108.40	4 697.50	435.65
LAND 2	591.41	2 970.90	2 675.40	-11 758.00	9 141.80	6 599.60	116 726.0	17 355.00	-2 079.80	8 837.70	-81 685.00	1 797.30
LAND 3	-35.90	-60.73	-126.46	-108.41	184.67	183.17	-1 053.60	-2 258.50	3.49	-271.99	2 421.60	-476.41
LAND 4	135.20	174.52	215.49	211.19	350.89	399.15	-475.45	-13.16	604.19	343.43	3 154.30	111.96
COAL	7.78	10.60	17.35	18.40	16.62	25.73	116.26	58.94	19.76	44.20	-98.10	34.42
MINERALS	-0.40	-1.14	-1.65	-3.64	-0.46	1.99	54.91	26.81	-9.27	5.01	-262.61	8.84
OIL	-1.81	-0.87	-1.01	-3.68	3.87	0.84	-5.51	-24.07	-1.50	-8.03	40.36	-17.43

Note: a Each column contains a set of estimates formed by minimisation of the residuals in the direction indicated.

The problem of chronic measurement errors is little discussed but by no means insignificant. In dealing with measurement error, Klepper and Leamer (1984) begin with the computation of direct and reverse regressions.[2]

Direct and reverse regressions for the 1988 cereals and machinery equations are reported in Tables 6.1 and 6.2. The first column in each table contains the usual least-squares estimates. The second column contains a reverse regression estimate formed by regressing CAPITAL on net exports of cereals (machinery) and on the other resource variables and then solving the estimated equation for cereals (machinery) in terms of all the resource endowments. Other columns follow the same procedure. Table 6.2 shows that, with the exception of CAPITAL and LABOUR 1, all other resource variables contain some adjusted estimates which have different sign patterns compared with the corresponding estimates based on direct regression (first column). If CAPITAL and LABOUR 1 alone are suspected to have measurement errors, there is no need to impose prior restrictions on them. This is because neither the CAPITAL nor the LABOUR 1 coefficient changes sign in the first two columns and therefore the set of maximum likelihood estimates remains bounded.

However, if any one of the other variables is thought to contain a measurement error, the set of feasible estimates becomes unbounded because of changes in sign. Prior information may then be useful in restricting these unbounded sets of estimates. The numbers of estimates that have sign changes vary across variables, ranging from as many as five (MINERALS) to as few as one (COAL).

It is also interesting to note that there is an exact symmetrical relationship between those variables in which changes in sign are observed. In addition to these two regressions, similar calculations have been done for all other equations, and the $\kappa+1$ regressions for each equation formed by minimising the sum of squares in the $\kappa+1$ possible orthogonal directions fail to conform in sign (not shown).

The question now is how to determine the extent of measurement errors in variables and the degree to which the true explanatory variables may be perfectly collinear. Table 6.3 reports the results of errors-in-variables diagnostics (g and $1-\lambda_1$). The g statistics are very small, which means that eliminating the measurement error could increase the R^2 by at most a very small amount; the $1-\lambda_1$ statistics are very large, which suggests that the squared correlation between the true and the measured explanatory variables exceeds 0.979 in 1965 and 0.998 in 1988. The latter indicates the possibility that correlations among the measured explanatory variables are so high that the true explanatory variables may be perfectly collinear. This possibility may justify the use of prior distribution, as prior distribution is not subject to the problem of perfect collinearity.

The next step is to determine prior distribution. Because of the identical model formulation being used, determination of prior means and standard errors for trade and GNP regressions is based mainly on reasoning provided by Leamer (1984), although some adjustment needs to be made for the four land variables, and prior means for GNP and net export equations in 1988 need to be determined. Prior means and standard errors for coefficients in the GNP regressions in 1965 and 1988 are reported in Table 6.4. These are the prior beliefs about the annual earnings of each factor. A brief explanation follows.

Table 6.3 Errors-in-variables diagnostics (g and $1 - \lambda_1$)[a]

	1965	1988
g		
GNP	0.0013	0.0150
PETRO	0.0522	0.0337
MAT	0.1184	0.0015
FOR	0.0022	0.0089
TROP	0.0070	0.0013
ANL	0.0005	0.0089
CER	0.0255	0.0620
LAB	0.0334	0.0090
CAP	0.0015	0.0409
MACH	0.0150	0.0072
CHEM	0.0004	0.0001
$1 - \lambda_1$	0.9780	0.9980

Note: a g is the proportion of the gap between estimated R^2 and 1 that can be attributed to measurement orror without allowing perfect collinearity in the data. $1 - \lambda_1$ is the minimum squared correlation between true variables and their measuremont, to ensure that the true variables are not perfectly collinear.

In principle, the coefficient of the CAPITAL variable is real interest rate plus rate of depreciation. Since a 15-year life and 13.3 per cent depreciation rate are assumed in the capital stock figures, plus a real rate of interest of 3–4 per cent, the coefficient would be around 0.17. Because of the possibility of underestimating the capital stock number,[3] the prior estimate of the capital coefficient is set at 0.5, with a large standard error of 0.5.

The annual earnings of the three categories of labour for 1965 are obtained by taking the averages used by Leamer (1984) of the prior means of corresponding variables between 1958 and 1975. These prior means are based on information obtained from US sources. For example, farm workers in the United States earned US$1,700 per annum in 1958 and US$5,200 in 1975. Workers in radio and television broadcasting earned US$7,100 per annum in 1958 and US$13,000 in 1975 (Leamer 1984, p. 145). Since most agricultural workers in the United States fall into the LABOUR 2 category, US agricultural earnings are used as the prior mean for the LABOUR 2 coefficient. The earnings of US broadcast workers are taken to be the prior mean for the LABOUR 1 coefficient. It is estimated that earnings of agricultural workers in developing countries are about one-tenth those of US workers.[4] Therefore, one-tenth of US agricultural annual earnings is taken to be the prior mean for unskilled workers. The annual earnings of the three categories of labour in 1988 are determined by calculating increases, based on the 1965 earnings of each group, at a rate slightly lower than the average growth rate of these earnings between 1958 and 1975.

Table 6.4 Prior means and standard errors for the GNP regressions[a]

	1965		1988	
	Mean	Standard error	Mean	Standard error
CAPITAL	500	500	500	500
LABOUR 1	10 050	5 025	20 000	10 000
LABOUR 2	3 450	1 725	9 000	4 500
LABOUR 3	345	1 725	900	450
LAND 1	52.5	26.3	157.5	78.8
LAND 2	30	60	90	180
LAND 3	20	10	60	30
LAND 4	10	20	30	60
COAL	1	0.1	1	0.1
MINERALS	1	0.1	1	0.1
OIL	1	0.1	1	0.1

Note: a All variables are measured in thousands — of US dollars, workers or hectares — except for CAPITAL, which is measured in millions of US dollars.

Prior means for the four land variables are based on information supplied by Leamer (1984).[5] Leamer (p. 145) says that, according to the US Department of Agriculture (1978), rent per acre of cropland in 1975 ranged from a high of US\$70 per acre for irrigated land to a low of US\$14.9 per acre. Pastureland varied from a high of US\$26.70 per acre to a low of US\$5.30 per acre. At 2.47 acres to the hectare, the average rental values that could be expected for LAND 1 and LAND 3 (as defined in the current study) in 1975 are US\$105 per hectare (\$42.45 × 2.47) and US\$40 per hectare (\$16 × 2.47) respectively. The prior standard deviation for these two variables has been set at one-half the prior means; this reflects a high degree of confidence in the signs of the coefficients based on the reliability of information about rents for these two types of land. The prior means for LAND 2 and LAND 4 in 1975 have been set at 60 and 20 respectively, with relatively large standard errors to reflect uncertainty about these coefficients.[6] Thus, the prior means for the four land variables in 1965 and 1988 have been obtained by multiplying prior means for 1975 by 0.5 (for 1965) and

1.5 (for 1988), based on approximate changes in asset values over the period 1958–75.[7]

Prior means for COAL, MINERALS and OIL have been fixed by applying the following simplified assumption (Leamer 1984): if these resources are traded freely and their production does not use other inputs, then every dollar produced by coal, minerals and oil will add approximately $1 to GNP. A relatively low level of standard error has been selected for these prior means to reflect considerable confidence in them.

According to Leamer (1984, p. 147), 'the choice of a prior distribution for the net export equations is much more difficult than the choice for the GNP equations because the coefficients do not have observable counterparts and because they are in theory a consequence of a rather complex computation'. Prior means for the net export equations have been obtained by taking the following steps, and the results are reported in Table 6.5. First, the effect that nontraded goods has on the derivatives of net exports is considered with respect to factor endowments. Based on the Heckscher–Ohlin theorem, the even model with nontraded goods and factor price equalisation can be written as $T = A^{-1}(E - \alpha E_w)$ or as $T = A^{-1}(E^* - \alpha E^*_w)$, where the asterisks indicate resources devoted to the traded goods sector. Based on the second form of the equation, the consumption effect can be written as $\alpha A^{-1} E^*_w = A^{-1} E^*_w Y/Y_w$, which is GNP times the share of the commodity in final output. Leamer (1984, p. 147) points out that 'the derivative of this consumption effect with respect to a factor endowment is just the consumption share times the effect of the resource on GNP'; the latter is predicted using the prior means in Table 6.4. To determine prior means for net export equations, the consumption shares have all been set to 1/20. It is assumed here that roughly half of final output is nontraded goods and services and that each of the 10 aggregates comprise roughly the same proportion of final output. With no production effect, then the expected effect of a resource on net exports would be the negative of its effect on GNP divided by 20. The prior means for other coefficients sum to zero across equations, as implied by balanced trade.

Discussion of estimates

Based on the HOV model, net exports of the 10 aggregate commodities measured in thousands of dollars can be explained in terms of the following 11 measured resources:

CAPITAL = millions of US dollars of discounted and accumulated investment flows;

LABOUR 1 = thousands of professional/technical workers;

LABOUR 2 = thousands of nonprofessional skilled workers;

LABOUR 3 = thousands of unskilled workers;

LAND 1 = thousands of hectares of arable land;

Table 6.5 Prior means, net export equations, 1965 and 1988[a]

	CAPITAL	LABOUR 1	LABOUR 2	LABOUR 3	LAND 1	LAND 2	LAND 3	LAND 4	COAL	MINERALS	OIL
1965											
PETRO	-25	-502	-172	-17.2	-0.17	-0.33	-3.33	-1.67	-0.05	-0.05	0.2
MAT	-25	-502	-172	-17.2	-0.17	-0.33	-3.33	-1.67	0.45	0.45	0.2
FOR	-25	-502	43	17.2	-0.17	-0.33	-3.33	15	-0.05	-0.05	-0.05
TROP	-25	-502	43	17.2	-0.17	2.99	-3.33	-1.67	-0.05	-0.05	-0.05
ANL	-25	-502	43	17.2	-0.17	-0.33	29.9	-1.67	-0.05	-0.05	-0.05
CER	-25	-502	43	17.2	1.51	-0.33	-3.33	-1.67	-0.05	-0.05	-0.05
LAB	37.5	-502	43	17.2	-0.17	-0.33	-3.33	-1.67	-0.05	-0.05	-0.05
CAP	37.5	-502	43	-17.2	-0.17	-0.33	-3.33	-1.67	-0.05	-0.05	-0.05
MACH	37.5	2 008	43	-17.2	-0.17	-0.33	-3.33	-1.67	-0.05	-0.05	-0.05
CHEM	37.5	2 008	43	-17.2	-0.17	-0.33	-3.33	-1.67	-0.05	-0.05	-0.05
1988											
PETRO	-25	-1 000	-450	-45	-0.5	-1	-10	-5	-0.05	-0.05	0.2
MAT	-25	-1 000	-450	-45	-0.5	-1	-10	-5	0.45	0.45	0.2
FOR	-25	-1 000	112.5	45	-0.5	-1	-10	45	-0.05	-0.05	-0.05
TROP	-25	-1 000	112.5	45	-0.5	9	-10	-5	-0.05	-0.05	-0.05
ANL	-25	-1 000	112.5	45	-0.5	-1	90	-5	-0.05	-0.05	-0.05
CER	-25	-1 000	112.5	45	4.5	-1	-10	-5	-0.05	-0.05	-0.05
LAB	37.5	-1 000	112.5	45	-0.5	-1	-10	-5	-0.05	-0.05	-0.05
CAP	37.5	-1 000	112.5	-45	-0.5	-1	-10	-5	-0.05	-0.05	-0.05
MACH	37.5	4 000	112.5	-45	-0.5	-1	-10	-5	-0.05	-0.05	-0.05
CHEM	37.5	4 000	112.5	-45	-0.5	-1	-10	-5	-0.05	-0.05	-0.05

Note: a Standard errors equal to means.

LAND 2 = thousands of hectares of land under permanent crops;

LAND 3 = thousands of hectares of permanent meadows and pastures;

LAND 4 = thousands of hectares of forests and woodland;

COAL = thousands of dollars of production of primary solid fuel;

MINERALS = value in thousands of dollars of production of minerals; and

OIL = thousands of dollars of production of oil and gas.

Weighted regression estimates of the trade and GNP equations are given in Table 6.6. In general, the squared multiple correlations (R^2) are quite high. It can also be seen that the R^2 values for some equations are higher in 1988 than in 1965 (GNP, ANL, CER, LAB and CAP), while others are lower in 1988 than in 1965 (PETRO, MAT, FOR, TROP, MACH and CHEM). The former case indicates the increased importance of these resources as determinants of trade, while the latter indicates the declining role of these resources in determining trade patterns. The heteroscedasticity adjustment factors, θ in the formula $\sigma^2 = \alpha GNP^{\theta}$, are given in the last column of the table. (For the GNP equation, the model is $\sigma^2 = \alpha CAPITAL^{\theta}$.) This adjustment factor would be 2 if the standard error were proportional to GNP. In two cases the adjustment factor exceeds 1 and in other cases ranges from as low as 0.20 to as high as 0.80.

It should be mentioned that the weighted least-squares estimates are still subject to the problem of chronic measurement errors. Even so, several findings of interest, which in general apply as well to the Bayes estimates to be discussed later, emerge with regard to these estimates. The first of these is that while the natural resources MINERALS and OIL contribute to comparative advantage in the natural resource products PETRO and MAT, as found by Leamer (1984), CAPITAL remains a source of comparative disadvantage in both products and LABOUR 1 changes from comparative disadvantage to comparative advantage during the period. As expected, one of the LAND variables creates comparative advantage in the four crops, FOR, TROP, ANL and CER (LAND 2 with TROP in 1988 is an exceptional case).

Second, abundance of arable land (LAND 1) is clearly a source of comparative disadvantage in all manufactures except LAB in 1988. As anticipated, CAPITAL is a source of comparative advantage in CAP, MACH and CHEM as well as GNP.

Third, the role of LABOUR 1 in contributing to comparative advantage in CAP and CHEM changes: the sign pattern for CAP changes from positive in 1965 to negative in 1988, while the sign pattern for CHEM changes from negative to positive. This suggests that professional/technical workers do contribute to comparative advantage in CHEM, which is in accordance with the hypothesis put forward in the original model (Leamer 1984). The roles of LABOUR 2 and 3 remain unchanged (although this is not the case with the Bayes estimates of LABOUR 3) during the period.

If, as Leamer (1984, p. 164) says, 'a t-value in excess of 2 is taken to mean that the coefficient is measurable in the sense of taking on the sign of its least-squares value with high probability', then Table 6.6 shows that the effects of CAPITAL, LAND 1

Table 6.6 Weighted least-squares estimates[a]

	CAPITAL	LABOUR 1	LABOUR 2	LABOUR 3	LAND 1	LAND 2	LAND 3	LAND 4	COAL	MINERALS	OIL	R^2	$wt(\theta)$
1965													
GNP	0.02	75.10**	-2.66**	-1.64**	1.05**	1.35*	-0.07*	0.001	0.01	-0.01	0.03**	.97	.41
PETRO	-0.13	-747.77**	17.93**	28.63**	-16.84**	12.87*	1.30**	-0.36*	0.02	-0.001	2.06**	.98	.48
MAT	-0.88**	-488.63**	-5.98*	7.23**	3.58**	8.61*	-0.35*	0.44**	0.38**	0.85**	0.08*	.98	.42
FOR	0.24	122.94	-17.23*	-1.64	7.21*	-40.08*	-1.47**	1.20**	-1.69**	0.52**	-0.16*	.75	.51
TROP	-1.71**	321.79*	-2.21	-11.16**	9.22**	27.27*	0.17	0.56*	-1.58**	-0.29**	0.05	.89	.49
ANL	-0.23	294.19	-10.57	-14.49*	15.85**	-44.33*	0.95*	0.05	-2.18**	-0.23*	0.08	.60	.61
CER	-2.74**	679.38**	-54.38**	-40.72**	38.19**	29.59*	1.21*	-0.55	-0.67*	0.08	0.34*	.91	.62
LAB	-1.12*	637.66**	9.25	-7.59*	-5.17*	-5.06	0.42	-0.69*	-1.39**	-0.25*	-0.13*	.75	.86
CAP	0.11	418.59*	39.94**	4.38	-19.23**	-46.45*	0.52	-0.29	-0.78*	-0.06	-0.29*	.78	.48
MACH	6.02**	-1 293.60**	41.65*	14.63*	-18.89**	21.98	-2.28**	0.58	6.02**	-0.66**	-0.02	.95	.29
CHEM	2.15**	-369.13**	-0.45	6.42**	-1.74	2.88	-0.64**	0.13	0.97**	-0.06*	0.01	.94	.25
1988													
GNP	1.27**	-18.58	-0.54	-1.85*	1.78*	-3.04	-0.4**	0.25*	0.05*	-0.02**	0.01*	.99	.28
PETRO	-19.74**	4 275**	-35.7	22.13	-69.85*	-351.64*	34.37**	-10.55*	-2.75**	0.55*	0.48**	.91	.88
MAT	-15.22**	2 119**	-69.1*	-6.13	-17.77	-20.15	14.3**	-3.68	-0.36	0.93**	0.21*	.86	1.12
FOR	0.57	-737.58	-80.12*	42.48	37.72	63.99	-17.20**	7.8*	-0.09	0.8*	0.16*	.65	.31
TROP	-6.1**	1 020.77**	23.83	-99.67**	110.55**	-11.85	5.14*	-11.35**	-1.34**	0.05	0.09*	.78	.53
ANL	-8.29**	758*	-24.1	-41.78	42.84	-159.07	2.13	-0.38	-0.06	0.1	0.03	.63	.20
CER	-2.98**	-182.8	-54.8*	-68.8**	101.7**	299.5**	-4.68*	-5.12*	0.59**	-0.17*	0.15**	.94	.54
LAB	-4.94*	583.4	232.43*	-100.1	16.74	187.1	16.86*	-14.6*	-1.69*	-0.26	0.35**	.81	.43
CAP	10.69**	-1 372*	47.1	96.6*	-118.2**	232.64*	-3.55	14.37**	0.59*	0.26	-0.46**	.83	.69
MACH	105.9**	-20 255**	602.5*	896.6**	-950.16**	658.1	-32.63	130.8**	7.55**	-0.18	-1.82**	.84	.58
CHEM	2.08	103.5	-70.63	70.51	-146.55**	371.16*	-15.48*	14.2*	2.32**	0.33	-0.48**	.48	1.07

Notes:
a GNP is scaled in thousands of US dollars; CAPITAL is in millions of US dollars.
* Indicates that $|t|>1$.
** Indicates that $|t|>2$.

Table 6.7 Bounds for weighted least-squares formed by omitting observations one at a time[a]

	CAPITAL	LABOUR 1	LABOUR 2	LABOUR 3	LAND 1	LAND 2	LAND 3	LAND 4	COAL	MINERALS	OIL
1965											
GNP	-.09/.12	**32.62/98**	**-3.06/-.96**	-2.42/2.25	-.85/1.96	-.92/2.86	-.12/.03	-.04/.07	-.01/.08	-.02/0.2	**.01/.13**
PETRO	-.55/.14	**-936/-567**	**11.3/29.2**	**18.75/31.2**	**-19.8/-9.0**	-16.8/22.0	**.37/1.44**	**-1.16/-.23**	-.14/.37	-.12/.10	**1.51/2.17**
MAT	**-1.64/-.73**	-537/230	**-11.6/-2.74**	**2.68/15.32**	**1.01/5.32**	**2.43/15.2**	**-1.02/-.17**	**.30/1.39**	**.04/.44**	**.72/.92**	**.05/.26**
FOR	-2.8/1.05	-218/1161	-39.8/2.25	-19.8/2.76	**2.58/13.56**	-48.1/7.24	**-4.43/-1.02**	**.69/3.45**	**-3.04/-1.2**	**.23/.85**	**-.25/-.10**
TROP	-2.74/.66	-488/445	-9.3/15.4	-16.4/3.01	-1.1/12.8	9.16/56.4	-2.78/.68	-1.1/1.04	**-1.85/-.54**	**-.4/-.03**	-.10/.27
ANL	-3.17/2.06	**37.4/1301**	**-56/-1.12**	**-32/-.41**	**5.02/22.0**	-83.5/15.8	**.37/4.9**	-.30/.25	**-3.5/-1.14**	**-.38/-.05**	-.08/.60
CER	**-5.63/-1.4**	**97/1668**	**-75.9/-33**	**-58/-5.4**	**13.6/46.6**	**.33/55**	**.63/4.17**	-.93/.04	-1.95/.61	-.22/.32	-.03/1.52
LAB	-2.74/2.3	-526/795	**.27/34.5**	-19.9/12.8	-12.3/1.28	-24.8/4.42	-.02/.68	**-1.97/-.28**	-2.04/.11	**-.39/-.09**	**-.53/-.03**
CAP	-.53/1.83	-169/685	**16.6/53.8**	-28.7/14.7	**-27.1/-8.0**	**-77/-19.3**	-.07/3.6	-1.89/.06	**-1.14/-.02**	-.24/.15	**-.87/-.12**
MACH	**1.6/7.38**	-1880/215	**8.5/63.2**	-11.8/46.8	**-43.6/-9.7**	—73/73.3	-3.14/7.34	-1.25/1.43	**4.1/7.1**	**-1.1/-.18**	-.38/1.16
CHEM	**1.28/2.51**	**-491/-76**	-7.78/4.1	**1.28/13.3**	-6.89/.05	-11.6/13.8	-.76/.82	-.04/.24	**.58/1.29**	-.10/.02	-.07/.32
1988											
GNP	**.98/1.36**	-45.6/29.8	-2.4/1.92	-4.1/1.1	-97/3.37	-9.2/4.05	-.64/.08	-.63/.59	**.002/.06**	**-.05/-.01**	-.002/.02
PETRO	-22.7/4268	-38/5240	-104/37.3	-99/81.6	-380/44	-570/35.2	-12.6/42.5	-19.1/7.9	-3.2/.52	-.27/1.28	-20/.81
MAT	**-17/-1.89**	-47/3013	-208/14.9	-83/120	-101/104	-265/332	-39/22.4	-12.3/14.6	-.88/.44	**.45/1.56**	-.02/.42
FOR	-3.8/4.33	-1536/398	**-156/-44**	-26/67.2	**16.2/104**	-30/255	**-42/-12.1**	-2.5/45	-.54/.23	**.10/1.56**	-.23/.27
TROP	**-7.5/-4.6**	**606/1470**	-19.7/47.5	**-132/-73**	**55/149**	-123/187	-24/8.2	**-14.9/-7.4**	**-1.69/-.57**	-.1/.23	-.09/.16
ANL	**-9.88/-2.6**	-173/1413	-101/12.3	**-68/-12.8**	**8.89/110**	-287/43	-6.38/5.94	-3.48/9.3	-.66/.29	-.1/.25	-.09/.18
CER	**-75/-.27**	-743/266	-126/234	**-94/-5.4**	-3.97/164	**.62/415**	-7.9/4.3	-7.82/.13	-3.17/.95	-172/.05	-44.7/.22
LAB	**-7.8/-1.53**	-328/1201	**133/379**	**-466/-49**	-112/55.9	-371/32.6	-15.8/23.6	**-26.5/-4.9**	**-2.29/-.81**	**-.46/-.03**	**-.56/-.11**
CAP	**8.97/12.3**	**-1958/-944**	**20.5/141**	-103/133	**-201/-46**	-118/354	-10/16.9	**9.24/24.7**	-.40/1.12	-.09/.45	**-.57/-.21**
MACH	**61.2/126**	**-25467/-12993**	**280/1440**	**170/1333**	**-1688/-523**	-155/2127	-74/295	**88/179**	**1.9/12.3**	-1.48/1.5	**-2.57/-.46**
CHEM	-.13/12.3	-1553/676	**-120/-7.39**	-14.3/138	-189/14	-147/596	-27/12.3	**2.89/27.4**	**.13/3.19**	-.21/.59	-.63/.05

Note: a Intervals that exclude zero are in boldface.

and COAL on trade are most measurable (12 out of 20). LABOUR 1 has 10 measurable effects, LABOUR 3 has eight, and both LAND 3 and OIL have seven. Among the effects with *t*-values greater than 2 in absolute value, the surprises in terms of signs are: LABOUR 1 (minus) for 1965 MACH and CHEM and 1988 MACH; LABOUR 2 and LABOUR 3 (minus) for 1965 CER; LABOUR 3 (minus) for 1988 CER; COAL and OIL (plus) for 1988 CER; and MINERALS (plus) for 1965 FOR. Finally, as observed by Leamer (1984), the results also show that several of the resources are estimated to have negative effects on GNP.

The approach proposed by Belsley, Kuh and Welsch (1980) has been used in detecting nonsystematic heteroscedasticity (outliers). Extreme estimates after individual observations have been omitted are given in Table 6.7. Estimates that have signs insensitive to these one-at-a-time omissions are printed in boldface. The coefficients that are most insensitive to the choice of observations are those of LABOUR 2, which has a total of 13 out of 22 insensitive coefficients. CAPITAL, LAND 1 and COAL each have 12 insensitive coefficients; LABOUR 3 and MINERALS have a total of 10 insensitive coefficients each. The most sensitive coefficients are those of LAND 2 and LAND 3, which respectively have only three and six insensitive signs.

It has been pointed out that 'the omission of a country will generate an extreme estimate for a coefficient in many different equations' (Leamer 1984, p. 166). The following is a list of countries that critically influence the estimates in that they often generate an extreme estimate if omitted. The number of times (out of 20) that the variable generates an extreme estimate in a trade equation is given in parentheses; five or more times is considered significant.

CAPITAL: GER (10), JAP (8), ITLY (6);

LABOUR 1: GER (9), US (6), JAP (5);

LABOUR 2: INDO (9), JAP (8), SWE (5), GER (5);

LABOUR 3: GER (9), INDA (9), US (6), MEX (5);

LAND 1: INDO (12), GER (8), US (8);

LAND 2: AUSL (13), LSAL (7), SPAN (5);

LAND 3: AUSL (20), CAN (5);

LAND 4: BRAZ (14), GER (6), CAN (5);

COAL: GER (17), UK (7);

MINERALS: CHLE (10), US (8), BRAZ (6), CAN (6), GER (5); and

OIL: VELA (9), US (8), GER (7).

To illustrate the concept of *information contract curve*, the MACHINERY equation in 1988 is chosen to demonstrate how prior variance can be constrained to an interval ($0.5 \leq \sigma_1 \leq 2$), and how a subset of points on the contract curve can be selected. Estimates of the 1988 MACHINERY equation using the prior information described in Table 6.5 are given in Table 6.8.

Following Leamer (1984, p. 150), the first row of this table contains values for σ_1, the scalar that multiplies all the prior standard errors. If $\sigma_1 = \infty$, the prior standard errors are infinite and the estimates are based on the data alone; the values for $\sigma_1 = \infty$ are recorded in the last column of the table. If $\sigma_1 = 0$, the prior standard errors are all set to zero and the coefficients are constrained to equal their prior means; the results when $\sigma_1 = 0$ are recorded in the first column. The column headed $\sigma_1 = 1$ contains the compromise estimates built on the prior means defined in Table 6.5 (which are the Bayes estimates reported later for all other equations). The value $\sigma_1 = 2$ uses a prior mean that is twice as diffuse (twice as close to sample information); the value $\sigma_1 = 0.5$ uses a prior mean that is twice as dogmatic (twice as close to prior information).

Table 6.8 Bayes estimates, MACHINERY equation, 1988

	$\sigma_1 = 0$	$\sigma_1 = 0.5$	$\sigma_1 = 1$	$\sigma_1 = 2$	$\sigma_1 = \infty$
CAPITAL	37.50	95.37	100.80	103.91	107.35
LABOUR 1	4 000.00	-4 270.98	-8 421.21	-12 581.31	-20 931.25
LABOUR 2	112.50	137.37	159.82	198.73	598.16
LABOUR 3	-45.00	-34.14	-23.53	-3.01	907.64
LAND 1	-0.50	-0.50	-0.50	-0.51	-940.05
LAND 2	-1.00	-1.00	-1.00	-1.00	591.41
LAND 3	-10.00	-10.77	-11.50	-12.83	-35.90
LAND 4	-5.00	-3.66	-2.34	0.22	135.20
COAL	-0.05	-0.05	-0.05	-0.04	7.78
MINERALS	-0.05	-0.05	-0.05	-0.05	-0.40
OIL	-0.05	-0.05	-0.06	-0.07	-1.81

As Table 6.8 shows, there is a difference in magnitude but not in sign between the least-squares estimate of the CAPITAL coefficient (107.35) and the prior estimate (37.5). The pooled estimate of the CAPITAL coefficient when $\sigma_1 = 1$ is close to the least-squares estimate (100.8). Similarly, the prior, least-squares and pooled estimates of the coefficients for LABOUR 2, LAND 1, LAND 3, MINERALS and OIL are similar; the signs of the prior estimates and data estimates remain the same.[8] With the other coefficients, however, the prior estimates and the data estimates disagree. For example, despite the prediction of the prior means, highly skilled workers (LABOUR 1) are estimated by the data to have a negative effect on MACHINERY net exports.

The negative sign remains even when σ_1 is as small as 0.5. While the LABOUR 3 coefficient is estimated by the data alone to be positive, it changes to negative even with a small dose of prior information, $\sigma_1 = 2$. Similar results can be observed for LAND 2 and COAL. In the case of LAND 4, when the prior information is further sharpened ($\sigma_1 = 1$), then the expected positive sign occurs.

The results given in Table 6.8 confirm Leamer's claim (1984, p. 151) that $0.5 \le \sigma_1 \le 2$, which allows prior information to be either twice as informed or twice as uninformed, is a reasonable interval of values for σ_1. This is because the results show that the estimates corresponding to this interval in general conform in sign to their prior values and the implausible least-squares estimates are eliminated. For example, the least-squares estimate for the OIL coefficient suggests that each extra dollar of OIL output will generate US$1.81 of MACHINERY imports. A fairly small dose of prior information ($\sigma_1 = 2$) produces a sensibly small coefficient; a further injection of prior information ($\sigma_1 = 1$) does in fact lead to a value very close to the prior expectation. To give another example, sharpening prior information not only changes the sign of the COAL coefficient (from positive to negative), but also produces the sensible coefficient, namely that each extra dollar of COAL output generates US$0.05 of MACHINERY imports.

Significantly, Table 6.8 confirms Leamer's (1984) finding that LABOUR 1 has a negative effect, contrary to the sign of the prior means and regardless of the value of σ_1 in the interval $0.5 \le \sigma_1 \le 2$. This result may bring under scrutiny once more the definition of this category of labour; or it may mean that the influence of human capital on comparative advantage does not take a linear form.

Tables 6.9 and 6.10 set out Bayes estimates and *t*-statistics based on the prior means reported in Tables 6.4 and 6.5. The justification for using Bayesian analysis here is that 'minor chronic measurement errors would render the least-squares estimates totally irrelevant, but leave the Bayes estimates relatively intact' (Leamer 1984, p. 170).

Table 6.9 shows clearly that in general the Bayes estimates conform to expectations based on the model specification: the natural resource products, PETRO and MAT, are related to the natural resources COAL, MINERALS and OIL; the four crops are positively related to the four respective LAND variables; and the four manufactured commodities are positively related to CAPITAL and LABOUR variables. There are also some discrepancies, which will be discussed later. The sign patterns of the CAPITAL and LABOUR 2 coefficients for all four manufactured aggregates are identical for both years. More specifically, as expected, CAPITAL contributes to comparative advantage in all manufactured commodities except LAB, and LABOUR 2 contributes to comparative advantage in the same commodity aggregates with the exception of CHEM.

It is interesting to observe the changing role of LABOUR 1 (highly skilled labour) from 1965 to 1988. In 1965, instead of being concentrated in MACH and CHEM as one would expect, LABOUR 1 is positively related to LAB and CAP. However, by 1988 it has converged to the prior expectation, being positively related to CHEM (the

Table 6.9 Bayes estimates[a]

	CAPITAL	LABOUR 1	LABOUR 2	LABOUR 3	LAND 1	LAND 2	LAND 3	LAND 4	COAL	MINERALS	OIL
1965											
GNP	0.02	75.25	-2.65	-1.64	1.06	1.43	-0.07	0.00	0.10	0.00	0.04
PETRO	-0.13	-738.53	18.43	28.15	-0.30	-0.31	1.34	-0.41	-0.05	-0.02	1.89
MAT	-0.88	-490.28	-5.52	7.30	-0.13	-0.30	-0.32	0.40	0.38	0.86	0.10
FOR	0.22	15.49	-10.31	1.18	-0.16	-0.34	-1.46	1.18	-0.07	0.00	-0.06
TROP	-1.74	65.12	5.24	-5.79	-0.16	3.29	0.05	0.23	-0.06	-0.06	-0.04
ANL	-0.25	44.89	-1.25	-8.12	-0.16	-0.33	1.09	-0.24	-0.07	-0.06	-0.04
CER	-2.78	364.12	-43.92	-33.51	4.15	-0.33	0.86	-0.60	-0.06	-0.06	-0.02
LAB	-1.12	468.86	10.49	-6.36	-0.18	-0.33	0.27	-0.71	-0.08	-0.08	-0.06
CAP	0.09	150.95	36.87	-1.60	-0.18	-0.34	0.02	-0.33	-0.06	-0.06	-0.07
MACH	5.99	-1 097.99	36.05	1.15	-0.17	-0.33	-2.97	0.26	-0.02	-0.07	-0.05
CHEM	2.13	-357.99	-1.52	4.64	-0.17	-0.34	-0.81	0.17	0.03	-0.08	-0.03
1988											
GNP	1.30	-27.76	-0.60	-1.69	1.96	-3.51	-0.44	0.31	0.05	-0.02	0.01
PETRO	-19.26	2 196.47	-45.63	-17.10	-0.51	-1.01	17.32	-6.41	-0.08	-0.03	0.39
MAT	-15.34	1 228.00	-74.45	-26.85	-0.50	-1.00	7.25	-4.52	-0.02	0.83	0.21
FOR	-1.67	-551.97	-33.80	41.10	-0.50	-1.00	-13.44	5.92	-0.05	-0.02	-0.02
TROP	-5.89	616.27	32.04	-49.53	-0.47	8.85	2.30	-8.56	-0.09	-0.04	-0.01
ANL	-9.55	501.66	9.70	5.09	-0.50	-1.00	5.18	-4.51	-0.05	-0.04	-0.04
CER	-2.59	-424.80	-43.60	-36.24	7.07	-0.98	-5.98	-4.35	-0.02	-0.07	0.02
LAB	-5.02	-376.00	169.39	21.39	-0.50	-1.00	-0.61	-6.54	-0.06	-0.05	-0.06
CAP	11.30	-1 403.04	60.68	16.37	-0.51	-1.00	-6.49	2.92	-0.04	-0.04	-0.10
MACH	100.80	-8 421.21	159.82	-23.53	-0.50	-1.00	-11.50	-2.34	-0.05	-0.05	-0.06
CHEM	2.52	210.98	-8.61	-10.76	-0.51	-1.00	-13.14	0.11	-0.03	-0.04	-0.08

Note: a Bayes estimates reported in this and other tables in this chapter are obtained using the author's own program.

Table 6.10 *t*-values for Bayes estimates[a]

	CAPITAL	LABOUR 1	LABOUR 2	LABOUR 3	LAND 1	LAND 2	LAND 3	LAND 4	COAL	MINERALS	OIL
1965											
GNP	0.37	**3.85**	-2.53	-3.58	2.97	0.87	-1.69	0.05	3.35	0.22	3.80
PETRO	-0.43	-7.00	3.18	11.26	-1.76	-0.94	5.48	-1.93	-0.95	-0.60	**30.99**
MAT	-3.91	-6.13	-1.27	3.87	-0.75	-0.92	-1.72	2.49	3.02	**16.91**	2.04
FOR	0.30	0.08	-0.76	0.20	-0.95	-1.02	**-2.46**	2.21	-1.47	-0.03	-1.25
TROP	-1.86	0.23	0.31	-0.81	-0.96	1.11	0.06	0.36	-1.27	-1.26	-0.90
ANL	-0.27	0.16	-0.07	-1.13	-0.93	-1.02	**1.43**	-0.39	-1.38	-1.16	-0.86
CER	-3.29	1.40	-2.86	**-5.07**	2.84	-0.99	1.27	-1.03	-1.13	-1.17	-0.50
LAB	-1.92	**2.41**	0.96	-1.34	-1.05	-1.01	0.56	-1.73	-1.60	-1.70	-1.34
CAP	0.10	0.55	**2.26**	-0.23	-1.07	-1.03	0.03	-0.54	-1.13	-1.20	-1.38
MACH	**4.51**	-2.36	1.63	0.12	-1.03	-1.00	-2.88	0.31	-0.47	-1.49	-1.04
CHEM	**7.18**	-3.35	-0.27	1.87	-1.00	-1.02	-3.33	0.82	0.68	-1.89	-0.88
1988											
GNP	**23.13**	-1.49	-0.38	-1.23	1.41	-0.65	-2.37	1.88	4.26	-3.15	2.12
PETRO	**-8.49**	3.64	-0.71	-0.49	-1.01	-1.01	2.86	-1.59	-1.64	-0.68	3.30
MAT	**-7.96**	2.27	-1.37	-0.82	-1.00	-1.00	1.33	-1.20	-0.07	4.01	2.01
FOR	-0.77	-0.94	-0.63	1.20	-0.99	-1.00	**-2.29**	0.93	-1.06	-0.32	-0.53
TROP	**-4.49**	1.54	0.91	-1.89	-0.95	0.99	0.57	-2.78	-1.92	-0.91	-0.30
ANL	**-4.44**	0.86	0.18	0.15	-0.99	-1.00	0.72	-1.14	-1.06	-0.80	-0.86
CER	**-2.33**	-1.23	-1.44	-1.55	1.59	-0.98	-1.72	-1.58	-0.34	-1.52	0.43
LAB	-1.19	-0.46	**2.06**	0.52	-1.00	-1.00	-0.07	-1.41	-1.12	-1.03	-1.22
CAP	**5.28**	-2.42	1.13	0.48	-1.02	-1.00	-1.11	0.74	-0.81	-0.85	-2.11
MACH	**8.78**	-2.97	1.50	-0.53	-1.01	-1.00	-1.18	-0.47	-0.93	-1.01	-1.15
CHEM	0.89	0.23	-0.13	-0.28	-1.01	-1.00	**-1.90**	0.03	-0.63	-0.87	-1.69

Note: a Largest value in row is in boldface.

most capital and human capital intensive product) and negatively related to LAB and CAP except MACH. This suggests a dramatic change in the role of human capital as a source of comparative advantage.

A similar trend is apparent with LABOUR 3 (unskilled labour), which can be expected to contribute positively to comparative advantage in LAB through its contribution to comparative advantage (disadvantage) in manufactured products. In 1965 LABOUR 3 was, contrary to expectation, positively related to MACH and CHEM and negatively related to LAB and CAP. By 1988, however, LABOUR 3 is positively related to LAB (as well as to CAP) and negatively related to MACH and CHEM. In the 1960s, LABOUR 3 and to a greater degree LABOUR 2 contributed to comparative advantage in the top three manufactured aggregates and particularly MACH; by the end of the 1980s, though, it was mainly the combination of CAPITAL and LABOUR 1 and to some extent LABOUR 2 which contributed to comparative advantage in the same three manufactured aggregates, particularly CHEM.

This phenomenon is consistent with the trend, particularly in developing countries, towards the rapid accumulation of capital (see Chapter 3) and with the changing proportions of the three types of labour in the total world labour force from the 1960s to the 1980s. In 1965, these proportions were 4.8 per cent, 59.9 per cent and 35.2 per cent respectively for LABOUR 1, LABOUR 2 and LABOUR 3 (3.1 per cent, 53.7 per cent and 43.1 per cent if China is included). In 1988 these percentages had changed to 7.7 per cent, 66.2 per cent and 26.1 per cent (6.7 per cent, 63.9 per cent and 29.3 per cent with China included), indicating increased literacy and an increased proportion of professional/technical workers.

Most of the other resource variables have the anticipated sign in relation to the four aggregates of manufacture, with the exception of COAL with CHEM in 1965, LAND 3 with LAB and CAP in 1965 and LAND 4 with CAP and CHEM in 1988. The economic interpretation of the sign pattern of these coefficients can be stated as follows. Each dollar of COAL extracted is estimated to generate US$0.033 of CHEM exports in 1965 but US$0.032 of CHEM imports in 1988. In the case of MINERALS and OIL, the variables all generate imports of all four manufactured aggregates in both years. For example, each dollar of MINERALS produced is estimated to generate US$0.076 of CHEM imports in 1965, while each dollar of OIL will generate US$0.099 of CAP imports in 1988. A close look at the magnitude of these coefficients also reveals the following interesting trends. The sizes of the COAL coefficients (absolute values) are in general lower in 1988 than in 1965 and the sign of COAL is reversed during the period. Meanwhile, the sizes of the OIL coefficients (absolute values) are not only in general higher in 1988 than in 1965, but also much higher than those of COAL in 1988. This suggests the increasing importance of OIL as a source of energy in the late 1980s.

The two natural resource products, PETRO and MAT, have their sources of comparative advantage in the three natural resources, COAL, MINERALS and OIL. The high negative signs of CAPITAL coefficients with high *t*-values (Table 6.9) show clearly that the CAPITAL variable creates demand (a large volume of imports) for these natural resource products. Contrary to prior estimates, LAND 3 is found to have a positive effect on net exports of PETRO and LAND 4 has a positive effect on net exports of MAT in 1965. While LAND 4 changes its sign in relation to MAT from positive in 1965 to negative in 1988, the sign pattern of LAND 3 in relation to PETRO remains unchanged with a high *t*-value; it becomes positive with MAT as well in 1988. One possible explanation for this is that 'the coverage of the MINERALS variable is incomplete and . . . land is where raw materials are found' (Leamer 1984, p. 176).

The other important finding with regard to PETRO and MAT concerns the reversed role of the three categories of LABOUR in contributing to comparative advantage (disadvantage) in these resource products during the period. In 1965, LABOUR 3 led to net exports in both PETRO and MAT while LABOUR 1 caused net imports in the same products. By 1988, however, the opposite is the case. It is also interesting to observe that the sign patterns of both LABOUR 1 and LABOUR 2 with either PETRO and MAT or MACH and CHEM are consistent in both years. In other words, these LABOUR variables were sources of comparative advantage in PETRO and MAT and in MACH and CHEM in each of these years. These two findings reflect, firstly, the increasingly important role played by professional/technical workers in developing more efficient uses of energy and raw materials during the period. In addition, the consistency of sign patterns indicates the strong complementary relationship between natural resource products (PETRO and MAT) and manufactured products (MACH and CHEM) in relation to LABOUR 1 and LABOUR 3.

As the four land variables are used for the first time in this model estimation, it is significant that the four crops, FOR, TROP, ANL and CER, are in general statistically positively related to the land variables. FOR is positively associated with LAND 4 (forests and woodland), TROP with LAND 2 (land under permanent crops), ANL with LAND 3 (permanent meadows and pastures) and CER with LAND 1 (arable land). Capital was, as expected, a source of comparative disadvantage in these crops, with the exception of FOR in 1965. Similarly, the natural resources, COAL, MINERALS and OIL, do in general contribute to comparative disadvantage in these crops, though OIL has a positive effect on CER only in 1988.

The major surprise is that LABOUR 1 contributes positively to all the crops in 1965, while LABOUR 2 is positively correlated only with TROP, and LABOUR 3 only with FOR; this despite the prior estimate for LABOUR 1 being negative and the prior estimates for LABOUR 2 and LABOUR 3 being positive for these crops. It was observed, however, that the sign patterns for the labour variables in relation to these crops began to converge towards the prior expectation of the labour variables in 1988: LABOUR 1 was positively correlated only with TROP and ANL, LABOUR 2 only with TROP and ANL, and LABOUR 3 only with FOR and ANL. One possible explanation for the negative contribution of labour variables to crops, particularly CER, can be explored by considering the demand effect of these relationships. From this perspective, it is not surprising to find labour variables, and especially LABOUR 2 and LABOUR 3, creating comparative disadvantage in CEREALS in both years and in ANL only in 1965. Moreover, changes in the sign patterns of LABOUR 2 and LABOUR 3 in relation to ANL during the period mean that the demand effect of labour variables on CER is larger than that on ANL. This is just commonsense.

The question now is whether the foregoing inferences are robust or fragile. They would seem robust in the sense that the Bayes estimates pool the data information with another source of information, namely prior information, and therefore estimates are relatively insensitive to such econometric problems as gross errors and chronic errors. However, they could be fragile if problems such as improper specification of the prior means occur in applying the Bayesian approach. A sensitivity study of the Bayesian estimates is therefore necessary; and, for this reason, the effect of perturbations of prior distribution will be studied.

To illustrate the effect, bounds for the Bayes estimates of the MACHINERY equation are first shown in Table 6.11. These intervals of estimates are generated from intervals of prior covariance matrices that range from one-quarter to four times the covariance matrices ($0.25\Omega_0 \leq \Omega \leq 4\Omega_0$). These were used to obtain the Bayes estimates in Table 6.9. 'This interval allows the standard error of any linear combination of parameters to be reduced or to be increased by a factor of two. This is a rather wide interval of variance matrices, reflecting great ambiguity in the choice of prior' (Leamer 1984, p. 177).

The results given in Table 6.11 show that eight out of 11 coefficients (CAPITAL, LABOUR 1, LABOUR 2, LAND 1, LAND 3, COAL, MINERALS and OIL) take on a single sign in this interval.[9] The fact that most of the estimates are insensitive to choice of Ω in the interval $0.25\Omega_0 \leq \Omega \leq 4\Omega_0$ suggests that much can be learned from the data about the determinants of MACHINERY net exports. It is, however,

Table 6.11 Estimates and bounds, MACHINERY equation, 1988[a]

	Prior estimate	Least squares	Bayes estimate	Lower bound	Upper bound
CAPITAL	37.5(37.5)	107(12.1)	101(11.5)	86.90	105.60
LABOUR 1	4 000(4 000)	-20 931(4 014)	-8 421(2 833)	-15 917.00	-958.00
LABOUR 2	112.5(112.5)	598(342)	160(107)	125.30	258.90
LABOUR 3	-45(45)	908(296)	-24(45)	-39.50	35.40
LAND 1	-.5(.5)	-940(299)	-.5(.5)	-0.51	-0.50
LAND 2	-1(1)	591(1184)	-1(1)	1.00	-1.00
LAND 3	-10(10)	-36(40)	-11.5(9.7)	-15.10	-10.40
LAND 4	-5(5)	135(36)	-2.34(4.9)	-4.33	5.06
COAL	-.05(.05)	7.78(2.4)	-.05(.05)	-0.05	-0.04
MINERALS	-.05(.05)	.4(1.46)	-.05(.05)	-0.05	-0.05
OIL	-.05(.05)	-1.8(.76)	-.06(.05)	-0.08	-0.05

Note: a Standard errors in parentheses.

necessary to go beyond a single-equation case to obtain a comprehensive view of the sensitivity issue.

The bounds in Table 6.12 indicate the sensitivity of the Bayes estimates to choice of prior variance matrix for GNP and net export equations in both 1965 and 1988. Leamer (1984, p. 177) points out that 'each such matrix in this interval implies a Bayes estimate, and from among this set of estimates the most extreme are selected and reported'. Those estimates that take on a single sign are not sensitive to the choice of prior distribution, and can be said to be independent of the choice of prior variance matrix.

As most coefficients take on a single sign, it would seem that a surprisingly high proportion of coefficients are insensitive to the choice of prior variance matrix. The insensitive coefficients are those of CAPITAL, LAND 1 and LAND 2, which do not encounter any sign change across equations. The most sensitive coefficients are those of LABOUR 3, with 12 out of 20 sets of estimates showing a sign change. LABOUR 1 and LABOUR 2 have seven sensitive coefficients each, while LAND 3, LAND 4, COAL and OIL have five each. MINERALS has only four sensitive coefficients. In comparison with the situation in 1965, the 1988 figures show a slight increase in the total number of sensitive coefficients.[10]

These sensitivity results have the following implications for the foregoing discussion of Bayes estimates. First, the results confirm the roles played by capital, arable land, tropical land and, to a lesser extent, natural resources, forest land and pasture, and semiskilled workers in determining trade patterns. Second, the sensitivity to choice of the prior variance matrix of LABOUR 1 and LABOUR 3 coefficients both in 1965 and 1988 casts doubt on the finding that the roles of human capital and of unskilled workers have changed.

The GNP equation is of particular interest because, as pointed out by Leamer (1984, p. 179), 'the same assumptions that imply our linear trade model also imply the linear GNP equation with coefficients equal to factor returns'. However, the results obtained from the current data point to a problem similar to that found by Leamer (1984) in his data, namely that some of the coefficients turn out to be negative. In several cases, the weighted regression estimates in Table 6.6 have negative coefficients. LABOUR 2 and LABOUR 3 in 1965 and LAND 3 and MINERALS in 1988 even have t-values of less than -2. The Bayes results in Table 6.9 also indicate that six coefficients remain negative even after the dose of prior information in 1988. Furthermore, the posterior t-values for LABOUR 2 and LABOUR 3 in 1965 are -2.5 and -3.6 respectively. LAND 3 and MINERALS in 1988 have significant negative coefficients, with t-values of -2.4 and -3.2 respectively. There is therefore evidence of a deficiency in the basic model, either because 'resources are left out or mismeasured or the model should be nonlinear' (Leamer 1984, p. 179).[11]

China is for the first time included in this cross-country analysis of the relationship between trade patterns and resource endowments. Because of its size and its increasing participation in world trade, it can be expected that the inclusion of China will have some impact on the results of the model estimation. In order to examine this impact,

Table 6.12 Bounds for Bayes estimates[a]

	CAPITAL	LABOUR 1	LABOUR 2	LABOUR 3	LAND 1	LAND 2
1965						
GNP	.0198/.0199	75.14/75.71	-2.656/-2.651	-1.641/-1.632	1.055/1.079	1.367/1.655
PETRO	-.1402/-.1269	-746.6/-710.9	17.784/18.593	25.451/28.884	-.6698/-.2021	-.3246/-.2447
MAT	-.88863/-.879	-491.1/-490	-5.835/-5.436	6.45/7.527	-.159/-.0063	-.3234/-.2245
FOR	.1572/.2395	-158.4/90.47	-14.62/1.9603	-.3527/5.316	-.168/-.1383	-.3601/-.3319
TROP	-1.835/-1.714	-208.2/236.96	.4412/16.98	-9.231/2.081	-.1683/-.1434	3.066/4.162
ANL	-.3518/-.2228	-218.7/210.6	-6.872/12.51	-11.91/.5489	-.1672/-.125	-.35/-.3313
CER	-2.859/-2.764	-23.54/584.1	-53.08/-19.91	-39.81/-17.96	2.204/10.258	-.3292/-.317
LAB	-1.128/-1.093	167.7/591.9	8.829/15.79	-7.788/-1.981	-.2019/-.172	-.3428/-.3308
CAP	.0777/.1598	-157.3/338.97	36.13/38.71	-6.778/.6116	-.2202/-.1731	-.3667/-.3323
MACH	5.962/6.11	-1229/-666.5	34.34/39.12	-7.514/6.437	-.1878/-.1711	-.3338/-.3302
CHEM	2.131/2.139	-363.02/-338.1	-2.119/.7077	3.36/4.989	-.1699/-.1687	-.3577/-.3317
1988						
GNP	1.295/1.295	-27.81/-27.547	.6013/-.5971	-1.699/-1.667	1.928/2.071	-3.846/-2.276
PETRO	-19.4/-19.223	525.5/3402	-68.78/-39.39	-35.12/6.244	-.5205/-.5013	-1.03/-1.002
MAT	-15.51/-15.3	186.4/1854.6	-90.26/-70.28	-37.97/-14.99	-.508/-.501	-1.002/-1.0
FOR	-2.179/-1.539	-778.7/-397.6	-64.26/25.896	38.07/43.58	-.4993/-.4889	-.9994/-.9906
TROP	-6.045/-5.849	91.34/837.2	25.59/50.45	-81.81/-1.832	-.4934/-.3943	8.42/8.963
ANL	-9.883/-9.462	-256.5/1015	-11.56/51.497	-25.72/30.45	-.4992/-.4876	-1.01/-1.001
CER	-2.718/-2.553	-577.3/-367.8	-52.62/-15.61	-56.76/.03003	5.155/14.031	-.994/-.9043
LAB	-5.421/-3.471	-791.6/244.5	134.4/207.2	-19.1/38.305	-.4999/-.4988	-1.004/-1.0
CAP	11.237/11.555	-1549/-1200	50.1/81.64	-22.55/63.324	-.5403/-.5025	-.9988/-.981
MACH	86.9/105.6	-15917/-958	125.26/258.96	-39.54/35.44	-.5105/-.5007	-.9999/-.99827
CHEM	2.37/3.115	53.26/733.2	-50.25/52.64	-34.04/28.003	-.5288/-.5018	-.9988/-.9815

Table 6.12 (continued)

	LAND 3	LAND 4	COAL	MINERALS	OIL
1965					
GNP	-.075/-.0732	.0017/.0024	.0358/.2882	-.009/.0457	.0343/.0808
PETRO	1.262/1.3544	-.474/-.3986	-.0488/-.0351	-.0413/.0002	1.524/2.0223
MAT	-.3426/-.3086	.3475/.4194	.371/.389	.8449/.8641	.0911/.1104
FOR-1	.-1.621/-1.413	1.169/1.234	-.1377/-.0556	-.037/.1069	-.0526/.0806
TROP	-.3925/.1765	-.3366/.4519	-.1022/-.0534	-.0887/-.0529	-.0483/-.0282
ANL	1.071/1.141	-.6676/-.0749	-.1229/-.0547	-.0726/-.0517	-.0479/-.0222
CER	.3955/.991	-.8783/-.4902	-.0742/-.0516	-.073/-.0518	-.0432/.0349
LAB	.0612/.321	-.8594/-.6667	-.1591/-.0574	-.1369/-.0582	-.0846/-.0534
CAP	-.3916/.1466	-.7163/-.1823	-.0741/-.0516	-.0786/-.0522	-.1074/-.0545
MACH	-3.05/-2.942	-.565/.7068	-.0434/.0545	-.1377/-.056	-.0548/-.0503
CHEM	-.8444/-.7951	.08888/.1975	-.0281/.2168	-.101/-.0589	-.0446/-.0211
1988					
GNP	-.4464/-.4358	.3137/.3179	.0384/.0813	-.0248/-.0075	.0065/.0112
PETRO	2.995/27.724	-7.751/-5.479	-.1716/-.0579	-.0458/.0097	.2917/.4487
MAT	-.849/12.143	-4.823/-4.161	-.2393/.2426	.6835/.9048	.2051/.2116
FOR	-14.63/-11.694	5.325/8.154	-.0597/-.051	-.0412/.0745	-.0431/.0247
TROP	-1.719/3.998	-9.986/-6.665	-.2095/-.0613	-.0482/-.0291	-.0384/.0323
ANL	4.769/6.771	-4.828/-4.074	-.0595/-.0506	-.0473/-.0116	-.0474/-.0222
CER	-7.055/-5.582	-4.663/-4.163	-.0413/.0675	-.1117/-.0558	-.0274/.0843
LAB	-6.872/8.792	-9.391/-5.43	-.074/-.052	-.0543/-.0503	-.0865/-.0526
CAP	-8.261/-5.29	-2.23/9.821	-.0475/-.0123	-.0478/-.0197	-.1934/-.0634
MACH	-15.11/-10.392	-4.326/5.057	-.0492/-.0365	-.0516/-.0501	-.08/-.0519
CHEM	-14.88/-11.29	-3.417/6.55	-.045/.0222	-.0482/-.0232	-.1531/-.0583

Note: a GNP is scaled in thousands of dollars; CAPITAL is in millions of dollars.

Table 6.13 Bayes estimates and *t*-values with China included, 1988

	CAPITAL	LABOUR 1	LABOUR 2	LABOUR 3	LAND 1	LAND 2	LAND 3	LAND 4	COAL	MINERALS	OIL
Estimate											
GNP	1.31	-29.71	-0.84	-1.65	2.19	-3.24	-0.46	0.30	0.04	-0.02	0.01
PETRO	-16.39	1 964.90	-100.81	-14.30	-0.50	-1.01	15.42	-7.22	-0.09	-0.04	0.44
MAT	-13.36	1 050.84	-112.49	-24.06	-0.50	-1.00	5.93	-5.22	-0.15	0.79	0.25
FOR	-4.36	-243.07	4.75	37.57	-0.50	-1.00	-11.63	8.17	-0.05	-0.01	-0.03
TROP	-6.93	788.30	50.10	-51.72	-0.47	8.72	3.25	-8.05	-0.09	-0.04	-0.02
ANL	-8.66	470.04	-9.77	5.75	-0.49	-1.00	4.32	-4.76	-0.05	-0.04	-0.04
CER	-4.50	-150.69	-8.72	-38.35	6.46	-0.98	-4.35	-3.29	-0.01	-0.06	0.00
LAB	-2.84	-469.80	151.10	22.39	-0.50	-1.00	-1.16	-6.88	-0.06	-0.05	-0.06
CAP	11.71	-1470.07	50.39	17.90	-0.51	-0.99	-6.72	3.04	-0.04	-0.04	-0.10
MACH	101.79	-9 057.56	177.37	-23.11	-0.50	-1.00	-11.47	-2.17	-0.05	-0.05	-0.06
CHEM	5.71	-307.16	-63.62	-8.50	-0.51	-0.99	-14.84	-0.60	-0.03	-0.04	-0.08
***t*-value**											
GNP	31.47	-1.70	-0.61	-1.22	1.91	-0.61	-2.51	1.87	4.30	-3.29	2.28
PETRO	-9.39	3.31	-1.74	-0.40	-1.00	-1.01	2.54	-1.79	-1.75	-0.74	3.77
MAT	-9.13	2.00	-2.31	-0.73	-0.99	-1.00	1.10	-1.38	-0.54	3.80	2.42
FOR	-2.62	-0.42	0.10	1.08	-1.01	-1.00	-1.97	1.27	-0.98	0.29	-0.70
TROP	-7.02	2.05	1.58	-1.97	-0.94	0.97	0.82	-2.63	-1.93	-0.85	-0.44
ANL	-5.41	0.84	-0.20	0.17	-0.99	-1.00	0.62	-1.22	-1.09	-0.81	-0.79
CER	-5.12	-0.43	-0.31	-1.58	1.46	-0.98	-1.21	-1.16	-0.14	-1.35	-0.01
LAB	-0.90	-0.59	1.96	0.54	-1.00	-1.00	-0.14	-1.48	-1.16	-1.04	-1.19
CAP	7.38	-2.64	1.05	0.53	-1.03	-0.99	-1.18	0.78	-0.80	-0.85	-2.18
MACH	11.70	-3.30	1.68	-0.52	-1.01	-1.00	-1.18	-0.44	-0.92	-1.01	-1.17
CHEM	2.63	-0.34	-1.04	-0.22	-1.01	-0.99	-2.15	-0.14	-0.66	-0.90	-1.58

the model estimation has been redone with the inclusion of 1988 data on China.[12] The Bayes estimates and their *t*-values are reported in Table 6.13.

The impact of the China factor can be seen by comparing Table 6.13 with Tables 6.9 and 6.10. The results are mixed. There are a few significant changes in estimation results for some coefficients when China is included. For example, the coefficients of LABOUR 1 in the CHEM equation, LABOUR 2 in the FOR and ANL equations and LAND 4 in the CHEM equation change signs. Some of the changes, such as LAND 4 and LABOUR 2 in FOR, are in accord with the prior estimate, and some, such as LABOUR 1 and LABOUR 2 in ANL, move away from the prior estimate.

Another important finding in a statistical sense is the reinforcement of the role of CAPITAL in contributing to comparative advantage in CAP, MACH and CHEM, regarded as the most capital intensive industries. The *t*-values of the CAPITAL coefficients increase substantially in all three equations. More significant is the increase in the *t*-value in the CHEM equation; this makes the coefficient of CAPITAL statistically significant at the 5 per cent level in the CHEM equation and reverses the decreasing trend (significant in a statistical sense) of the CAPITAL coefficient from 1965 to 1988, as demonstrated in Table 6.10.

Several conclusions can be drawn from the preceding model estimation. First, the 11 measured resources in general do a good job of explaining the trade patterns of the 10 commodity aggregates, especially agricultural and natural resource commodities, and of providing information about sources of comparative advantage. This supports the conclusion reached by Leamer (1984) that the simple linear model of trade and factor endowments largely explains the variability of net exports across countries and identifies sources of comparative advantage, even though problems such as measurement errors and nonlinearities still exist in the current data sets.

Second, the Bayes estimates indicate that structural changes in the relationship between certain factor endowments and trade aggregates may have taken place during the period 1965 to 1988. These structural changes can be regarded as evidence for changes in the patterns (or sources) of international comparative advantage during the period. Of interest in this regard is the altered role from 1965 to 1988 of human capital as a source of comparative (dis)advantage in manufactured products: in 1965, the most highly skilled workers (LABOUR 1) contributed to comparative advantage in LAB and CAP and to comparative disadvantage in MACH and CHEM; but in 1988 these workers contributed positively only to the most skill-intensive manufactured aggregate (CHEM).

Another finding with regard to structural change is the altered role of unskilled workers (LABOUR 3) as a source of comparative advantage in the top two manufactured aggregates, MACH and CHEM; unskilled workers contributed to comparative advantage in MACH and CHEM in 1965 but contributed to comparative disadvantage in these two manufactured aggregates in 1988. The changing role over time of resources in determining trade patterns can also be seen in the relationship between COAL and MAT: in 1965 COAL contributed positively to MAT, while in 1988 it became a source of comparative disadvantage in MAT. While MINERALS remained the main source of comparative advantage in MAT, the positive role of OIL in this regard increased rapidly during the period.

In contrast to LABOUR 1 and LABOUR 3, the role of semiskilled workers (LABOUR 2) in relation to the four manufactured aggregates remains stable over the period; in both 1965 and 1988, semiskilled workers contributed to comparative advantage in LAB, CAP and MACH, and to comparative disadvantage in CHEM.

Third, some changes in the Bayes estimates over time, although not in the form of changes in sign, are still statistically significant: there are substantial increases in the *t*-values of certain coefficients over time, for example. These indicate that statistically more robust estimation results have been obtained, increasing the credibility of the inferences drawn from the model estimation with regard to the coefficients concerned.[13]

For example, although the role of CAPITAL in determining the trade patterns of manufactured products remains the same from 1965 to 1988 (contributing positively to CAP, MACH and CHEM and negatively to LAB), the statistical significance levels change markedly during the period; while the *t*-value of the CAPITAL coefficient in the MACH equation remains at the 5 per cent level over time, the *t*-value in the CAP equation reaches the 5 per cent level and the *t*-value in the CHEM equation actually drops substantially. This means that CAPITAL contributes solidly to comparative advantage in capital-intensive products and machinery in 1988.

Fourth, in general the four new land variables perform well in the model estimation. As a result, the link between each land variable and its corresponding agricultural aggregate is established.

Finally, continuing on from Leamer's (1984) results, the 1988 estimation results show that in the late 1980s human capital (LABOUR 1) is still the most important source of comparative advantage in chemicals, while physical capital and skilled and unskilled workers are the main sources of comparative advantage in machinery and in capital intensive and labour intensive manufactures. It was also observed that natural resources are still sources of comparative advantage in natural resource products.

7 Shifting international comparative advantage from the 1960s to the 1980s

This study set out to examine to what extent the trends identified by Leamer (1984) in the data for the period 1958–75 continued into the 1980s, the central question being: what resource supplies have determined comparative advantage and has there been a structural change in patterns of trade and resource endowments over time?

Summary and conclusions

Three approaches to the preceding question were adopted. First, the relationship between trade patterns and resource endowments was described in the form of trade dependence profiles and resource abundance profiles. Second, sign patterns of trade in factor services based on the Heckscher–Ohlin–Vanek (HOV) model were used to measure relative factor abundance in a cross-country setting. Third, econometric analysis of the trade dependence model using the Bayesian econometric method was applied to cross-country trade and resource data for two points in time; this was done to measure further the accuracy of the HOV model and to examine structural changes in the relationship between trade patterns and resource endowments over the new period of time covered in this book. In addition, the book previewed different forms of data. This not only laid the foundation for the analysis described above but, because the preview contains rich information about the international economy, was in itself a useful exercise.

Principal findings

First, through its preview of trade and resource data, Chapter 3 provided information about resource endowments and their changes over time, presenting the absolute values and quantities of key resource supplies such as capital and labour, and their ranking and growth rates from 1965 to 1988 (including the two subperiods 1965–74 and 1974–88). The results showed that, in general, developed countries ranked high with regard to capital per worker and skilled labour per worker, although some developing economies, particularly East Asian economies, including the NIEs, witnessed rapid growth in capital and labour skills.

As reported in Chapter 3, changes in the international distribution of key resource endowments (skilled labour, semiskilled labour, unskilled labour and arable land) provided initial indications of changes in patterns of world trade. This was supported by the results of cross-country correlations between trade and resource endowments.

The ladder of development formed by sorting the signs of net exports of four manufactured aggregates demonstrated how countries have changed their composition of trade and upgraded themselves along the development path. Perhaps the most dramatic change observed during the period under study was the shift of a large number of countries one step up from the bottom of the ladder, achieved by exporting labour intensive products by the 1980s. Many developing countries remained at the initial stages of development.

Second, trade and resource data in the form of trade dependence profiles and resource abundance profiles clearly supported the view that there was, in general, a linkage between patterns of trade and patterns of resource endowments, as implied by the Heckscher–Ohlin theorem (Chapter 4). In general, countries with similar trade dependence profiles did in fact tend to have similar resource abundance profiles. Exporters of machinery and chemicals, for example, tended to be relatively more abundant in capital and highly skilled labour. Further evidence for this linkage was provided by cross-country comparison of productivity in key factor endowments.

Third, empirical study of the factor content of trade in a cross-country setting based on the HOV model revealed that sign patterns of trade in factor services can provide another criterion for measuring the relative abundance of resource endowments (Chapter 5). The results showed that cross-country analysis of the factor content of trade is of greater benefit in uncovering factor abundance rankings than single-country analysis. The empirical results reinforced the evidence provided by the trade dependence and resource abundance data displays. Also, based on comparison of developed and developing countries, the results indicated that in general no 'Leontief Paradox' exists. This finding is of significance in that it approaches the controversial Leontief Paradox from a different perspective, namely cross-country analysis.

Fourth, econometric analysis using the Bayesian econometric method showed that, in general, the 10 trade aggregates are well explained by the 11 resource endowments (Chapter 6). The inclusion of the four land variables derived from standard sources was justified by their statistical performance in the model. Furthermore, the estimation results seemed to indicate that natural resource aggregates and aggregates of different agricultural products were best explained by comparing them with the four aggregates of manufactured products.

Finally, it was observed from the estimation results reported in Chapter 6 that the roles of several resource endowments — including highly skilled labour and unskilled labour — in determining the trade patterns of certain trade aggregates changed over the period under study. Although capital remained unchanged throughout the period with respect to sign, in a statistical sense its role in determining trade patterns of manufactured products, particularly capital intensive products and machinery, strengthened. This and the evidence provided by trade dependence profiles and resource abundance profiles for the rapid accumulation of certain factor endowments (Chapter 4) indicated that shifting comparative advantage with respect to some factor endowments (certain categories of labour and to some extent capital) might have taken place during the period.

The theoretical significance of the above findings is twofold. First, the empirical verification of the HOV model establishes that there are general relationships between patterns of trade and patterns of resource endowments. These relationships are significant because they provide information about sources of international comparative advantage and their changes over time.

Second, the original form of the Leontief Paradox is no longer relevant, as proved in Leamer (1980); this claim is verified by the empirical results on cross-country factor abundance ranking obtained in Chapter 5. Factor abundance revealed by analysis of net exports of factor services within the framework of the HOV model partly explains controversial issues related to the Leontief Paradox. For example, comparing country i's world share of capital K_i/K_w with its world share of labour L_i/L_w confirmed that most developed countries are characterised by $K_i/K_w > L_i/L_w$, while the reverse is true for all developing countries.

However, comparison of K_i/K_w and L_i/L_w was based on the linkage of $K_x/L_x > K_m/L_m$ and $K_i/K_w > L_i/L_w$. This linkage breaks when there is a 'sufficiently large' trade surplus (so that $K_T > 0$ and $L_T > 0$) and when there is a 'sufficiently large' trade deficit (so that $K_T < 0$ and $L_T < 0$). The empirical results in Chapter 5 showed that $K_T > 0$ and $L_T > 0$, and $K_T < 0$ and $L_T < 0$, may be compatible respectively with either $K_i/K_w > L_i/L_w$ or $K_i/K_w < L_i/L_w$, as argued by Aw (1983). This implies that the Leontief-type measure, namely K_x/L_x and K_m/L_m, may not be used under such circumstances.

Empirical findings

This book makes an empirical contribution in a number of areas. First, the trade dependence model specified by Leamer (1984) was re-estimated using up-to-date data sets. The time span covered in these data sets allowed comparison of this study's results with those of Leamer, as well as comparison of different points of time within the new time span. The results in general confirmed Leamer's findings and showed evidence of structural changes in the relationship between trade and resource endowments during the new period studied.

Second, it was a useful and worthwhile exercise to apply the Bayesian econometric method, an approach that represents the process of learning and that requires prior information to be incorporated into the model estimation. With the Bayesian approach, prior information must change when changes associated with the parameters take place. Repeated estimation is therefore needed to incorporate these changes into model estimation and to establish the credibility of the model.

Third, the study provided comprehensive data displays, which constitute a convenient and up-to-date array of information about the international economy. Trade dependence profiles illustrated the composition of net exports of the 10 trade aggregates relative to GNP; resource abundance profiles illustrated the relative abundance of 11 resources hypothesised to be the sources of international comparative advantage. All 61 economies under study were included in these profiles, thus presenting a clear and accurate picture of the world's trading relations.

Finally, the data sets covered the period from the mid-1960s to the late 1980s, a period in which many economies, and East Asian economies in particular, underwent dramatic changes in their economic and trade structures. Empirical study can help to explain these changes (see the next section).

A note of caution should be added here. The approach used by Leamer (1984) and applied in this study is intended not to test but to measure the accuracy of the HOV model (Chapter 2). Measuring the accuracy of the HOV model is based on the following assumption: that 'the demonstration of the accuracy of the estimated linear trade model [is] necessarily a demonstration of the accuracy of the HOV model' (Leamer 1984, p. 59).[1]

A certain degree of accuracy of the HOV model does not mean that the model captures all of the elements that determine patterns of trade, nor does it suggest that the model explains all trade equations equally well. Two examples are the lack of statistical significance in important relationships between variables (such as the trade aggregates of manufactured products and highly skilled labour) and the better performance of trade equations for nonmanufactured aggregates over those of manufactured aggregates.

The existence of a number of sensitive coefficients in the model estimation was also observed (Chapter 6). This is mainly because 'the many potential explanatory variables are highly collinear and because the prior distribution cannot be selected with much precision. As a consequence it is difficult to disentangle one effect from another' (Leamer 1984, p. 178).

Some of the above-mentioned empirical findings and the problems associated with the approach adopted in this book have wider theoretical implications. Specifically, the overall performance of the trade dependence model with regard to the aggregates of four manufactured products leads to speculation that other theoretical explanations of trade patterns of manufactured products (for example, factors which explain intra-industry trade, such as product differentiation, scale economies and imperfect competition) may play a part in determining trade patterns. Future research could focus on widening the scope of the theoretical framework, in addition to correcting existing problems in the approach and improving the analytical techniques used in this approach.[2]

Nevertheless, two general conclusions stand out. First, cross-country differences in resource endowments still play an important role in determining patterns of trade, although there is evidence to suggest that a substantial amount of trade in commodities, particularly manufactured commodities, is explained by factors that go beyond the Heckscher–Ohlin framework. Second, structural change took place in the relationship between patterns of trade and certain resource endowments — for example, skilled labour, unskilled labour and capital — from the 1960s to the 1980s, providing further evidence for shifts in sources of international comparative advantage during the period.

Implications for Asia–Pacific economies

Work of this type has significant implications for the group of Asia–Pacific economies consisting of Indonesia, Malaysia, the Philippines, Singapore, Thailand, Hong Kong, Korea, Taiwan, China and Japan.[3] What are the distinguishing features of the structure of factor endowments in these Asia–Pacific economies? How have these features, from a dynamic point of view, affected these economies' patterns of trade, particularly manufacturing trade? Does dynamic change in factor endowments and trade patterns in these economies support the hypothesis of shifting comparative advantage, which says that shifts take place as endowments change? What are the implications of shifting comparative advantage for further industrialisation in these economies?

This study has found that the structure of factor endowments in these Asia–Pacific economies has certain characteristics, which can be summarised as follows.

First, rapid increases in capital accumulation were observed in these economies from the 1960s to the 1980s. Average annual growth rates of capital stock from 1965 to 1988 in these economies were much higher than the world average in terms of both the absolute value of capital stock (10 per cent compared with 5.4 per cent [Table 3.12]) and capital per worker (6.8 per cent compared with 3.1 per cent [Table 3.13]). As a result, the capital stock and capital per worker ranking of most of these economies rose substantially during this period, as shown in Tables 3.12 and 3.13. Rapid increases in capital accumulation in these economies were also reflected in remarkable changes in their world capital shares, reported in Table 3.16. The results of cross-country factor rankings over time, reported in Tables 5.5 and 5.6, provide additional evidence for this (see Chapter 5).

Second, in contrast with the increase in capital, average annual growth rates for skilled labour in these economies during the period were only slightly higher than the world average in absolute terms (6.8 per cent compared with 5.3 per cent [Table 3.14]) and almost the same as world average annual growth rates in terms of share of skilled labour in total labour (3.6 per cent compared with 3 per cent [Table 3.15]).[4] As a result, with respect to skilled labour as a percentage of total labour, the ranking of about half of these economies in 1988 had worsened compared with 1965 while the remaining economies had increased their ranking only slightly (China, Hong Kong and Taiwan were the exceptions). This situation is also reflected in mixed changes (some increases and some decreases) in these economies' shares of world skilled labour from 1965 to 1988, as reported in Table 3.16. This may indicate that these economies were on average doing a better job of accumulating physical capital than of producing highly skilled labour from 1965 to 1988.

Third, in contrast to the situation in developed countries, these economies, together with some other developing economies, increased their world shares of semiskilled labour from 1965 to 1988, as reported in Table 3.16 (Japan, as a developed country, is the exception). Although, as Table 3.16 shows, most of these economies experienced a decline in their world shares of unskilled labour during the period, this group of economies can be regarded as a densely populated one. This may have some effect on the competitiveness of these economies' manufactured products, as will be discussed later.

How have the resource patterns described above affected the development of trade, particularly trade in manufactured products, in these economies? The question can be approached using the three propositions most commonly put forward with respect to shifts in comparative advantage. These propositions are based on changes in commonly used but broadly defined capital/labour ratios as indicators for changes in resource supplies; they are supported by the results on sources of comparative advantage and their changed role over time reported in Chapter 6.[5]

The first proposition is that an increase in the capital/labour ratio will lead to an increase in the size of the manufacturing sector as a proportion of the total economy. The second proposition is that a further increase in the capital/labour ratio will enhance production of more capital intensive products within the manufacturing sector. The third proposition is that an increase in the ratio of skilled labour to worker, together with an increase in the capital/labour ratio, will be conducive to more sophisticated manufacturing production with greater value-added.

In a dynamic context, these three propositions can be considered as three stages of structural change in the process of development (of course, overlapping between stages may exist), and they can thus be used to examine trade development in Asia–Pacific economies based on the characteristics of their resource patterns.

First, rapid increases in capital/labour ratios from the 1960s to the 1980s led to a continuous expansion of the manufacturing sectors of these economies. In most cases, this took place in sectors where labour intensive manufactured products were being produced. This was partly because 'the process of capital accumulation and rising per capita incomes forces changes in the industrial composition of manufacturing activity through its effect on the wage level' (Garnaut and Anderson 1980, p. 386).[6] The expansion of the manufacturing sectors in these economies can be seen in Table 1.3, which shows exports of manufactured products as a share of the total exports of selected developing economies from 1965 to 1990. All the economies experienced dramatic increases in manufactured exports as a share of total exports during the period.

The impact of changes in resource supplies on trade patterns of manufactured products in these economies can also be seen in the growth rate of exports. Table 7.1 lists the average annual growth rates of GDP, total exports and exports of manufac-

Table 7.1 Annual real growth rates of GDP, total exports and manufactured exports for selected Asia–Pacific economies, 1970–80 and 1980–90 (%)[a]

	GDP		Total exports		Exports of manufactures	
Country	1970–80	1980–90	1970–80	1980–90	1970–80	1980–90
Indonesia	7.24	5.61	7.56	3.27	13.64	34.96
Malaysia	7.86	5.99	3.88	10.51	14.20	20.12
Philippines	5.86	1.60	5.79	3.66	23.90	9.15
Singapore	8.91	7.04	4.88	8.50	11.05	11.76
Thailand	6.69	7.82	10.78	13.65	25.59	23.46
Hong Kong	9.27	7.13	8.41	4.29	8.50	4.31
Korea	8.60	9.31	22.62	11.89	24.66	12.31
Taiwan	9.25	7.89	14.78	13.44	16.17	13.98
China	5.77	8.92	10.01	10.45	10.02	10.96
Japan	4.51	4.14	9.49	4.21	9.73	4.41
United States	2.74	2.90	6.64	3.06	6.24	4.57

Note: a Growth rates of GDP are based on the constant price in the local currency; growth rates of total exports and exports of manufactures are obtained by adjusting total exports and exports of manufactures against the US dollar-based export price index (1987=100). Annual growth rates of both total exports and exports of manufactures are based on 1972–80 for the first period for Taiwan and on 1980–89 for the second period for Hong Kong.

Source: GDP and trade figures were obtained from *World Tables 1992*, International Economic Databank, the Australian National University.

tures in these Asia–Pacific economies and in the United States for two periods: 1970–80 and 1980–90 (the United States is included in this table as a reference).

It can be seen from Table 7.1 that annual real growth rates of manufactured exports were considerably higher than the growth rates of total exports throughout the two periods, providing further evidence for the expansion of the manufacturing sector in these Asia–Pacific economies. It has been observed that the more advanced an economy becomes, the narrower the gap between the growth rate of its total exports and that of its manufactured exports. Thus the potential for revealing comparative advantage (gaining in market share) in manufactured products is relatively large for less developed economies. Fulfilment of this potential and the structural changes that accompany this process will have important implications for market and policy issues as these economies industrialise further.

Second, 'over time, as the per worker endowment of capital increases, the comparative advantage within the manufacturing sector will shift towards more capital-intensive activities' (Anderson and Smith 1981, p. 296). The changes that took place in the ladder of development over time for these economies (Chapter 3) and in the trade dependence profiles (Chapter 4) provide evidence to support this argument.

All except Japan ranked low in terms of capital per worker in 1965 (Table 3.13). Only Hong Kong, Korea and Taiwan were on the rung of the development ladder as net exporters of labour intensive manufactured products (Table 3.8). In 1974, Korea and Taiwan had improved their rankings of capital per worker (Table 3.13), and by 1980 both had become net exporters of capital intensive manufactured products. Taiwan's progress up the ladder of development was even more obvious in 1988, by which time it had become a net exporter of labour intensive, capital intensive manufactured products and machinery after rapidly improving its capital per worker ranking.

The shift towards more capital intensive production as capital/labour ratios increase can also be approached by increasing export dependence and reducing import dependence on manufactured products, particularly capital intensive manufactured products and to some extent machinery, over time.[7] This will be reflected in trade dependence profiles.

The trade dependence profiles show that the majority of these Asia–Pacific economies are net exporters of labour intensive manufactured products and that a few are net exporters of capital intensive manufactured products. However, their dependence on trade in manufactured products shows different patterns with regard to import dependence on manufactured products on the one hand and export dependence on manufactured products on the other.

For example, of these economies, only Korea and Taiwan increased their export dependence on capital intensive manufactured products over the period. Import dependence on capital intensive manufactured products (another sign of a shift towards production of more capital intensive manufactured products) declined in two economies, Malaysia and Thailand. While Japan's and China's export dependence on capital intensive products fell, the import dependence on capital intensive products of all other economies increased. This suggests that most of these economies have the potential to develop capital intensive manufactured production by further increasing their capital/labour ratios; it would seem, therefore, that the region could support a larger scale of capital flows.

Third, one of the propositions that emerged from the model estimation reported in Chapter 6 was that, within its manufacturing sector, a country tends to specialise in the production and export of more sophisticated manufactured products with high value-added such as machinery and chemicals, and that this is mainly attributable to an increase in the country's skilled labour endowment together with an increase in its capital/labour ratio. Discussion of this proposition in the context of Asia–Pacific economies will have important implications for further industrialisation in the region.

Relatively high growth rates in physical capital and semiskilled rather than skilled labour indicate that much of the change in trade structure (reflected in rapid increases in labour intensive and capital intensive manufactured products) in these economies during the period under study was driven by the accumulation of physical capital and semiskilled labour. This is reflected in the changing structure of trade in manufactured products, particularly machinery and chemicals, in these economies. For example, by

1988 only Japan and Taiwan were net exporters of machinery. This suggests the huge potential to be realised in these Asia–Pacific economies by increasing skilled labour as physical capital increases.

This is true for Japan as well: Japan ranked much higher than the United States in terms of capital per worker in 1988 (Table 3.13), but much lower than the United States in terms of skilled labour per worker in the same year (Table 3.15).

The implications of shifting comparative advantage for further industrialisation in the Asia–Pacific region mainly affect three areas: market competition, international capital flows and demand for highly skilled labour.

First, as Rana (1990) says, 'shifts in comparative advantage are . . . not smooth and could involve considerable frictions in adjustment' (p. 244). For example, the upgrading of developing countries on the ladder of development requires that there be sufficient market capacity to absorb developing countries' exports of manufactured products.

Market constraints on the process of development have been aggravated by structural adjustment in developed countries, and this could lead to a resurgence of trade protectionism. Any such movement would undoubtedly affect the development process. As economies become more integrated, the sustained growth of the world economy depends very much upon whether countries can properly settle this market issue.[8]

Second, further industrialisation requires the continual injection of large quantities of capital into an economy. Thus, capital flows on a larger scale and in various forms can be anticipated within Asia–Pacific economies.

Third, the estimation results in Chapter 6 suggest that it is the combination of highly skilled labour and physical capital which contributes to comparative advantage in producing advanced manufactured products such as machinery and chemicals. Therefore, further industrialisation in Asia–Pacific economies will definitely lead to production of these highly sophisticated products, and this in turn will generate demand for a highly skilled labour force.

The conclusion reached in Chapter 4 — that, driven by demand, international migration of highly skilled labour will take place on a larger scale in areas experiencing rapid economic growth — is therefore warranted. Of course, for the same reason, it can be anticipated that Asia–Pacific economies will direct greater efforts towards education and training.

By successfully resolving the issue of market competition, enhancing international as well as regional capital flows and facilitating the movement of skilled labour in the region, shifts in comparative advantage in the Asia–Pacific region can be facilitated in such a manner that the region's resources are utilised most efficiently. A natural consequence of this would be that the degree of integration in the Asia–Pacific region would increase.

This book included China in its cross-country analysis, marking the first time that China has been included in a cross-country study of this type. This is a significant undertaking in that it provides the opportunity to examine China's trade patterns and the structure of its resource supplies from an internationally comparable perspective. More importantly, because of the country's size, including China changes the overall structure of trade and resource supplies in the world economy, and consequently the relative positions of other countries with respect to trade and resource supplies also change.

The results provided in this study demonstrate that remarkable changes have taken place in China's resource supplies, especially capital and skilled labour. For example, the growth rate of capital in China from 1965 to 1988 ranks second only to Korea in absolute terms and ranks top and equal with Korea in per capita terms (per worker). China ranked fourth in absolute terms in 1988 for capital stock endowment, although its ranking for capital per worker remained low due to its large population and high labour participation rate. A little progress was made in this area in relative terms from 1974 to 1988 due to China's rapid accumulation of capital. China also dramatically increased its world share of capital, skilled labour and semiskilled labour and decreased its share of unskilled labour and arable land (Table 3.16).

It is interesting to note that over the period under study, China's patterns of trade have come to conform more closely to its patterns of resource endowments. This is at least in part due to the ongoing institutional change and economic reform, which have been conducive to China's achieving its true comparative advantage.

Such conformity can be reflected in changes over time in manufactured products as a proportion of total exports. As shown in Table 1.3, in 1965 manufactured products constituted 45.8 per cent of China's total exports; this figure dropped slightly to 45.1 per cent in 1970. In the decade from 1970 to 1980, there was an unimpressive increase in the share of manufactured products, from 45.1 to 48.7 per cent. However, the share increased remarkably from 48.7 per cent in 1980 to 80.3 per cent in 1990, corresponding to the changes in resource endowments reported in this study. This is still lower than Hong Kong (96 per cent), Israel (97 per cent), Korea (94 per cent) and Taiwan (93 per cent), and slightly lower than Portugal (81 per cent), but is higher than all other developing countries. Furthermore, a prominent feature with respect to changes in resource supplies is that China's rapid accumulation of capital and increase in skilled labour are accompanied by a large unskilled labour force. There is, then, a huge potential for China to gain a greater market share of manufactured products in world trade, not only in labour intensive products but also in capital and human capital intensive products.

The discussion of the implications for Asia–Pacific economies confirms the role of trade in East Asian industrialisation resulting from the changing pattern of factor endowments in these economies. It also suggests that trade will continue to contribute to the ongoing economic development and modernisation of these economies.

Appendix A

Country list

The following economies are included in this book (abbreviations in parentheses):[1]

Argentina (ARG), Australia (AUSL), Austria (AUST), Belgium–Luxembourg (BLUX), Brazil (BRAZ), Burma (BURM), Canada (CAN), Chile (CHLE), China (CHNA), Colombia (CLUM), Costa Rica (CSTA), Cyprus (CYPR), Denmark (DEN), Dominican Republic (DORE), Ecuador (ECUA), Egypt (EGPT), El Salvador (LSAL), Finland (FIN), France (FRA), Germany, West (GER), Ghana (GANA), Greece (GRCE), Honduras (HOND), Hong Kong (HOKO), Iceland (ICE), India (INDA), Indonesia (INDO), Ireland (IRE), Israel (ISRL), Italy (ITLY), Jamaica (JAMC), Japan (JAP), Korean Republic (KOR), Liberia (LIBR), Libyan Arab Republic (LIBY), Malaysia (MALY), Malta (MLTA), Mauritius (MAUR), Mexico (MEX), the Netherlands (NETH), New Zealand (NUZE), Nicaragua (NIGR), Norway (NOR), Panama (PANM), Paraguay (PRGY), Peru (PERU), the Philippines (PLIP), Portugal (PORT), Singapore (SING), Spain (SPAN), Sri Lanka (SRIL), Sweden (SWE), Switzerland (SWITZ), Taiwan (TAIW), Thailand (THAI), Turkey (TURK), the United Kingdom (UK), Uruguay (URGY), the United States (US), Venezuela (VELA) and Yugoslavia (YUG).

Data sources and methods

All trade data were obtained from the International Economic Data Bank at the Australian National University. All price data are reported in thousands of current US dollars. Exports are recorded at FOB (free on board) prices, while imports are recorded at CIF (customs, insurance and freight) prices. Quantities are measured in a variety of units depending on the commodity. Net exports or trade balance is defined as the value of exports of a commodity minus the value of imports of that commodity. All resource data were assembled by the author from various sources.

Trade and resource data for 1965 and 1988 respectively are listed in Tables A.1 and A.2. Abbreviations for the 61 economies are given in the first columns in these tables. The columns labelled AGG1–AGG10 in Table A.1 refer to the ten aggregates of net export data in thousands of US dollars. The columns for resource variables in Table A.2 are labelled according to the resource names used in the book; other columns indicate country attributes, which are described in Table A.3. Units and primary sources are also listed in Table A.3.

Table A.1 **Data set (net export data), 1965 and 1988**

Country	AGG1	AGG2	AGG3	AGG4	AGG5	AGG6	AGG7	AGG8	AGG9	AGG10
1965										
ARG	-79 575	-123 779	-131 177	-18 297	405 000	868 329	-30 927	-208 479	-300 018	-82 012
AUSL	-257 237	235 385	-169 741	102 701	482 565	1282 282	-243 425	-415 943	-1 161 728	-237 191
AUST	-54 432	-94 812	184 068	-131 264	-9 762	-159 048	102 649	109 223	-342 003	-105 228
BLUX	-198 151	-333 712	-123 702	-171 050	-44 344	-424 371	287 286	1 248 274	-197 502	-34 629
BRAZ	-193 235	30 982	55 537	829 380	66 945	119 285	-8 143	-4 520	-237 585	-159 585
BURM	-7 124	5 624	21 856	11 303	-18 695	143 417	-10 124	-100 678	-48 286	-20 628
CAN	-163 843	1 479 328	1 762 066	-281 708	302 692	829 623	-723 763	-668 196	-2 214 762	-200 215
SRIL	-23 145	-7 140	-9 638	300 586	-30 698	-6 226	-8 513	-52 308	-39 337	-30 834
CHLE	-31 839	592 943	5 343	-30 780	-37 173	-47 041	-29 483	-55 998	-216 386	-65 929
CHNA	18 150	1 564	9 262	-10 128	279 685	-228 288	169 432	270 599	-132 673	-120 037
CLUM	90 013	-12 854	-15 941	352 234	9 628	-20 312	-12 865	-26 435	-211 475	-66 347
CSTA	-8 518	-2 848	-9 440	79 778	4 949	-8 537	-6 250	-35 539	-54 308	-25 687
CYPR	-9 601	24 039	-8 144	21 193	-7 948	-5 797	-16 254	-29 596	-37 792	-13 118
DEN	-211 213	-134 260	-155 473	-81 252	971 515	-163 896	-3 437	-387 071	-240 930	-131 947
DORE	-8 590	11 222	-3 449	93 548	-6 873	42	-3 740	-14 707	-20 579	-9 411
ECUA	-11 778	-2 313	-4 178	110 962	5 633	-14 213	-8 535	-29 199	-56 524	-22 989
LSAL	-6 513	-2 792	-8 035	91 445	-1 834	30 072	-10 156	-22 628	-57 136	-26 132
FIN	-113 966	-83 723	924 720	-110 958	43 913	-6 708	-32 618	-192 777	-442 017	-144 311
FRA	-925 830	-632 791	-221 631	-452 656	-229 088	-156 642	368 347	1 094 285	560 542	307 777
GER	-1 044 056	-966 040	-809 698	-1 791 197	-1 073 741	-1 503 823	-704 163	766 575	6 308 785	1 237 514
GANA	-15 096	26 034	27 050	198 687	-21 715	-24 764	-48 162	-119 178	-154 683	-27 860
GRCE	-84 265	-14 754	-66 771	68 947	-92 396	50 365	-23 683	-140 556	-407 436	-95 415
HOND	-6 617	6 772	1 391	76 685	4 143	7 206	-9 794	-28 531	-32 742	-13 880
HOKO	-47 869	-20 022	-49 960	-113 661	-188 620	-202 016	343 329	-119 978	-182 791	-107 564
ICE	-12 100	-2 431	-11 224	-7 893	81 696	34 991	-11 517	-24 238	-45 866	-9 029
INDA	-128 780	-41 149	-39 527	338 310	55 079	-515 122	31 085	401 547	-1 036 593	-195 693
INDO	252 107	31 981	-11 167	289 305	2 225	38 292	-29 774	-238 884	-252 228	-54 433
IRE	-57 029	-40 125	-46 307	-19 620	260 988	-84 802	-21 344	-101 577	-242 961	-77 281
ISRL	-43 371	-13 577	-38 859	71 004	-29 043	-93 823	42 272	-46 526	-236 048	-18 323
ITLY	-607 201	-715 681	-348 308	285 361	-746 219	-947 899	912 572	764 670	1 120 879	122 614

Table A.1 (continued)

Country	AGG1	AGG2	AGG3	AGG4	AGG5	AGG6	AGG7	AGG8	AGG9	AGG10
JAMC	-17 275	47 315	-20 934	75 898	-25 438	-29 404	-13 111	-53 317	-69 729	27 059
JAP	-1 309 427	-1 568 403	-400 860	-445 882	3 588	-1 938 420	1 026 252	2 649 990	2 127 136	138 770
KOR	-28 882	5 729	-13 213	-6 978	19 727	-106 343	32 825	-16 717	-57 964	-103 047
LIBR	-8 138	96 682	-1 818	26 908	-3 914	-9 084	-11 394	-17 595	-34 823	-5 956
LIBY	772 873	-3 849	-8 221	-15 588	-10 432	-14 861	-45 671	-65 068	-121 974	-17 962
MALY	-70 001	298 900	98 657	422 832	-53 077	-82 678	-72 635	-134 888	-226 249	-66 822
MLTA	-6 018	82	-3 763	-7 277	-8 959	-16 403	-9 542	-6 140	-16 213	-6 416
MAUR	-3 654	-585	-2 489	58 257	-6 596	-17 254	-8 124	-11 632	-12 885	-9 886
MEX	15 427	101 978	-44 603	182 351	71 193	212 896	-22 264	-70 543	-805 258	-195 027
NETH	-192 824	-209 412	-282 622	160 568	853 531	-429 129	-301 056	-217 139	-542 629	146 976
NUZE	-66 464	-58 050	993	-43 926	581 848	267 177	-53 720	-244 794	-367 930	-80 622
NIGR	-7 609	4 569	-1 754	29 415	4 687	67 909	-10 861	-29 755	-50 009	-28 675
NOR	-117 307	91 896	148 259	-123 657	193 312	-35 009	-96 813	-150 968	-629 829	-43 005
PANM	-19 340	-1 233	-14 265	26 636	2 533	-9 123	-22 205	-33 846	-47 593	-19 836
PRGY	-7 776	-884	8 596	5 965	19 356	9 733	-2 633	-10 063	-20 850	917
PERU	-13 185	282 825	-22 944	51 763	-28 425	193 726	-27 354	-105 582	-303 876	-79 518
PLIP	-82 353	51 071	162 089	164 710	-50 605	150 761	-34 518	-110 089	-298 652	-79 107
PORT	-53 181	-37 178	79 566	34 398	31 599	-184 401	47 105	19 980	-243 012	-41 995
SING	27 767	-2 308	-9 955	22 108	-27 070	-69 335	-15 183	-71 563	-98 076	-26 167
SPAN	-232 842	-180 460	-81 908	216 277	-100 521	-383 344	-24 412	-281 397	-776 874	-191 468
SWE	-398 315	-37 275	1 041 120	-307 398	-54 406	-106 806	-241 279	-122 576	20 018	-198 250
SWITZ	-188 781	-105 823	-101 549	-255 670	-116 197	-193 152	-207 383	-218 333	414 264	240 494
THAI	-63 309	49 512	-5 617	132 113	-3 586	305 918	-57 434	-183 981	-261 790	-75 007
TURK	-51 391	18 833	-12 903	109 711	36 122	190 368	-11 237	-79 880	-225 481	-87 173
EGPT	-27 963	-17 548	-52 751	-17 728	-26 790	176 999	-3 148	-20 218	-221 685	-118 733
UK	-1 395 728	-1 123 763	-1 381 999	-1 304 116	-2 018 120	-1 715 519	402 584	1 221 400	3 967 077	437 165
US	-1 675 763	-790 607	-1 041 634	-2 192 216	-751 804	4 451 262	-1 444 098	-567 908	8 029 147	1 620 535
URGY	-24 020	-5 487	-9 613	-9 118	74 425	91 381	-4 174	-9 966	-38 619	-24 061
VELA	2 662 925	114 651	-46 311	-22 492	-55 536	-96 503	-91 659	-237 924	-653 672	-107 773
YUG	-22 782	-9 874	68 224	-16 937	148 197	-193 771	98 790	-92 227	-118 042	-58 739
TAIW	-25 943	-31 582	20 438	173 843	-7 226	-73 733	39 348	-1 500	-151 639	-49 645

Table A.1 (continued)

Country	AGG1	AGG2	AGG3	AGG4	AGG5	AGG6	AGG7	AGG8	AGG9	AGG10
1988										
ARG	-66 010	-357 541	17 243	319 774	907 235	4 246 125	-10 275	696 722	-1 350 937	-589 671
AUSL	394 043	8 111 693	-561 176	386 389	2 558 408	3 040 132	-2 072 098	-1 587 333	-11 535 785	-629 614
AUST	-157 753	125 064	498 224	-177 073	-247 797	-250 718	-670 024	145 637	-5 312 242	-1 219 373
BLUX	38 648	-1 344 731	-568 120	-21 146	13 422	-1 271 146	386 361	2 245 810	-8 481 395	-1 152 133
BRAZ	791 437	2 530 742	884 719	3 630 495	697 483	1 923 182	1 414 550	3 021 638	-1 543 605	-288 827
BURM	-6 573	4 756	52 068	11 642	9 714	-3 866	2 690	-60 213	-174 906	-35 274
CAN	4 048 176	9 598 893	13 606 072	-353 575	2 605 185	1 415 343	-12 641 710	-736 240	-6 782 500	205 638
SRIL	-13 687	7 403	-31 042	339 233	-2 622	-90 200	507 592	-277 046	-293 745	-127 728
CHLE	-16 413	1 920 672	340 588	697 655	327 970	212 048	-133 786	-210 450	-1 325 176	-342 971
CHNA	2 982 213	1 162 073	-961 265	1 586 976	2 453 087	-129 935	14 442 349	-260 587	-9 886 447	-3 344 308
CLUM	883 355	166 404	-58 135	1 840 133	278 895	-155 642	243 999	-59 098	-1 477 844	-670 222
CSTA	-13 291	-5 108	-61 234	627 610	158 094	-68 802	131 687	-87 977	-205 620	-157 068
CYPR	-1 294	1 719	-47 343	35 756	-8 871	-94 364	-63 963	-101 969	-403 880	-44 987
DEN	-618 526	-691 348	-991 418	-430 862	4 958 330	452 956	990 279	-1 252 265	-494 076	-565 482
DORE	-29 243	-5 053	-46 355	289 726	8 986	-156 712	324 868	-6 998	-353 019	-147 886
ECUA	480 442	-7 493	-36 456	684 181	478 466	-65 670	-45 146	-93 053	-499 578	-200 525
LSAL	-9 371	-8 622	-25 988	375 775	21 722	-104 996	-2 242	-24 808	-216 219	-89 169
FIN	-1 059 521	-839 562	8 165 797	-672 510	126 576	-207 195	-536 179	-515 237	-2 718 120	-1 016 107
FRA	-277 141	-478 622	-1 968 274	2 880 890	-1 170 285	1 885 565	-353 032	794 029	-12 340 026	1 691 224
GER	-12 726 094	-6 415 068	-2 376 740	-9 773 762	-2 438 558	-2 633 358	-8 550 457	11 900 331	87 523 496	19 078 172
GANA	-9 041	248 950	76 663	151 965	19 466	-37 477	-14 084	-36 480	-150 228	-80 989
GRCE	133 088	101 726	-280 497	377 846	-994 228	-117 670	1 033 120	-469 736	-2 227 541	-676 953
HOND	-11 025	5 214	-12 622	485 482	122 694	-41 482	-4 405	-57 691	-198 467	-115 582
HOKO	-896 095	-1 400 366	-1 425 751	-1 731 491	-2 777 600	-1 911 905	-469 608	-8 495 535	-11 668 242	-5 235 341
ICE	-92 541	136 367	-103 450	-70 149	936 548	71 116	-240 757	-100 048	-548 751	-144 894
INDA	208 674	217 670	-147 496	318 199	510 525	-491 808	3 005 961	519 061	-4 589 692	-1 260 085
INDO	4 958 976	3 849 784	1 833 317	1 649 990	649 435	-83 761	596 542	-382 691	-3 457 039	-918 896
IRE	-534 211	-335 117	-497 259	-36 433	2 512 238	575 858	249 839	-340 135	871 277	712 213
ISRL	-309 754	16 992	-192 735	178 996	90 373	-336 350	1 967 494	-170 937	-1 636 767	38 572
ITLY	427 489	-2 136 523	-1 237 664	2 039 079	-5 112 338	-1 881 872	14 273 834	3 810 610	-5 373 550	-3 530 776

Table A.1 (continued)

Country	AGG1	AGG2	AGG3	AGG4	AGG5	AGG6	AGG7	AGG8	AGG9	AGG10
JAMC	-64 969	104 598	-61 104	41 615	-53 061	-99 476	72 232	-133 488	-207 027	55 100
JAP	-25 416 908	-29 227 674	-10 808 539	-6 914 450	-16 533 669	-11 151 658	3 220 680	17 760 424	161 648 672	-1 057 018
KOR	23 613	-1 343 427	-672 347	87 200	888 454	-1 802 354	15 561 720	3 053 304	-1 286 232	-3 153 382
LIBR	1 857	161 130	27 146	101 669	-12 437	-38 002	-222 545	-36 385	-833 382	-12 093
LIBY	2 331 563	56 488	-40 129	-18 409	-75 193	-124 884	-211 476	-266 903	-1 077 929	-65 984
MALY	1 201 400	1 164 527	2 832 155	1 984 499	478 261	465 244	1 153 593	-742 970	-1 215 043	-880 500
MLTA	6 053	-4 012	-12 490	-8 053	-21 188	-15 812	85 045	-54 358	-59 594	-32 501
MAUR	- 612	-2 404	-9 353	22 509	-2 947	-18 535	203 677	-156 116	-234 167	-21 154
MEX	4 989 825	768 410	-467 880	1 593 035	-120 219	-1 311 525	595 587	-780 483	-1 429 074	-1 146 583
NETH	-1 381 634	1 101 680	-1 977 656	1 500 359	8 913 959	-1 476 478	-1 885 791	-1 195 658	-6 627 159	6 490 176
NUZE	-297 993	337 353	479 500	306 637	3 420 737	1 151 994	-457 222	-445 864	-2 615 647	-658 447
NIGR	-1 207	-69	-5 314	83 512	-25 256	32 156	-7 691	-47 941	-45 871	-34 843
NOR	2 445 282	2 265 397	-219 609	-283 163	920 172	-209 934	-1 920 660	-734 273	-4 104 226	1 501
PANM	-79 551	3 762	-48 490	307 967	131 777	-94 718	-485 934	-142 976	-3 013 208	-157 055
PRGY	-29 563	2 768	11 239	93 291	4 216	270 647	-96 656	-23 956	-241 065	-32 319
PERU	81 814	657 807	-15 056	146 235	-11 511	-130 251	57 993	-1 965	-460 859	-275 905
PLIP	-946 514	328 967	190 899	472 879	202 754	-161 024	1 021 464	-844 401	-1 129 360	-870 379
PORT	-32 170	-125 222	447 441	59 201	-266 867	-471 835	1 755 709	-429 133	-2 729 799	-488 887
SING	-1 347 519	-226 949	3 026	79 284	-353 946	-209 217	650 126	-2 304 548	-692 445	-157 393
SPAN	-4 358 254	-2 180 398	-934 666	2 572 669	-2 087 316	-1 205 961	892 405	1 013 722	-11 211 984	-2 476 718
SWE	-1 839 883	-522 883	8 133 367	-1 412 441	-515 148	-354 650	-3 010 781	886 012	3 656 476	-945 495
SWITZ	-1 745 370	17 716	-1 273 428	-1 740 402	-758 090	-425 199	-5 749 119	-781 715	2 461 132	4 312 322
THAI	-857 558	15 218	62 861	2 151 604	1 355 868	211 105	1 937 603	-956 271	-4 172 169	-1 153 263
TURK	312 741	-170 303	-108 556	627 799	19 230	-35 734	1 293 471	474 813	-2 804 781	-730 454
EGPT	1 529 674	43 290	-2 073 235	-829 699	-1 665 424	-3 000 638	-665 395	-1 462 708	-6 593 569	-2 873 888
UK	5 964 381	915 457	-5 351 736	-911 774	-3 278 400	-868 781	-3 147 860	-1 534 374	-21 953 792	1 742 978
US	-37 364 216	-3 554 456	-4 313 155	-10 570 886	-3 104 918	26 584 572	-52 657 392	-21 509 988	-59 058 696	10 247 488
URGY	-15 016	-8 211	7 531	13 112	126 729	100 810	112 077	24 490	-140 247	-90 252
VELA	5 378 435	744 375	-166 238	-53 115	-184 219	-708 708	-225 027	-199 781	-3 720 326	-961 881
YUG	15 281	96 005	214 451	127 787	9 940	-135 974	1 822 420	-292 750	-1 039 248	-515 226
TAIW	-2 468 424	-3 268 205	-518 622	-23 285	1 157 941	-2 219 921	17 355 120	5 389 345	4 738 568	-4 344 074

Table A.2 **Data set (resource data), 1965 and 1988**

Country	GNP	CAPITAL	LABOUR 1	LABOUR 2	LABOUR 3	LAND 1	LAND 2	LAND 3	LAND 4	COAL	MINERALS	OIL
1965												
ARG	21 556	81 814	459	6 418	647	19 598	8 500	146 500	59 934	1 661	25 987	115 853
AUSL	22 981	96 824	452	4 356	49	33 534	179	445 908	137 700	164 231	532 257	2 198
AUST	9 438	47 187	229	3 107	34	1 669	66	2 275	3 161	12 361	41 732	28 842
BLUX	17 687	60 914	291	3 315	36	957	50	812	687	87 850	60 218	968
BRAZ	23 012	57 692	702	13 115	8 834	22 400	7 854	131 880	526 800	9 706	194 690	30 059
BURM	1 602	815	218	5 690	3 988	10 090	268	336	45 274	67	10 880	3 605
CAN	50 897	130 113	690	5 690	130	42 079	80	20 994	322 271	40 617	1785 348	513 126
SRIL	1 786	1 052	145	2 449	865	709	1 027	213	3 458	0	506	0
CHLE	6 000	12 058	117	1 879	392	4 007	199	9 850	20 686	6 984	860 434	20 837
CHNA	75 049	54 041	991	156 819	209 190	117 493	558	204 000	106 629	1327 560	774 906	70 294
CLUM	5 664	13 806	200	3 034	1 900	3 545	1 506	16 682	77 190	12 432	8 909	72 336
CSTA	580	1 414	21	329	46	285	199	969	2 848	0	12	0
CYPR	409	522	9	169	57	367	66	93	171	0	37 681	0
DEN	10 175	46 833	214	2 015	23	2 749	12	337	438	3 121	0	0
DORE	945	1 080	23	506	291	580	280	1 020	1 100	0	13 003	0
ECUA	1 126	4 317	45	929	469	2 112	543	2 200	18 800	0	520	2 557
LSAL	789	1 128	20	375	412	489	166	606	230	0	1 058	0
FIN	8 145	36 228	167	1 846	20	2 714	0	111	21 779	67	81 690	0
FRA	98 704	380 128	1 804	17 826	198	19 293	1 774	13 221	11 905	236 798	705 592	53 569
GER	114 550	579 844	1 958	23 547	258	7 835	591	5 731	7 144	742 359	278 920	71 559
GANA	2 027	6 025	60	675	1 988	830	1 711	12 210	2 484	0	5 002	0
GRCE	6 113	16 327	124	2 801	713	2 941	859	5 100	2 545	7 459	24 294	0
HOND	496	970	14	241	312	682	139	2 000	7 100	0	6 985	0
HOKO	1 910	8 753	74	1 009	371	13	1	0	10	0	1 257	0
ICE	495	1 839	4	63	1	1	0	2 279	116	0	0	0
INDA	50 273	84 778	3 206	49 217	136 148	157 185	4 813	14 293	58 207	301 569	215 814	20 593
INDO	89 695	13 194	804	13 448	22 291	12 240	4 500	11 400	123 800	1 248	76 590	174 985
IRE	2 756	9 288	87	997	34	1 314	4	3 314	188	8 716	4 440	0
ISRL	3 547	11 112	86	547	119	316	85	751	94	0	23 505	1 758
ITLY	62 821	331 021	1 056	17 012	1 853	12 691	2 763	5 096	5 984	3 343	113 500	61 046

Table A.2 (continued)

Country	GNP	CAPITAL	LABOUR 1	LABOUR 2	LABOUR 3	LAND 1	LAND 2	LAND 3	LAND 4	COAL	MINERALS	OIL
JAMC	950	3 084	19	517	119	187	46	256	508	0	118 770	0
JAP	90 711	440 142	2 655	44 552	1 062	5 448	445	124	25 558	220 770	309 649	16 055
KOR	3 026	8 722	225	5 885	2 544	2 059	74	7	6 663	45 528	18 774	320
LIBR	220	1 000	7	29	375	135	240	240	3 869	0	149 531	0
LIBY	1 339	8 075	12	72	304	2375	134	7 400	491	0	82	381 764
MALY	2 911	7 024	118	1 177	1 158	507	2 133	35	14 784	0	333 261	0
MLTA	160	531	11	57	34	15	1	0	0	0	18	0
MAUR	226	936	9	105	73	91	2	7	64	0	24	0
MEX	20 048	51 859	408	7 003	3 921	23 486	1 422	73 820	80 620	8 907	297 016	162 406
NETH	19 904	120 269	383	3 743	42	954	38	1 293	280	50 820	11 066	26 192
NUZE	5 537	15 689	105	911	10	726	11	12 847	7 403	9 026	229	4
NIGR	556	855	12	223	239	710	155	1 710	6 432	0	13 255	0
NOR	7 000	42 893	112	1 279	14	837	13	172	6 883	1 927	56 468	0
PANM	644	1 391	15	232	90	437	124	899	4 100	0	65	0
PRGY	439	818	19	418	149	737	115	13 800	20 828	0	0	0
PERU	4 814	18 977	103	1 803	1 218	2 171	180	27 977	73 800	573	433 808	23 363
PLIP	5 982	14 573	379	7 883	3 229	4 840	1 967	812	14 700	422	98 667	0
PORT	3 857	14 101	92	2 061	1 270	3 732	600	530	3 165	2 100	20 173	0
SING	987	2 108	23	308	149	4	10	0	4	0	0	0
SPAN	23 247	99 259	477	9 610	1 547	16 126	4 583	12 300	13 160	59 660	159 624	457
SWE	21 703	93 899	521	2 895	35	3 352	45	554	26 216	262	356 016	373
SWITZ	14 221	91 555	216	2 271	25	402	13	1 755	981	0	2 521	0
THAI	4 053	8 930	180	9 188	4 469	11 279	1 360	308	24 070	182	88 029	13
TURK	8 522	18 274	299	5 962	7 351	23 541	2 234	28 451	20 170	23 172	64 241	10 008
EGPT	5 338	6 711	347	1 734	5 800	2 470	78	0	2	89	0	42 606
UK	100 485	361 269	2 386	21 724	746	7 299	108	12 330	1 761	849 336	201 525	1718
US	694 500	1 384 608	7 547	61 632	699	178 453	1 878	261 235	307 600	2 114 306	3 220 463	2 816 403
URGY	1 000	3 331	57	864	91	1 726	53	13 769	588	0	19	0
VELA	7 587	51 059	127	1 361	863	4 580	637	14 229	47 970	138	163 730	1 236 811
YUG	12 027	51 750	467	5 913	1 960	7 656	693	6 472	8 744	66 880	197 554	15 531
TAIW	2 802	6 728	172	2 722	860	827	62	0	2 551	22 369	6445	478

Table A.2 (continued)

Country	GNP	CAPITAL	LABOUR 1	LABOUR 2	LABOUR 3	LAND 1	LAND 2	LAND 3	LAND 4	COAL	MINERALS	OIL
1988												
ARG	84 562	118 263	845	9 730	687	26 000	9 750	142 400	59 400	17 671	66 685	3 275 861
AUSL	236 109	225 473	822	6 935	0	46 806	167	425 060	106 000	5019 466	5 366 541	2 623 619
AUST	126 057	116 970	492	3 101	0	1 433	74	1 982	3 200	33 046	59 861	215 430
BLUX	160 753	143 354	665	3 571	0	804	16	688	699	93 275	995	2 400
BRAZ	341 926	263 093	3643	37 434	11 721	66 500	12 050	169 000	555 560	208 321	3 667 516	575 265
BURM	8 093	3 114	418	11 934	5 045	9 557	490	362	32 384	1 763	82 071	186 285
CAN	474 065	394 572	2157	10 836	0	45 900	80	32 500	356 000	2 258 157	9 846 410	15 772 680
SRIL	6 908	6 636	292	5 093	819	923	975	439	1 747	0	2 179	0
CHLE	20 339	23 255	318	3 766	399	4 120	245	13 400	8 800	78 720	5 446 585	189 534
CHNA	372 393	888 738	33 405	395 620	225 975	92 590	3 161	319 080	114 564	27 690 048	4 864 017	2 844 714
CLUM	36 547	38 626	962	7 485	1467	3 850	1 497	40 200	50 900	574 902	249 375	788 160
CSTA	4 315	6 144	93	831	74	285	243	2 310	1 640	0	5 400	0
CYPR	4 213	4 534	27	259	30	104	53	5	123	0	4 077	0
DEN	103 213	78 643	607	2 228	0	2 566	4	217	493	0	10 530	383 513
DORE	4 315	9 612	86	1 403	669	1 120	355	2 092	619	0	405 682	0
ECUA	9 960	13 613	242	2 246	614	1 726	950	5 050	11 500	0	492	82 071
LSAL	5 355	2 767	55	1 005	515	565	168	610	104	0	54	0
FIN	103 182	84 622	583	1 940	0	2 441	0	127	23 222	61 049	336 256	0
FRA	946 728	885 194	3552	21 640	0	18 267	1 280	11 740	14 700	577 977	564 720	512 053
GER	1 205 568	1 032 054	4187	25 511	0	7 261	205	4 449	7 360	4299 834	786 045	2 078 823
GANA	5 095	5 311	210	1 374	3 660	1 150	1 720	3 390	8 210	0	5 660	0
GRCE	52 326	45 937	454	3 056	368	2 880	1 049	5 255	2 620	368 221	282 166	27 708
HOND	4 156	2 788	61	820	600	1 575	210	2 540	3 420	0	44 286	0
HOKO	54 497	59 447	217	2 054	667	6	1	1	12	0	0	0
ICE	5 776	4 713	15	117	0	8	0	2 274	120	0	36	0
INDA	265 539	274 769	8 398	118 508	184 139	165 950	3 500	12 040	66 600	6 536 917	1 311 992	1 198 111
INDO	74 024	159 525	1 984	44 055	22 370	15 800	5 420	11 800	113 433	112 381	1 486 365	5 677 614
IRE	28 480	28 691	199	1 192	0	960	3	4 688	339	70 028	282 569	309 840
ISRL	43 529	30 456	384	1 161	138	343	90	148	110	0	221 139	6 676
ITLY	823 225	659 636	2 661	19 785	694	9 104	3 045	4 907	6 735	16 113	223 345	2 328 528

Table A.2 (continued)

Country	GNP	CAPITAL	LABOUR 1	LABOUR 2	LABOUR 3	LAND 1	LAND 2	LAND 3	LAND 4	COAL	MINERALS	OIL
JAMC	2 793	2 945	84	1 053	46	207	62	195	187	0	111 426	0
JAP	2 860 773	2 278 775	6 331	55 139	0	4 170	511	636	25 105	404 260	327 132	342 490
KOR	168 946	167 346	1 143	14 755	2 250	1 997	141	88	6 491	654 565	66 423	0
LIBR	1 063	905	35	142	725	128	245	240	2 103	0	185 516	0
LIBY	23 514	30 490	105	308	646	1 800	345	13 300	680	0	234	1 326 933
MALY	32 747	48 269	505	4 122	2 021	1 040	3 840	27	19 340	902	368 812	2 234 421
MLTA	1 924	1 963	14	95	21	12	1	0	0	0	0	0
MAUR	1 910	2 368	30	392	0	100	6	7	57	0	126	0
MEX	169 131	215 663	2 142	24 350	2 846	23 150	1 560	74 499	43 540	330 214	1 802 531	4 710 631
NETH	226 899	204 026	1 306	4 770	0	902	29	1 081	300	0	2 484	943 122
NUZE	38 306	36 630	208	1 280	0	487	22	13 770	7 290	75 112	30 952	700 069
NIGR	2 946	2 580	58	583	473	1 095	173	5 300	3 600	0	306	0
NOR	89 003	105 148	445	1 645	0	862	0	102	8 330	9 799	147 565	5169 545
PANM	4 462	5 050	85	644	98	440	135	1 330	3 930	0	198	0
PRGY	5 826	6 230	143	1 062	172	2 100	116	20 500	14 950	0	0	0
PERU	24 332	26 755	513	5 015	1 222	3 400	325	27 120	68 900	5 207	1 937 314	129 918
PLIP	39 071	41 507	1 092	16 748	3 577	4 550	3 420	1 220	10 750	37 023	958 825	1 283
PORT	40 873	42 587	311	3 583	742	2 040	710	530	3 641	5 535	32 411	0
SING	24 808	36 668	141	912	217	2	0	0	3	0	0	0
SPAN	336 638	296 754	1 213	12 044	1 013	15 580	4 800	10 210	15 670	563 299	845 132	148 588
SWE	177 928	171 421	1 182	3 147	0	2 935	0	562	28 020	1148	946 897	12
SWITZ	194 822	178 008	498	2 797	0	391	21	1 609	1 052	0	7 776	1 200
THAI	56 955	58 586	824	24 177	3 409	17 900	2 250	760	14 165	110 987	285 313	809 140
TURK	68 568	83 729	1 099	16 247	6 031	24 750	2 980	8 600	20 199	627 669	274 034	26 154
EGPT	34 096	41 942	1 568	3 732	8 575	2 410	173	0	31	0	47 434	961 248
UK	830 232	615 780	4 488	23 741	0	6 930	58	11 560	2 364	3 408 494	286 572	7 687 923
US	4 880 600	2 913 986	18 524	101 944	605	187 881	2 034	241 467	265 188	29 799 948	6 637 165	69 840 368
URGY	7 639	5 796	106	1 030	60	1 280	44	13 520	669	0	0	0
VELA	61 810	92 078	761	5 350	342	3 200	690	17 600	30 755	2 665	311 587	3 890 220
YUG	49 782	160 971	1 054	8 485	1 107	7 037	723	6 347	9 358	924 304	787 296	374 058
TAIW	124 404	77 746	555	7 204	349	755	139	0	2 551	50 225	2 214	545 489

Table A.3 Variables and sources: country attributes

Variable	Description	Unit	Primary source
GNP	Gross national product at current market prices	Millions of US dollars	World Bank, *World Tables 1990*
LABOUR	Numbers of economically active population	Thousands	ILO, *Yearbook of Labour Statistics 1990*
CAPITAL	Capital stock at constant market prices assuming 15-year average life of assets	Millions of US dollars	Derived from World Bank, *World Tables 1990*
SKILL 1	Professional, technical and related workers as a percentage of economically active population	Percentage	ILO, *Yearbook of Labour Statistics*, various years
OIL	Crude oil production plus production of natural gas	Thousands of US dollars	UN, *Energy Statistics Yearbook*, various years
COAL	Production of primary solid fuels (coal, lignite, and brown coal) plus natural gas	Thousands of US dollars	Bureau of Mines, *Minerals Yearbook*, various years UN, *Energy Statistics Yearbook 1990*
PYRITE	Production of pyrite (sulphur content)	Metric tons	Bureau of Mines, *Minerals Yearbook*, various years
SALT	Production of salt	Thousands of metric tons	As above
TIN	Production of tin	Metric tons	As above
LEAD	Production of lead-bearing ores	Metric tons	As above
COPPER	Production of copper-bearing ore	Metric tons	As above
IRONORE	Production of iron ore (metal content)	Thousands of metric tons	As above
PHOSPHATE	Production of phosphate rock	Metric tons	As above
NICKEL	Production of nickel-bearing ore	Metric tons	As above
BAUXITE	Production of bauxite	Thousands of metric tons	As above
POTASH	Production of potash	Metric tons	As above
FLUOR	Production of fluorspar	Metric tons	As above
ZINC	Production of zinc-bearing ores	Metric tons	As above
MANGANESE	Production of manganese-bearing ores	Metric tons	As above

Table A.3 (continued)

LAND 1	Arable land	Thousands of hectares	FAO, *Production Yearbook*, various years
LAND 2	Land under permanent crops	Thousands of hectares	As above
LAND 3	Permanent meadows and pastures	Thousands of hectares	As above
LAND 4	Forests and woodland	Thousands of hectares	As above
LIT	Literacy rate	Percentage	World Bank, *World Tables* The Third Edition, Vol. II Social Data 1984 UNESCO, *Statistical Yearbook* 1989
MINERALS	Composite of 12 kinds of major minerals	Thousands of US dollars	Bureau of Mines, *Minerals Yearbook*, various years
ILLIT	Illiteracy rate	Percentage	Derived from LIT
LABOUR 1	LABOUR * SKILL 1	Thousands	
LABOUR 2	LABOUR-LABOUR 1-LABOUR 3	Thousands	
LABOUR 3	LABOUR * ILLIT	Thousands	

Notes:

1 Gross domestic investment (GDI) in the domestic currency is given annually for the period 1968–88. GDI in real terms is based on the 1980 price. In order to have a consistent and comparable data set for capital stock, average annual growth rates of real GDI for the periods 1950–60 and 1960–70 (given in *World Tables*, Third Edition, Volume 1, Economic Data from the Data Files of the World Bank 1984) were used to obtain annual data for the period 1950–68. Correspondingly, annual data in nominal terms for the same period were calculated based on average growth rates between 1968 and 1974 for each country. Implicit GDI deflators were computed directly from the two sets of data.

2 Figures for skilled labour (LABOUR 1) may have been undercalculated for some countries due to the unavailability of data on skill 1 for particular years under study.

3 Skilled labour (LABOUR 1) for China was calculated based on the numbers of professional and technical workers per 10,000 workers (*Statistical Yearbook of China*, various years).

4 Data for Taiwan were obtained primarily from Taiwan's *Statistical Yearbook*, various years.

Characteristics of manufactured aggregates

Table A.4 shows the means, standard deviation, maximum and minimum value of manufactured aggregates 7 to 10 (labour intensive manufactures, capital intensive manufactures, machinery and chemicals).

Table A.4 Characteristics of manufactured aggregates 7 to 10, 1965, 1971, 1980 and 1988 (thousands of US dollars)[a]

	Aggregate 7	Aggregate 8	Aggregate 9	Aggregate 10
1965				
Mean	-16 302	37 249	121 541	7 503
Standard deviation	309 201	485 096	1 497 624	287 128
Maximum	1 026 252	2 649 990	8 029 147	1 620 535
Minimum	-1 444 098	-668 196	-2 214 762	-237 191
1971				
Mean	-14 414	58 365	222 960	9 742
Standard deviation	748 842	999 590	2 340 281	469 131
Maximum	2 534 788	6 288 640	12 356 360	2 360 881
Minimum	-4 319 119	-2 855 452	-2 136 569	-488 072
1980				
Mean	-747	388 965	1 243 507	108 485
Standard deviation	3 527 328	3 449 603	11 948 411	2 313 277
Maximum	14 559 060	23 198 420	68 226 780	11 199 360
Minimum	-17 199 040	-4 816 185	-1 148 106	-2 738 412
1988				
Mean	-148 605	19 921	433 896	-18 699
Standard deviation	8 168 314	4 215 243	25 235 297	3 258 629
Maximum	17 355 120	17 760 420	161 648 700	19 078 170
Minimum	-52 657 390	-21 509 990	-59 058 700	-5 235 341

Note: a Manufactured aggregates 7 to 10 are labour intensive manufactures, capital intensive manufactures, machinery and chemicals.

Composition of skilled labour (LABOUR 1)

Table A.5 lists those categories of labour which consist of skilled labour (LABOUR 1) used in this study.

Table A.5 International Standard Classification of Occupations (ISCO), major group 0/1 — professional, technical and related workers (LABOUR 1), 1968

0–1	Physical scientists and related technicians
0–2/3	Architects, engineers and related technicians
0–4	Aircraft and ships officers
0–5	Life scientists and related technicians
0–6/7	Medical, dental, veterinary and related workers
0–8	Statisticians, mathematicians, systems analysts and related technicians
0–9	Economists
1–1	Accountants
1–2	Jurists
1–3	Teachers
1–4	Workers in religion
1–5	Authors, journalists and related writers
1–6	Sculptors, painters, photographers and related creative artists
1–7	Composers and performing artists
1–8	Athletes, sportspeople and related workers
1–9	Professional, technical and related workers not elsewhere classified

Source: Leamer (1984, Table 4.7).

Appendix B

Comparisons of the three measurements of capital stocks

Following the discussion in Leamer (1984, 1988a), three methods are used to calculate capital stock figures. The first method accumulates real investment in the local currency deflated by the home country price deflator for gross national investment and then translates the result into US dollars using the base year (1980) exchange rate. The second method translates foreign currencies into US dollars in each year using the current exchange rate and then divides by the US deflator for gross investment to form a series on real investment. The third method substitutes the purchasing power parity rates from Summers and Heston (1984) for observed exchange rates. The above three methods take the following forms:

$$R_t(1) = I_t(P_b/P_t)/S_b, \tag{B.1}$$

where R is a mnemonic for real investment; I_t is gross domestic investment in the home country currency, referred to here as 'pounds'; P_t is the home country investment price index (P_b represents the base year price index); and S_t is the exchange rate in pounds per US dollar (S_b is the base year exchange rate).

$$R_t(2) = (I_t/S_t)(P_b(\$)/P_t(\$)), \tag{B.2}$$

where $P_t(\$)$ is the US investment price index.

$$R_t(3) = (I_t/PPP_t)(P_b(\$)/P_t(\$)), \tag{B.3}$$

where PPP_t is the purchasing power parity exchange rate in pounds per US dollar, namely the pound price of a commodity bundle divided by the dollar price of the same bundle. 'The investment series $R(1)$ and $R(3)$ can be thought to correct the investment series $R(2)$ for misalignment of the exchange rate. The first investment series is equal to the second divided by an index of the real exchange index: $R_t(1) = R_t(2)/(r_t/r_b)$, where the "real exchange rate" is $r_t = S_tP_t(\$)/P_t$. These real investment series would be identical if the real exchange rate were constant, $r_t = r_b$, that is, if variation in the relative price of investment goods were exactly offset by variation in the exchange rate' (Leamer 1988a, p. 480).

Based on the above definitions, three different capital stock measures are computed and accumulated, assuming exponential survival profiles, to form three capital stock series in year b dollars:

$$K_t^b(j) = \sum_{j=t-\theta}^{t}(1-\delta)^{t-j}R_t(j) \quad j = 1, 2, 3, \tag{B.4}$$

where δ is the rate of depreciation, assumed to be 13.3 per cent, and θ is the length of asset life, assumed to be 15 years.

The estimates of capital stock for 62 countries end in 1974.[1] The correlations between *K(1)*, *K(2)* and *K(3)* are $(\rho_{12}, \rho_{13}, \rho_{23}) = (0.98, 0.97, 0.98)$. The statistics for these three capital stocks are given in Table B.1.

Table B.1 1974 statistics: capital stocks (62 economies)

	Mean	Standard deviation	Minimum value	Maximum value
K(1)	143 539	337 925	922	2 017 665
K(2)	127 180	315 034	707	2 017 665
K(3)	165 269	350 219	1 394	2 017 665

As Table B.1 shows, *K(3)* has a larger mean, a larger standard deviation and a smaller range than the other two measures. *K(2)*, on the other hand, has a smaller mean, a smaller standard deviation and a larger range than the other two measures, implying that *K(2)* is performing reasonably well in 1974.[2] This is understandable given that the world economy had not yet experienced any dramatic fluctuations in exchange rates and that the other two measures, which could be thought to correct *K(2)* for erratic swings in exchange rates, had not yet been given full play.

However, before that conclusion can be reached, further adjustment needs to be made to allow cross-country comparison. The identical numbers given for maximum value in Table B.1 imply that country size matters. The effects of country size can be eliminated by dividing capital stocks by total population. The corresponding correlations between these three capital stocks are $(\rho_{12}, \rho_{13}, \rho_{23}) = (0.98, 0.96, 0.98)$. The statistical results are shown in Table B.2.

Table B.2 1974 statistics: capital/population (62 economies)

	Mean	Standard deviation	Minimum value	Maximum value
K(1)/POP	5.436	5.690	22.320	0.032
K(2)/POP	4.771	4.635	17.143	0.045
K(3)/POP	6.258	4.738	17.873	0.131

Based on capital per person, *K(2)* still performs relatively well in terms of its smaller standard deviation. However, further examination may still be necessary; this can be achieved by identifying outliers.

Potentially unusual observations are identified first by regressing the 1974 figures for capital per person for each of the three methods of measuring capital against each other. The regression of *K(1)/POP* on *K(2)/POP* has an R^2 of 0.96. The largest Studentised residuals of this regression are: Canada (-4.98), the United Kingdom (2.76), Australia (2.59), Switzerland (2.28), Germany (2.25), Brazil (-2.21), Chile (-1.77) and the United States (-1.60). The figures show that, compared to the capital stock measure using current exchange rates, developed countries rank at the top for being both upward and downward measured when the current exchange rates are used.

The regression of *K(1)/POP* on *K(3)/POP* has an R^2 of 0.88. The largest Studentised residuals of this regression are: Switzerland (4.97), Sweden (4.19), Germany (3.45), Chile (-3.21), Uruguay (-3.12), Israel (-3.02), Norway (2.98), Iceland (2.88) and Greece (-2.81). Thus, compared to the third capital stock measure using purchasing power parity exchange rates, the first measure of capital per person *(K(1)/POP)* is significantly higher for Switzerland, Sweden, Germany, Norway and Iceland, and significantly lower for Chile, Uruguay, Israel and Greece. In comparison with the previous result, this suggests that there is a relative upward adjustment of the capital stock figures for developed countries and a relative downward adjustment for developing countries when purchasing power parity exchange rates are used.

The largest Studentised residuals of the regression of *K(2)/POP* on *K(3)/POP* with R^2 of 0.93 are Sweden (2.68), Iceland (2.55), Spain (-2.47), Switzerland (2.26), Canada (2.11), Uruguay (-1.87), Norway (1.78) and Greece (-1.60). Compared with the results derived from the regression of *K(1)/POP* on *K(3)/POP*, the capital stock measure using current exchange rates *K(2)* is probably preferable since it substantially reduces the Studentised residuals when *K(2)/POP* regresses on the measure using purchasing power parity, *K(3)/POP*.

Potentially unusual observations are also identified by regressing per capita GNP on capital per labour. 'If capital and labour were the only factors of production, and if factor prices were equalised internationally, then GNP/LABOUR = $w + r \times$ CAPITAL/LABOUR, where w is the wage rate and r is the rental rate of capital in suitable units. An outlying country in the bivariate scatter of GNP/LABOUR and CAPITAL/LABOUR can therefore be explained by reference to either: 1) other factors which contribute substantially to GNP, 2) differences in factor prices, or 3) mismeasurement of CAPITAL, GNP or LABOUR' (Leamer 1988a, p. 481).

Regression of per capita GNP on capital per labour in 1974 yields coefficients for the three capital series: (w, r) = (0.69, 0.40); (0.07, 0.51); (-1.44, 0.47). The R^2s for *K(1)*, *K(2)* and *K(3)* respectively are 0.88, 0.93 and 0.86. The negative estimate of the constant when *K(3)/LABOUR* is the explanatory variable casts some doubt on this measure of capital. This confirms Leamer's result using 1980 data. However, it should be noted that GNP uses the current exchange rate, not the purchasing power parity rate.

The unusual observations are reported in Table B.3, where Studentised residuals are used as measures of unusualness.

Table B.3 Largest Studentised residuals, 1974[a]

K(1)		*K(2)*		*K(3)*	
Libya	8.60	Libya	5.80	United States	6.91
Canada	6.36	United States	4.67	Venezuela	-5.07
United States	6.27	Norway	-3.18	Japan	-4.36
Australia	4.24	Japan	-3.01	Libya	4.21
Switzerland	-3.81	Venezuela	-2.73	Canada	3.76
Norway	-3.43	Switzerland	-2.55	Iceland	3.68

Note: a Regression of *GNP/LABOUR* on *K(j)/LABOUR*.

As Table B.3 shows, Libya and Venezuela are the only developing countries among those having large Studentised residuals. It is quite likely that the large residuals of these two countries are due to the omitted factor of oil reserves, since both are major oil-producing and oil-exporting countries, and as no other such countries are included in the sample.

This leaves some developed countries, almost the same group in each category, with unusualness spreading in both directions. Based on this, it would seem that *K(2)* can be preferred to *K(1)*. However, it should be noted that the comparison is based on capital stocks discounted and accumulated up to 1974, when changes in the exchange rate system had just begun. The advantage of using *K(1)* might show up clearly during periods of erratic change in exchange rates.

The above examination of the three measures of capital sheds light on the relative accuracy of each measure, but is inconclusive in choosing among them. Further evidence can be obtained using the Heckscher–Ohlin–Vanek model, in which the relationship between trade and endowment variables is formulated as follows (Leamer 1988a, p. 482):

$$T_{ij} = \beta_j X_i + \theta_j K_i + GNP_j \varepsilon_{ij}, \qquad \text{(B.5)}$$

where j is the commodity subscript, i is the country subscript, X is a vector representing the supply of m factors other than capital, K is the supply of capital, GNP is gross national product, T is the vector of net export and β, θ and ε are unobservable, the latter assumed to be normally distributed with mean zero and variance σ^2_j. This model is intended to explain cross-country variability in the commodity composition of trade at one point in time.

The above theoretical model was estimated using each of the three capital stock figures separately; the corresponding R^2s in the ten regressions are reported in Table B.4.

Table B.4 **R^2 in linear trade system using different capital stocks with unweighted data**

	K(1)	*K(2)*	*K(3)*
PETRO	.989	.988	.988
MAT	.938	.955	.960
FOR	.653	.639	.684
TROP	.899	.905	.898
ANL	.439	.417	.444
CER	.945	.922	.954
LAB	.688	.695	.692
CAP	.778	.860	.888
MACH	.870	.907	.946
CHEM	.840	.831	.853

The figures in Table B.4 show that, if unweighted models are used, *K(3)* gives the highest R^2 in seven of the 10 regressions, though the differences are not substantial. When the data are weighted by GNP or by population, as shown in Table B.5, each of the measures of capital stock performs about the same.

The results in Tables B.4 and B.5 seem to confirm Leamer's conclusion that 'more careful consideration of the method of translating investment into a common currency does not produce dramatic improvements in our understanding of the determinants of the commodity structure of trade' (Leamer 1988, p. 482). Therefore, *K(1)* has been selected as the measure of capital stock for this study.

Table B.5 **R^2 in linear trade system using different capital stocks with data weighted by GNP and population**

	K(1)/GNP	*K(2)/GNP*	*K(3)/GNP*	*K(1)/POP*	*K(2)/POP*	*K(3)/POP*
PETRO/GNP, POP	.949	.953	.952	.985	.985	.985
MAT/GNP, POP	.965	.966	.968	.711	.711	.739
FOR/GNP, POP	.117	.109	.134	.515	.494	.486
TROP/GNP, POP	.272	.298	.246	.392	.391	.389
ANL/GNP, POP	.076	.079	.096	.537	.523	.583
CER/GNP, POP	.317	.322	.337	.573	.563	.614
LAB/GNP, POP	.143	.143	.170	.305	.310	.302
CAP/GNP, POP	.068	.089	.114	.236	.228	.243
MACH/GNP, POP	.152	.158	.194	.519	.432	.435
CHEM/GNP, POP	.110	.099	.116	.305	.262	.291

Appendix C

Trade dependence and resource abundancc profiles

This appendix contains graphs describing composition of trade and relative abundance of resources for each of the 61 economies studied in each of the two years under study. Detailed discussion of these graphs can be found in Chapter 4. Full descriptions of the 10 trade categories and the 11 resource categories can be found in Chapter 3. The 'resource' labelled SIZE in the resource abundance profiles refers to GNP, which is obtained by calculating the country's GNP divided by GNP averaged over all countries in the given year.

In order to form comparable graphs for all countries, the trade data have been transformed according to the function sign $(T/Y) \times \ln(1 + 100|T/Y|)$, where T refers to net export data and Y refers to GNP. The resource data have been transformed according to the function $(5x - 5)/(x + 5)$, where x is either the resource abundance ratio (resource share divided by GNP share) or the GNP ratio (ratio of GNP to average GNP). Correspondences between the original numbers and the graphed numbers can be found in Tables C.1 and C.2.[1]

Table C.1 **Correspondence between graphed numbers (z) and trade shares (T/Y)[a]**

z	.5	.7	1.0	1.1	1.5	2.0	3.0	4.0
$100\|Y/T\|$	.65	1.00	1.72	2.00	3.48	6.39	19.09	53.60

Note: a $z = \ln(1 + 100|T/Y|)$.

Table C.2 **Correspondence between graphed numbers (z) and resource ratios (x)[a]**

z	-1	-.8	-.6	-.4	-.2	0.0	0.5	1.0	2.0	3.0	4.0	5.0
x	0	.17	.36	.56	.77	1.0	1.7	2.5	5.3	10.0	25.0	∞

Note: a $z = (5x - 5)/(x + 5)$.

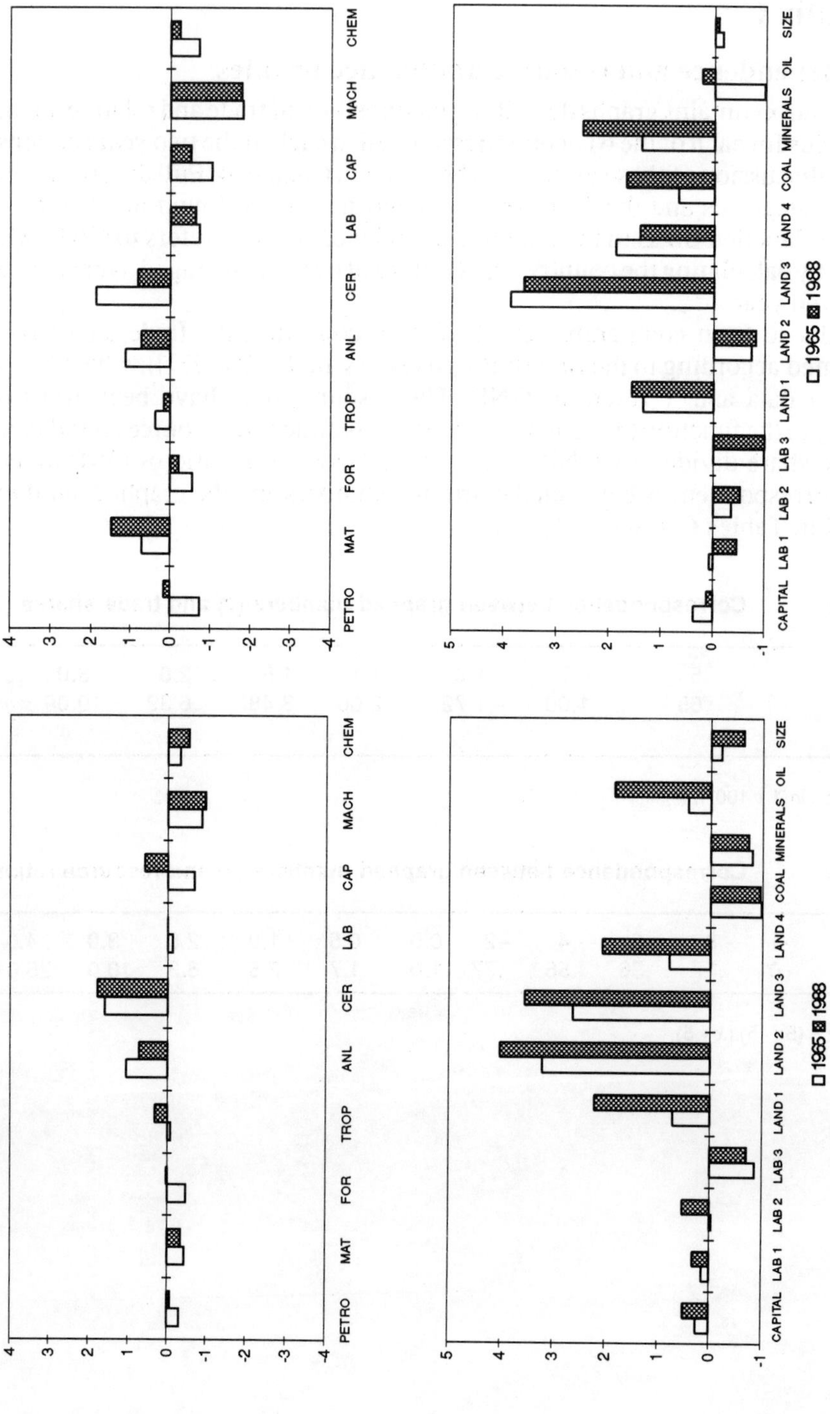
ARGENTINA
AUSTRALIA
PETRO MAT FOR TROP ANL CER LAB CAP MACH CHEM
CAPITAL LAB 1 LAB 2 LAB 3 LAND 1 LAND 2 LAND 3 LAND 4 COAL MINERALS OIL SIZE
1965 1988

BELGIUM–LUXEMBOURG

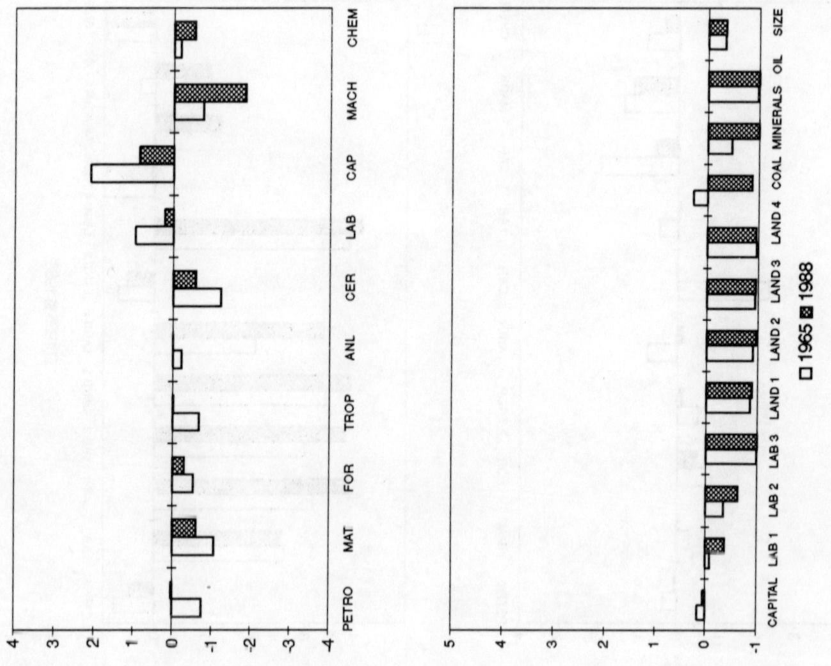

AUSTRIA

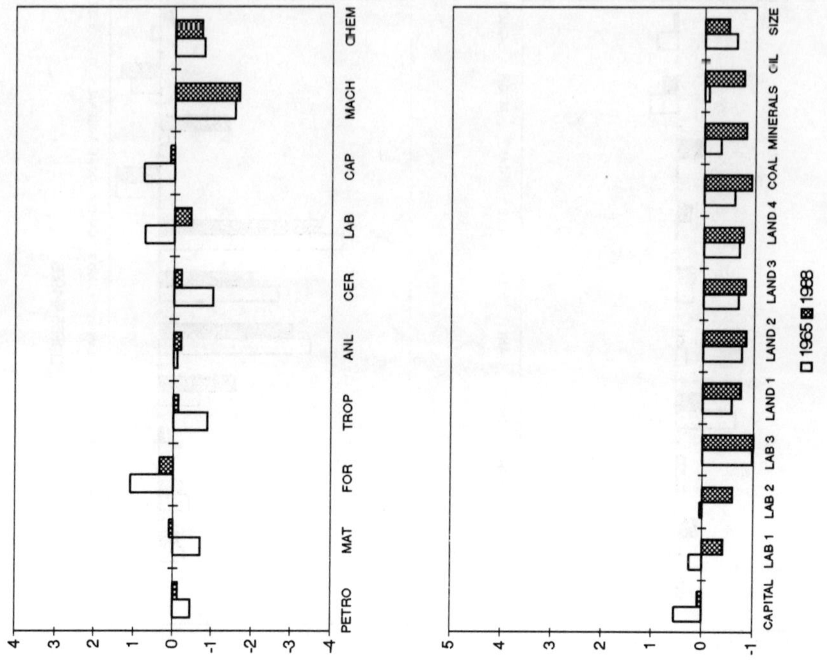

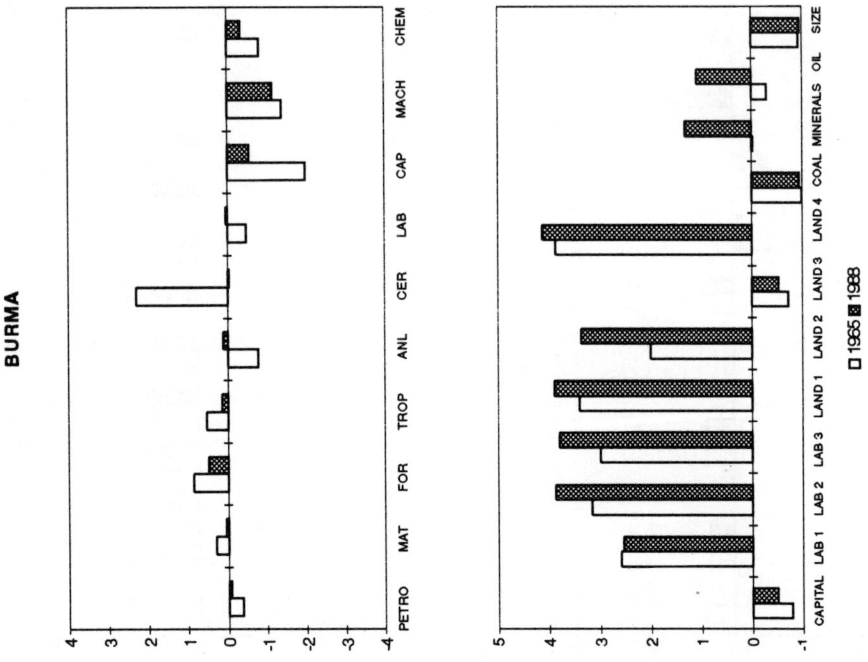
BURMA
PETRO
MAT
FOR
TROP
ANL
CER
LAB
CAP
MACH
CHEM
CAPITAL
LAB 1
LAB 2
LAB 3
LAND 1
LAND 2
LAND 3
LAND 4
COAL
MINERALS
OIL
SIZE
1965
1988

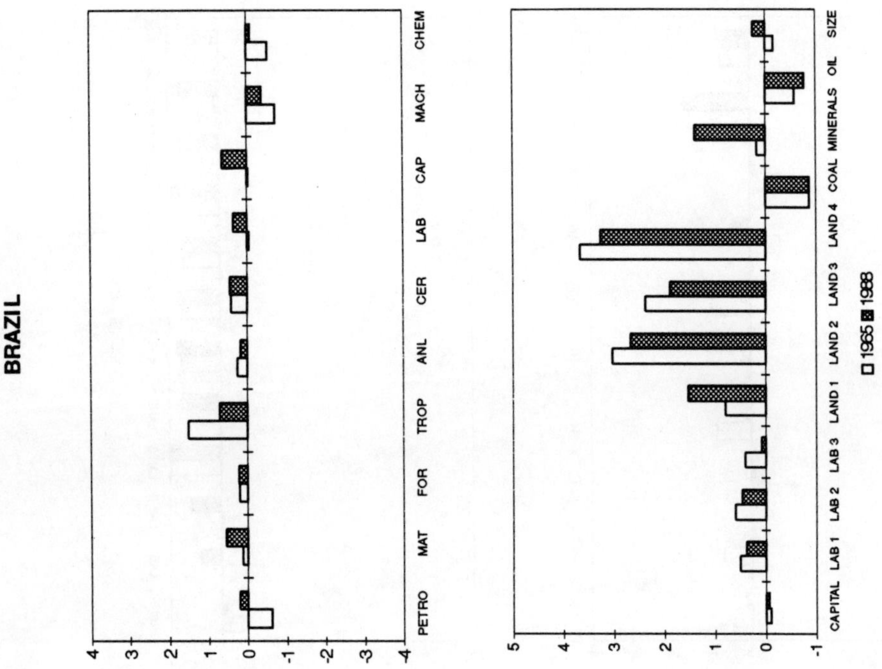
BRAZIL
PETRO
MAT
FOR
TROP
ANL
CER
LAB
CAP
MACH
CHEM
CAPITAL
LAB 1
LAB 2
LAB 3
LAND 1
LAND 2
LAND 3
LAND 4
COAL
MINERALS
OIL
SIZE
1965
1988

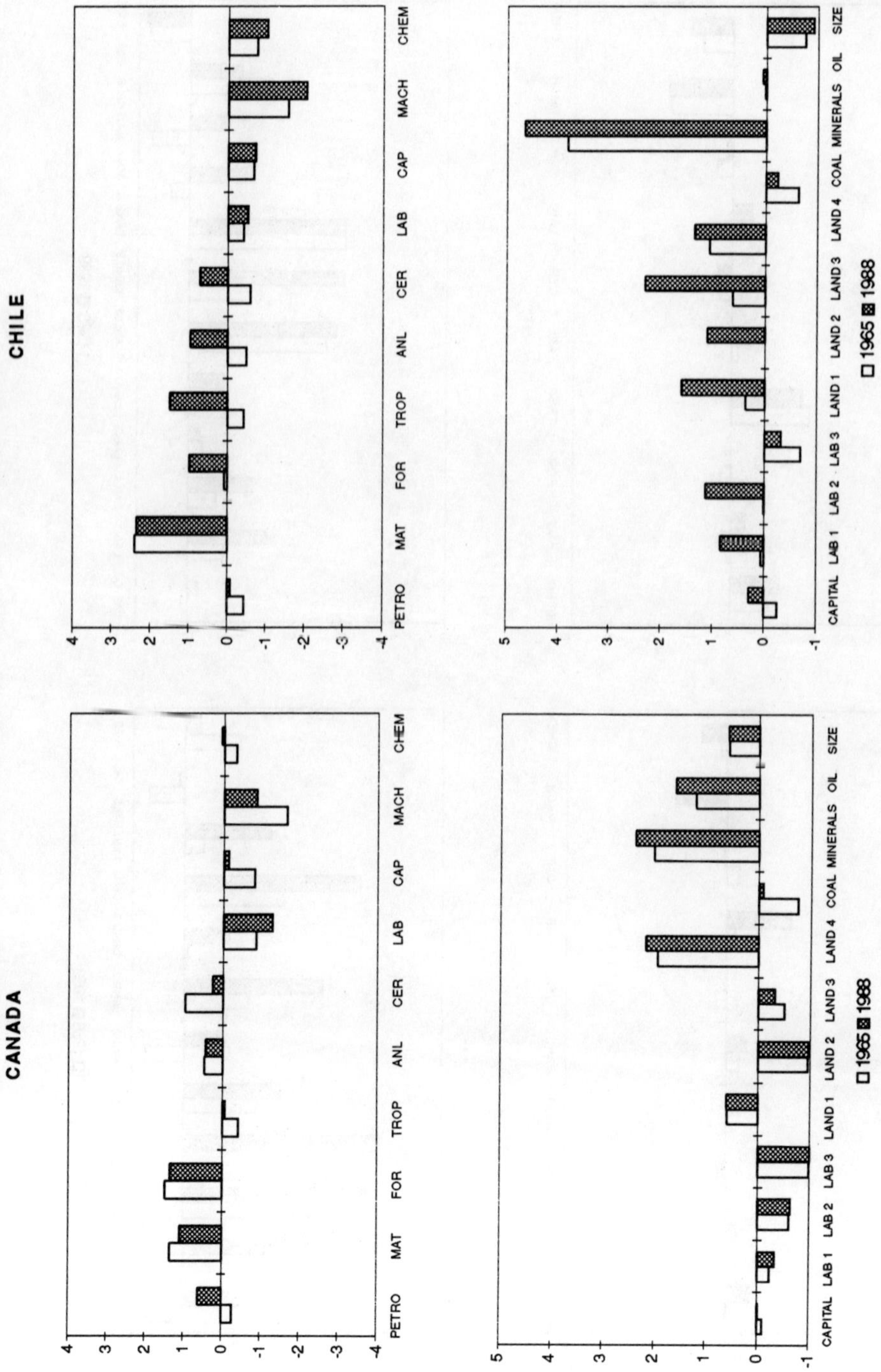
CANADA
CHILE
PETRO MAT FOR TROP ANL CER LAB CAP MACH CHEM
CAPITAL LAB 1 LAB 2 LAB 3 LAND 1 LAND 2 LAND 3 LAND 4 COAL MINERALS OIL SIZE
1965
1988

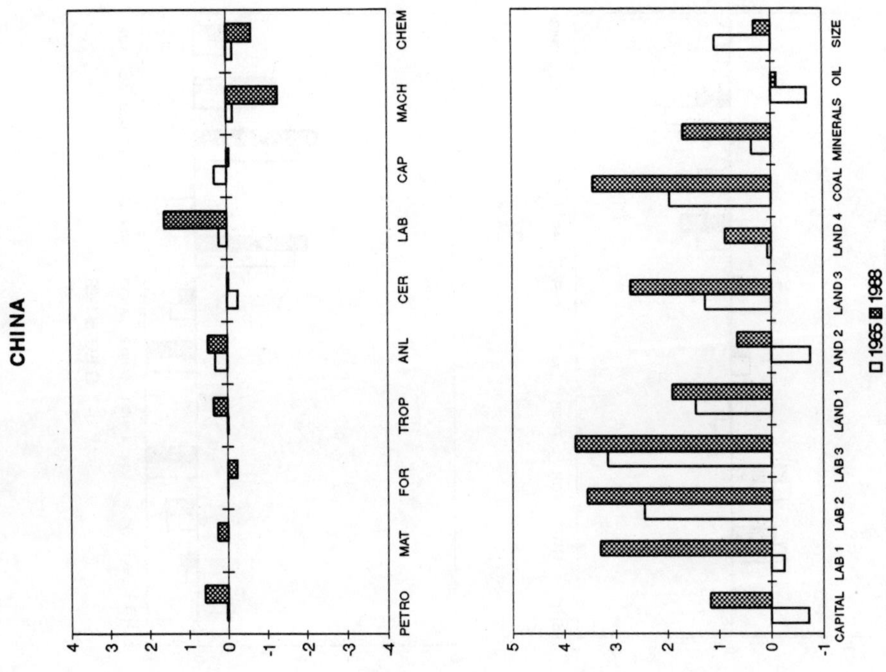
CHINA
PETRO MAT FOR TROP ANL CER LAB CAP MACH CHEM
CAPITAL LAB 1 LAB 2 LAB 3 LAND 1 LAND 2 LAND 3 LAND 4 COAL MINERALS OIL SIZE
1965 1988

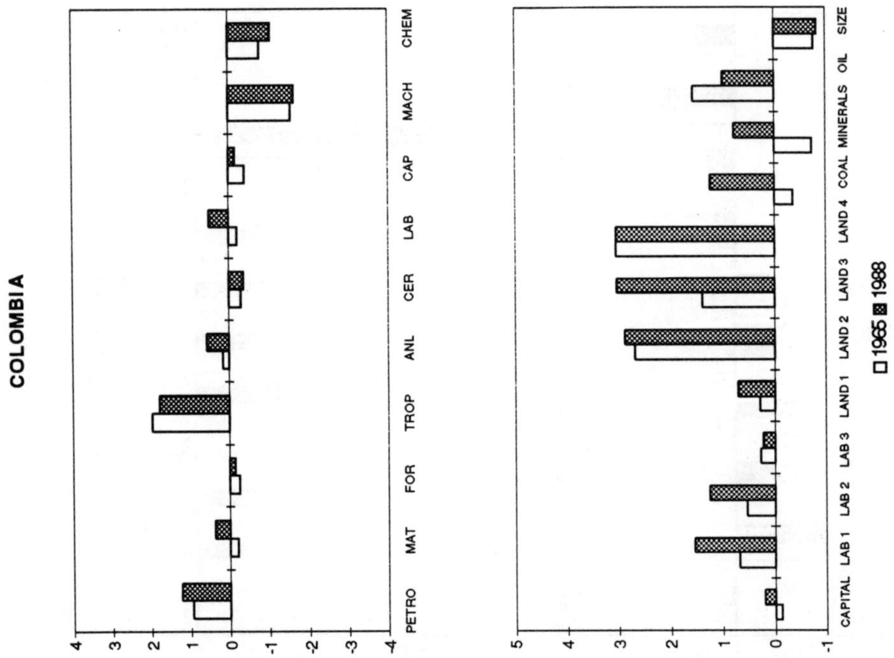
COLOMBIA
PETRO MAT FOR TROP ANL CER LAB CAP MACH CHEM
CAPITAL LAB 1 LAB 2 LAB 3 LAND 1 LAND 2 LAND 3 LAND 4 COAL MINERALS OIL SIZE
1965 1988

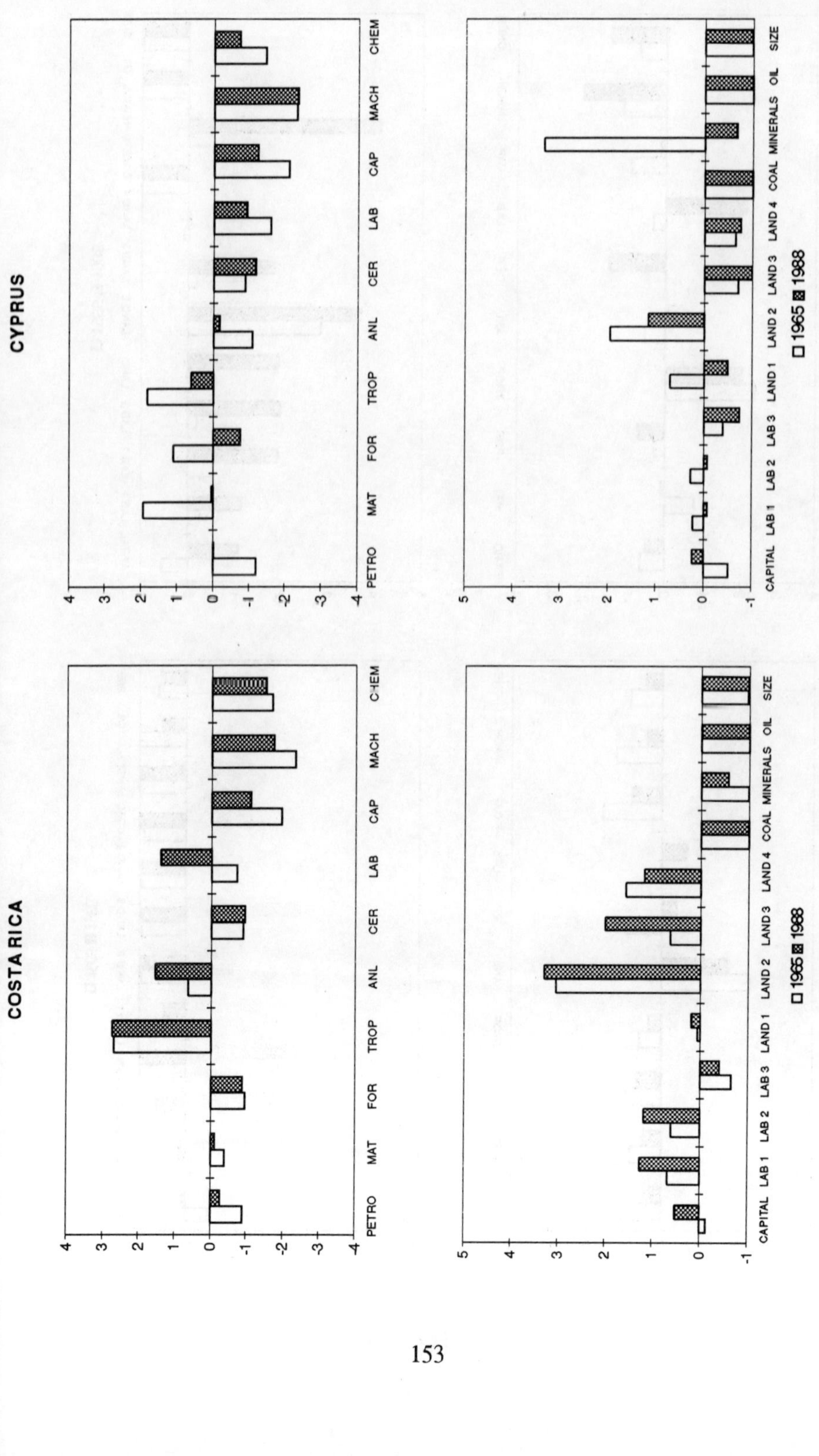
COSTA RICA
CYPRUS
PETRO MAT FOR TROP ANL CER LAB CAP MACH CHEM
CAPITAL LAB 1 LAB 2 LAB 3 LAND 1 LAND 2 LAND 3 LAND 4 COAL MINERALS OIL SIZE
1965 1988
4 3 2 1 0 -1 -2 -3 -4
5 4 3 2 1 0 -1

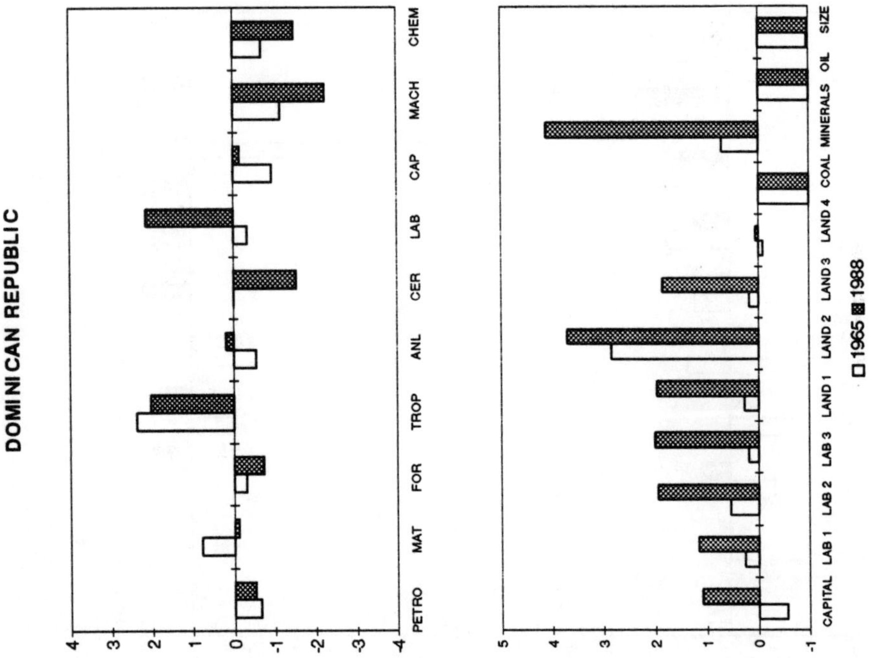
DOMINICAN REPUBLIC
4
3
2
1
0
-1
-2
-3
-4
PETRO
MAT
FOR
TROP
ANL
CER
LAB
CAP
MACH
CHEM
5
4
3
2
1
0
-1
CAPITAL
LAB 1
LAB 2
LAB 3
LAND 1
LAND 2
LAND 3
LAND 4
COAL
MINERALS
OIL
SIZE
1965 1988

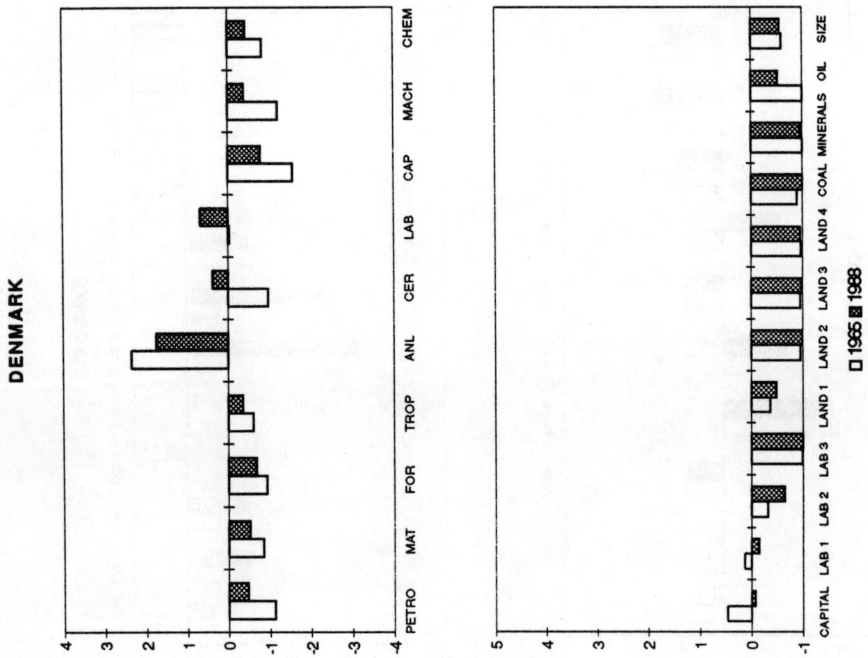
DENMARK
4
3
2
1
0
-1
-2
-3
-4
PETRO
MAT
FOR
TROP
ANL
CER
LAB
CAP
MACH
CHEM
5
4
3
2
1
0
-1
CAPITAL
LAB 1
LAB 2
LAB 3
LAND 1
LAND 2
LAND 3
LAND 4
COAL
MINERALS
OIL
SIZE
1965 1988

ECUADOR

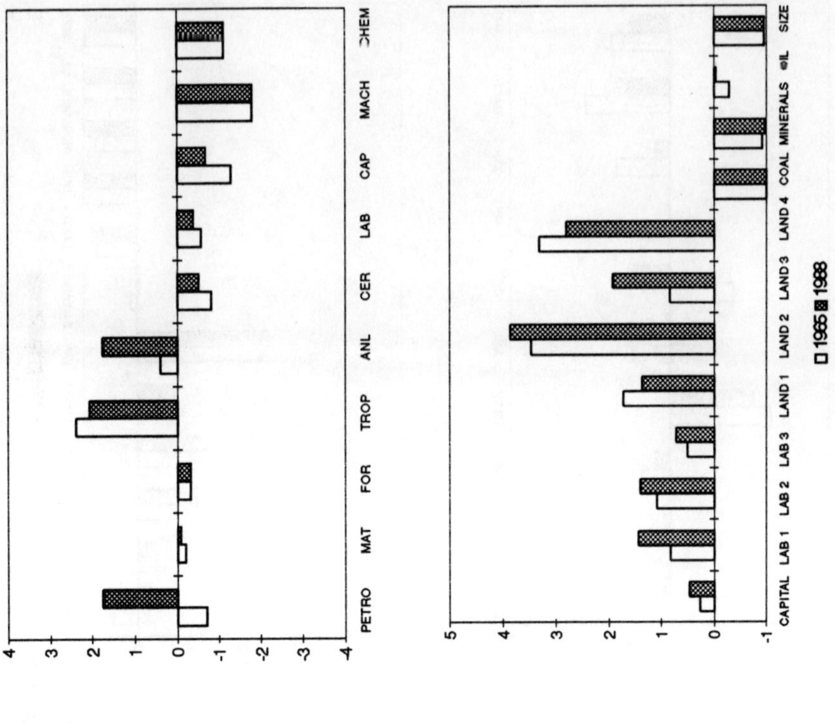

EGYPT

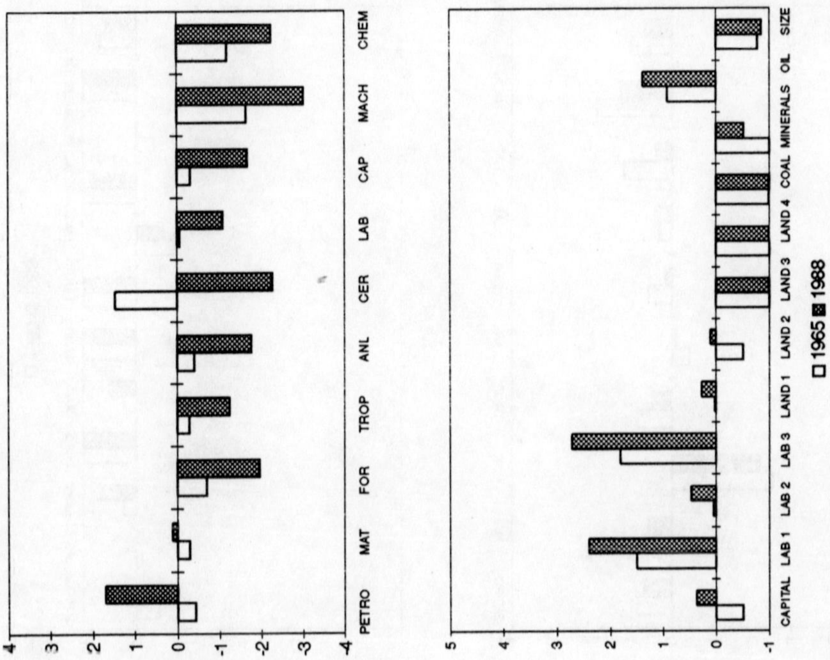

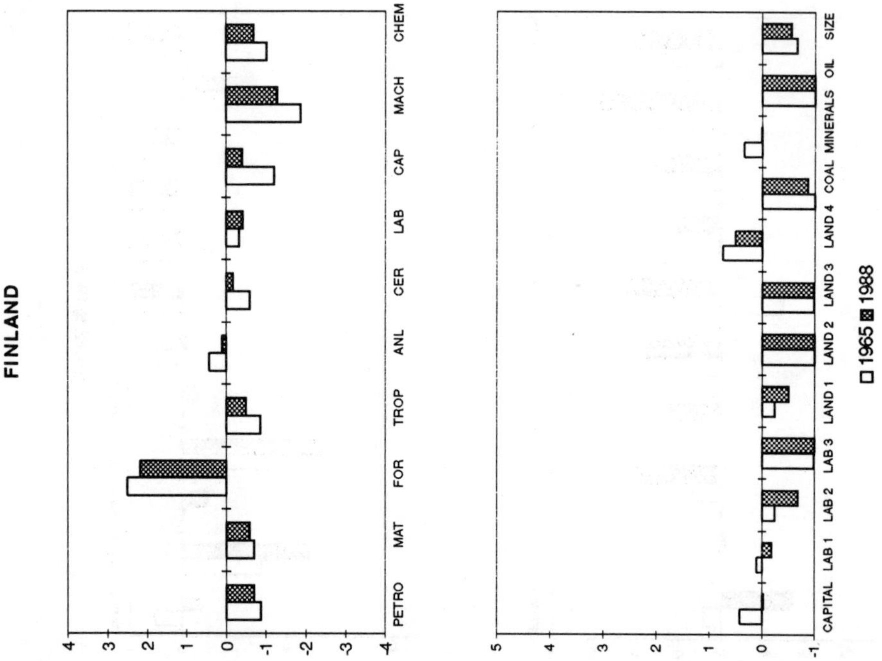
FINLAND
PETRO
MAT
FOR
TROP
ANL
CER
LAB
CAP
MACH
CHEM
CAPITAL
LAB 1
LAB 2
LAB 3
LAND 1
LAND 2
LAND 3
LAND 4
COAL
MINERALS
OIL
SIZE
1965
1988

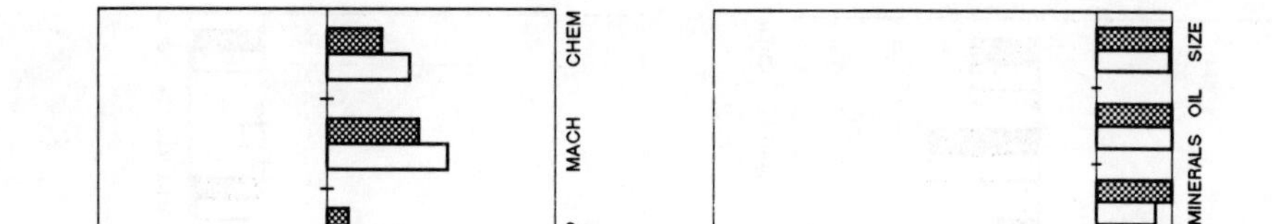
EL SALVADOR
PETRO
MAT
FOR
TROP
ANL
CER
LAB
CAP
MACH
CHEM
CAPITAL
LAB 1
LAB 2
LAB 3
LAND 1
LAND 2
LAND 3
LAND 4
COAL
MINERALS
OIL
SIZE
1965
1988

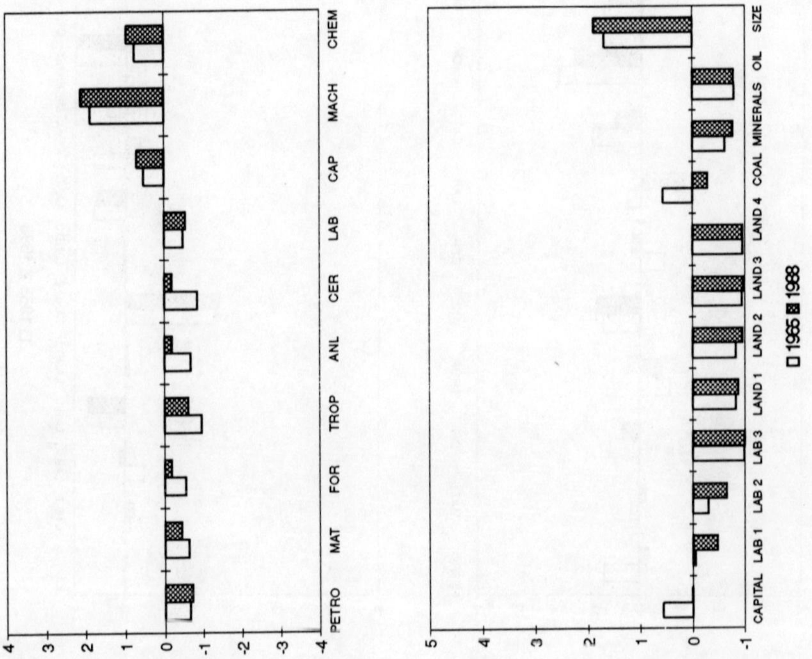
GERMANY
PETRO
MAT
FOR
TROP
ANL
CER
LAB
CAP
MACH
CHEM
CAPITAL
LAB 1
LAB 2
LAB 3
LAND 1
LAND 2
LAND 3
LAND 4
COAL
MINERALS
OIL
SIZE
1965
1988

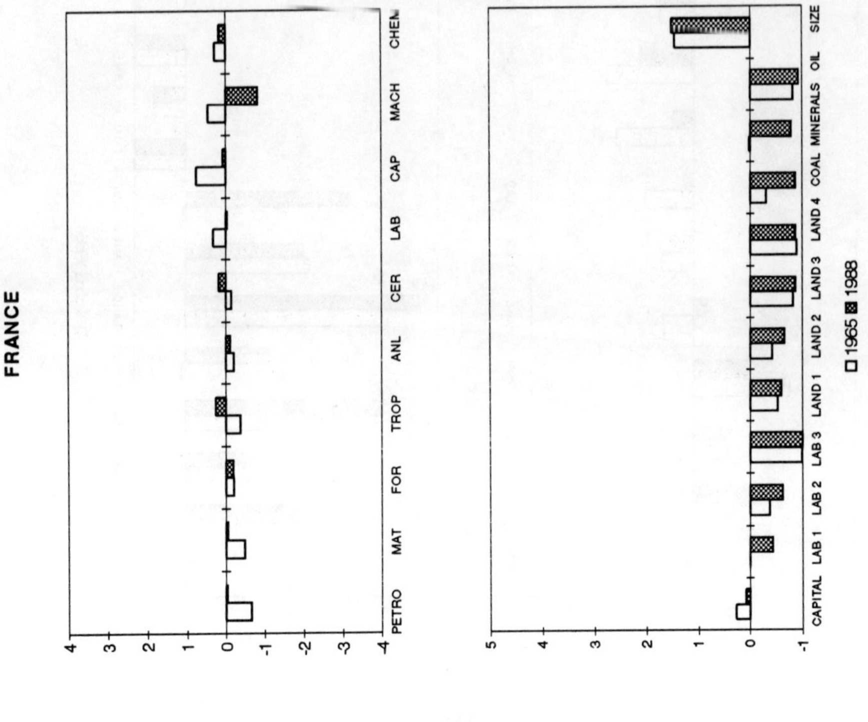
FRANCE
PETRO
MAT
FOR
TROP
ANL
CER
LAB
CAP
MACH
CHEM
CAPITAL
LAB 1
LAB 2
LAB 3
LAND 1
LAND 2
LAND 3
LAND 4
COAL
MINERALS
OIL
SIZE
1965
1988

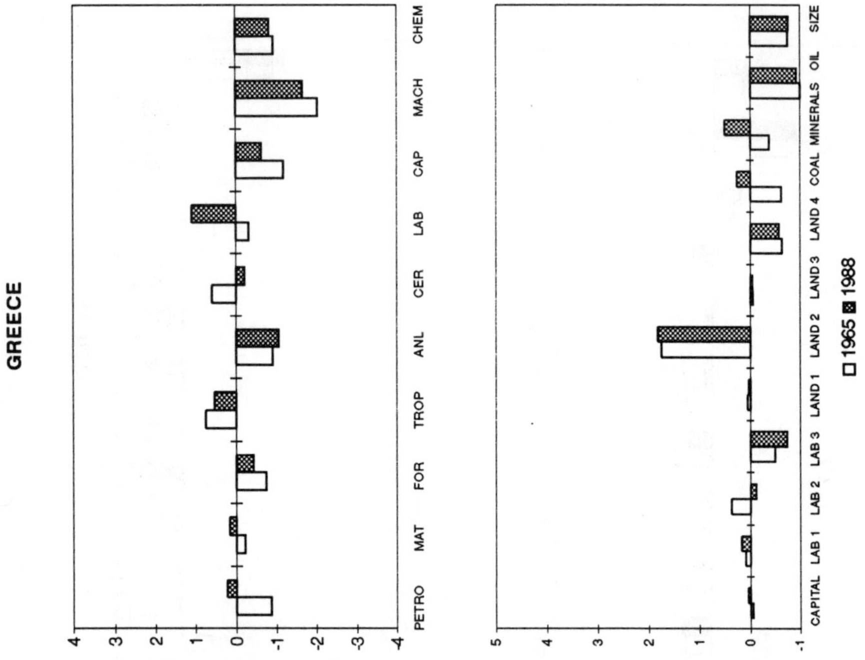
GREECE
PETRO
MAT
FOR
TROP
ANL
CER
LAB
CAP
MACH
CHEM
CAPITAL
LAB 1
LAB 2
LAB 3
LAND 1
LAND 2
LAND 3
LAND 4
COAL
MINERALS
OIL
SIZE
1965
1988

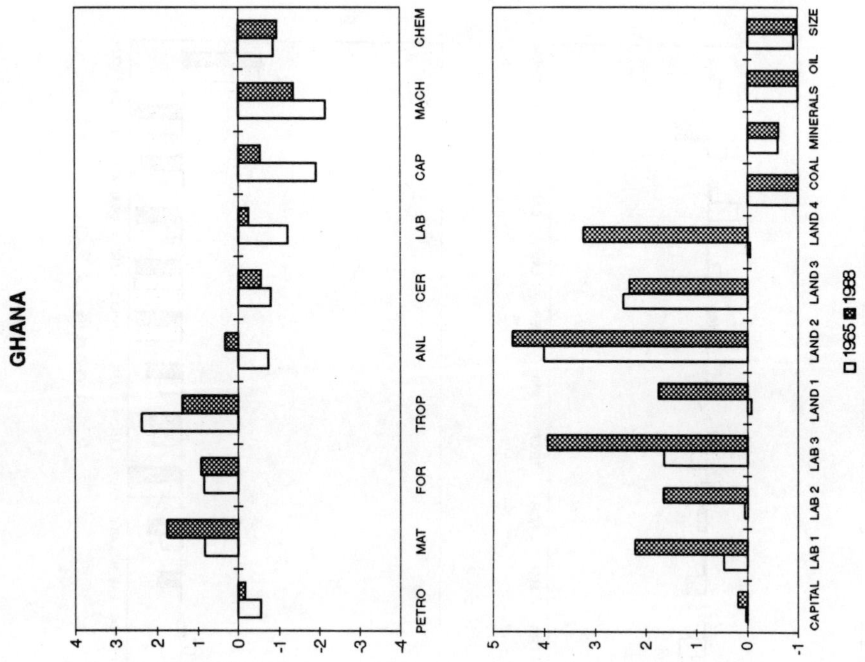
GHANA
PETRO
MAT
FOR
TROP
ANL
CER
LAB
CAP
MACH
CHEM
CAPITAL
LAB 1
LAB 2
LAB 3
LAND 1
LAND 2
LAND 3
LAND 4
COAL
MINERALS
OIL
SIZE
1965
1988

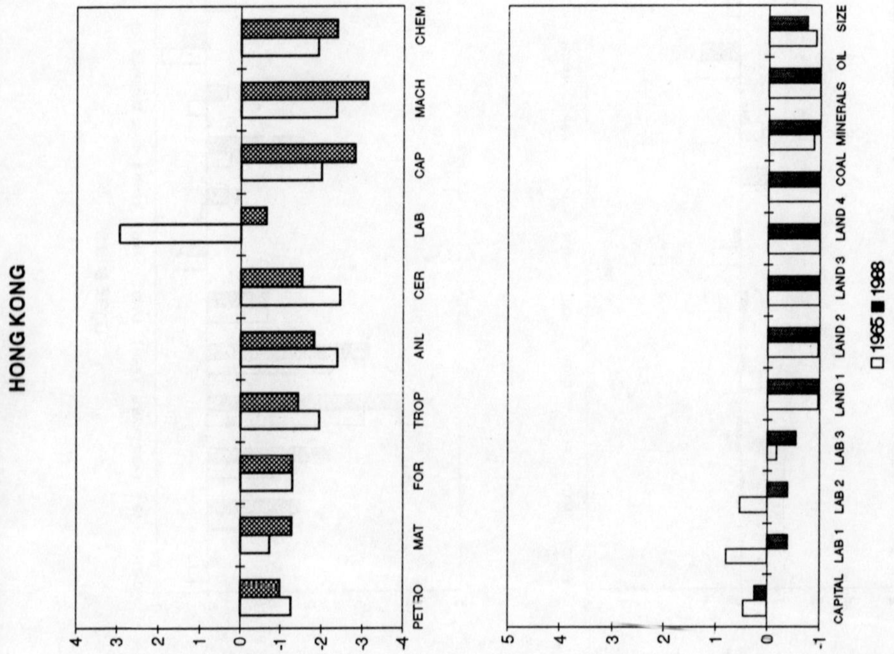
HONG KONG
PETRO
MAT
FOR
TROP
ANL
CER
LAB
CAP
MACH
CHEM
CAPITAL
LAB 1
LAB 2
LAB 3
LAND 1
LAND 2
LAND 3
LAND 4
COAL
MINERALS
OIL
SIZE
1965
1988

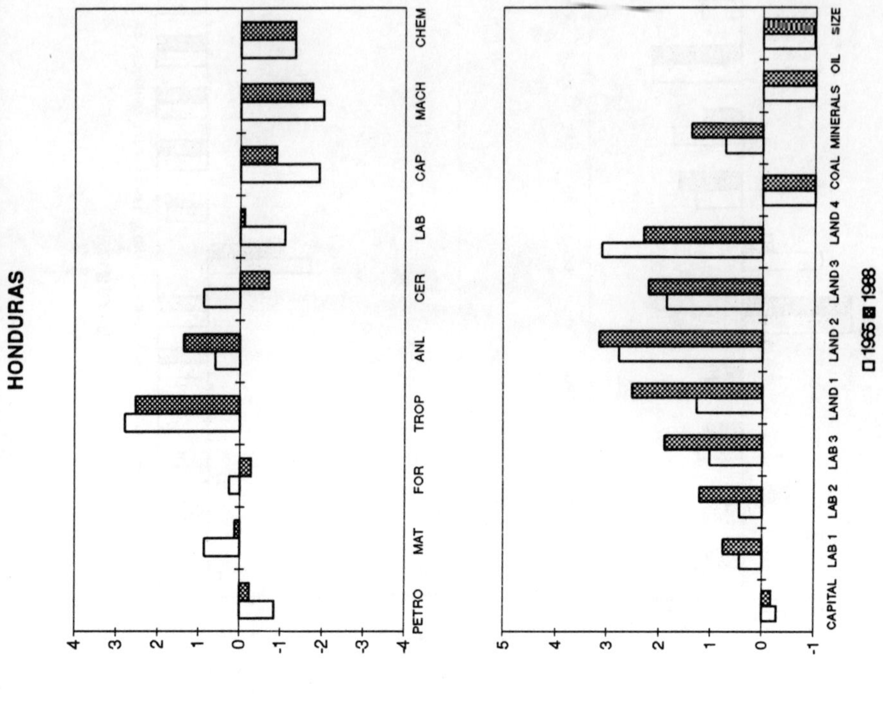
HONDURAS
PETRO
MAT
FOR
TROP
ANL
CER
LAB
CAP
MACH
CHEM
CAPITAL
LAB 1
LAB 2
LAB 3
LAND 1
LAND 2
LAND 3
LAND 4
COAL
MINERALS
OIL
SIZE
1965
1988

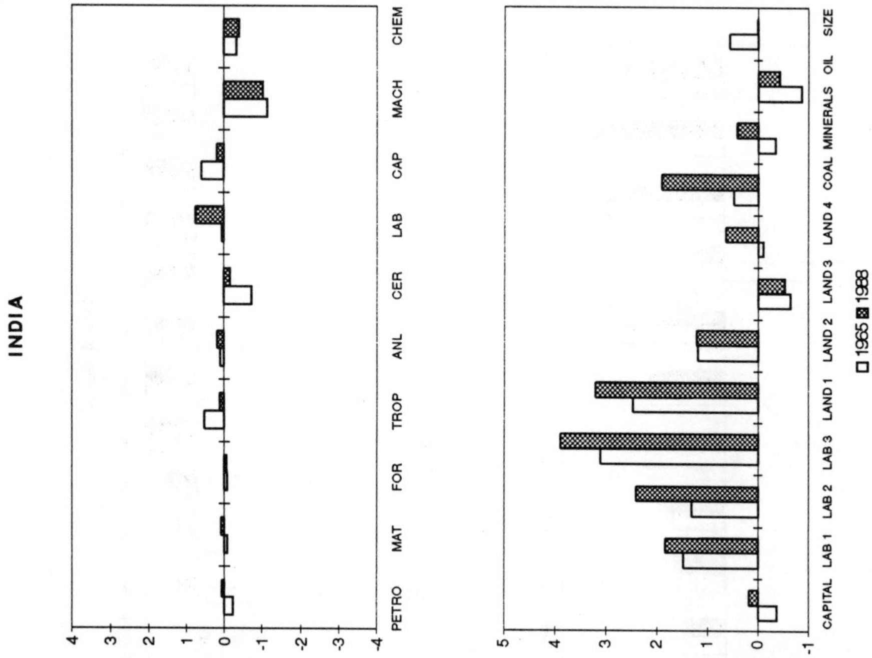
INDIA
4
3
2
1
0
-1
-2
-3
-4
PETRO MAT FOR TROP ANL CER LAB CAP MACH CHEM
5
4
3
2
1
0
-1
CAPITAL LAB 1 LAB 2 LAB 3 LAND 1 LAND 2 LAND 3 LAND 4 COAL MINERALS OIL SIZE
1965 1988

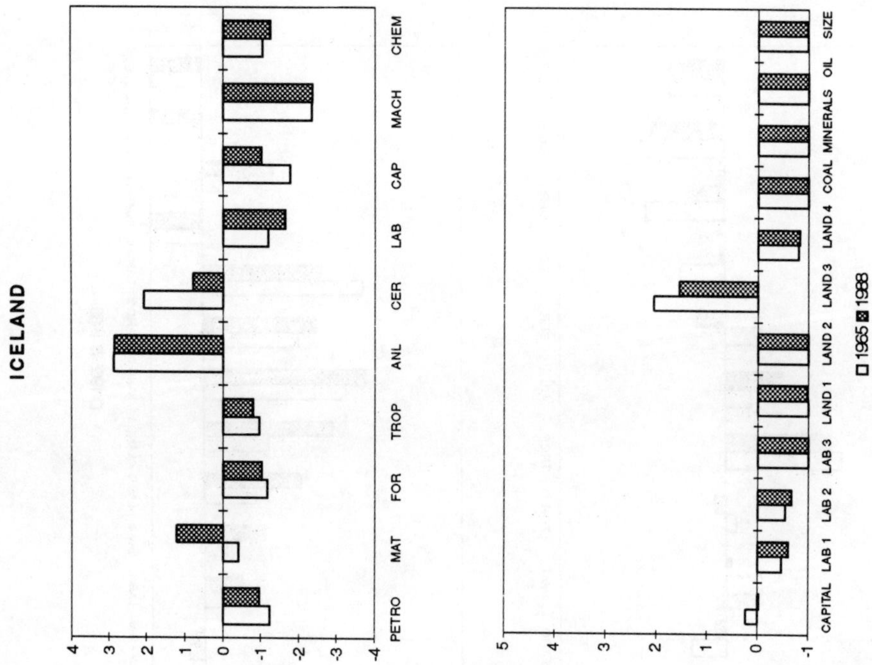
ICELAND
4
3
2
1
0
-1
-2
-3
-4
PETRO MAT FOR TROP ANL CER LAB CAP MACH CHEM
5
4
3
2
1
0
-1
CAPITAL LAB 1 LAB 2 LAB 3 LAND 1 LAND 2 LAND 3 LAND 4 COAL MINERALS OIL SIZE
1965 1988

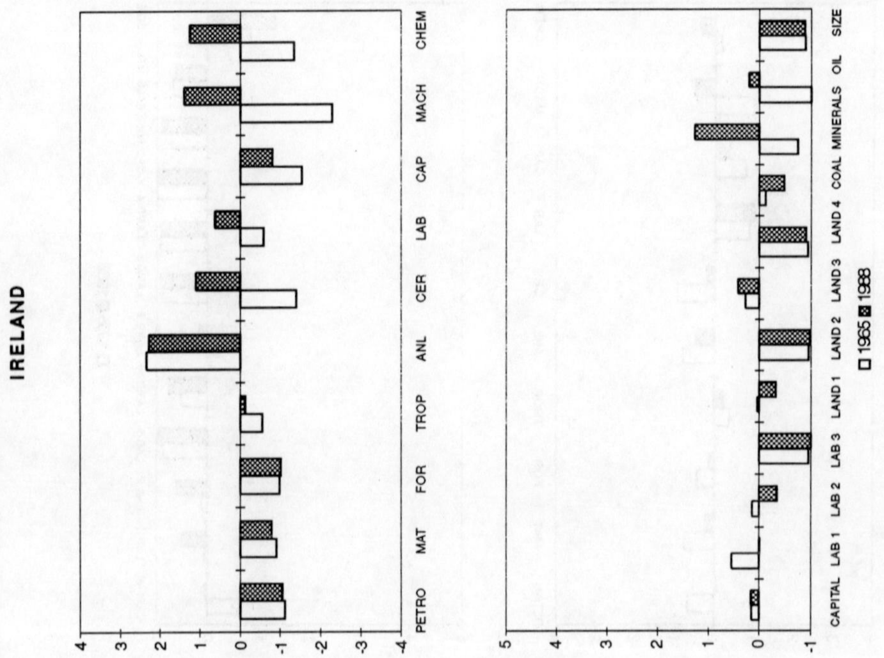
IRELAND
4
3
2
1
0
-1
-2
-3
-4
PETRO
MAT
FOR
TROP
ANL
CER
LAB
CAP
MACH
CHEM
5
4
3
2
1
0
-1
CAPITAL
LAB 1
LAB 2
LAB 3
LAND 1
LAND 2
LAND 3
LAND 4
COAL
MINERALS
OIL
SIZE
1965
1988

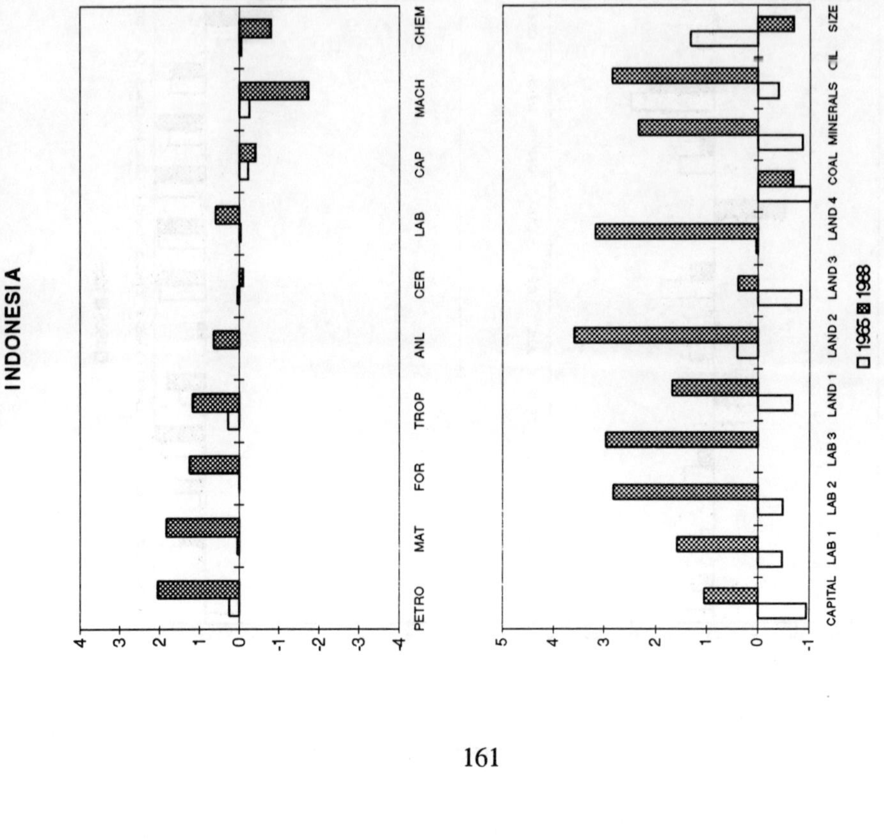
INDONESIA
4
3
2
1
0
-1
-2
-3
-4
PETRO
MAT
FOR
TROP
ANL
CER
LAB
CAP
MACH
CHEM
5
4
3
2
1
0
-1
CAPITAL
LAB 1
LAB 2
LAB 3
LAND 1
LAND 2
LAND 3
LAND 4
COAL
MINERALS
CIL
SIZE
1965
1988

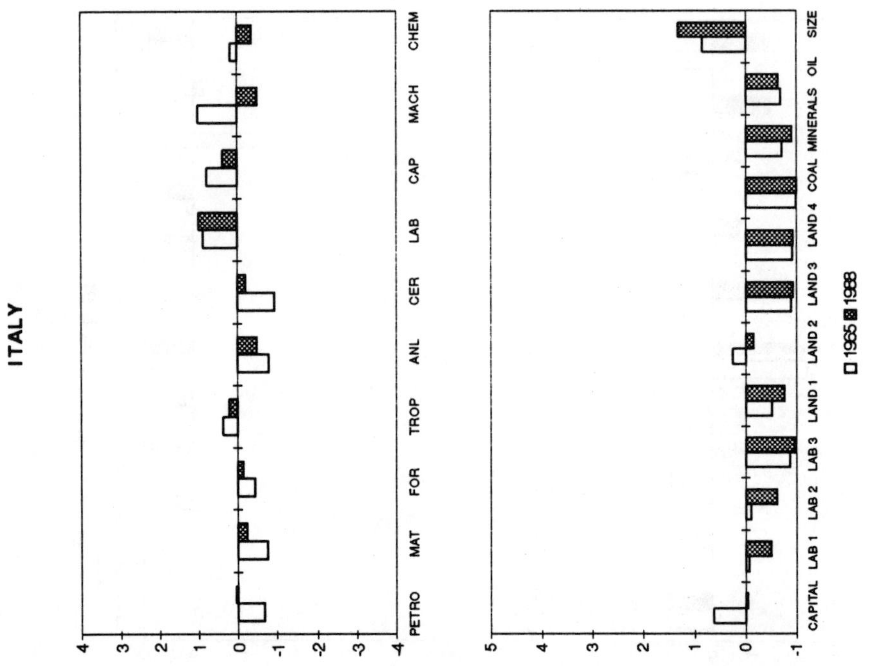
ITALY
PETRO MAT FOR TROP ANL CER LAB CAP MACH CHEM
CAPITAL LAB 1 LAB 2 LAB 3 LAND 1 LAND 2 LAND 3 LAND 4 COAL MINERALS OIL SIZE
1965 1988

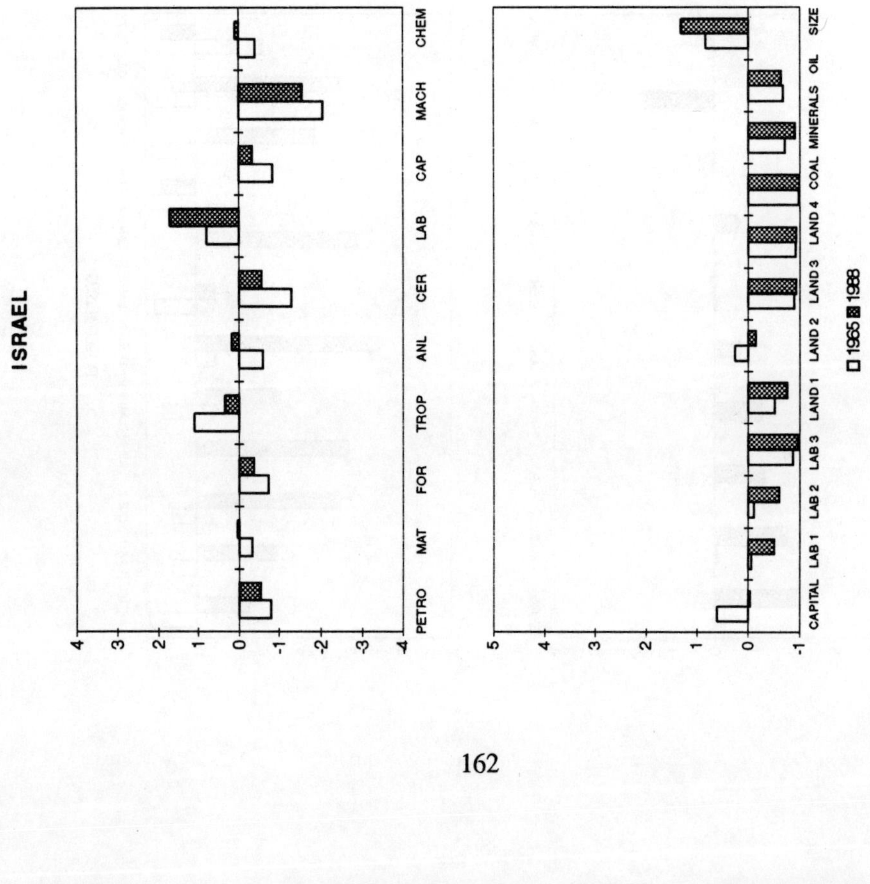
ISRAEL
PETRO MAT FOR TROP ANL CER LAB CAP MACH CHEM
CAPITAL LAB 1 LAB 2 LAB 3 LAND 1 LAND 2 LAND 3 LAND 4 COAL MINERALS OIL SIZE
1965 1988

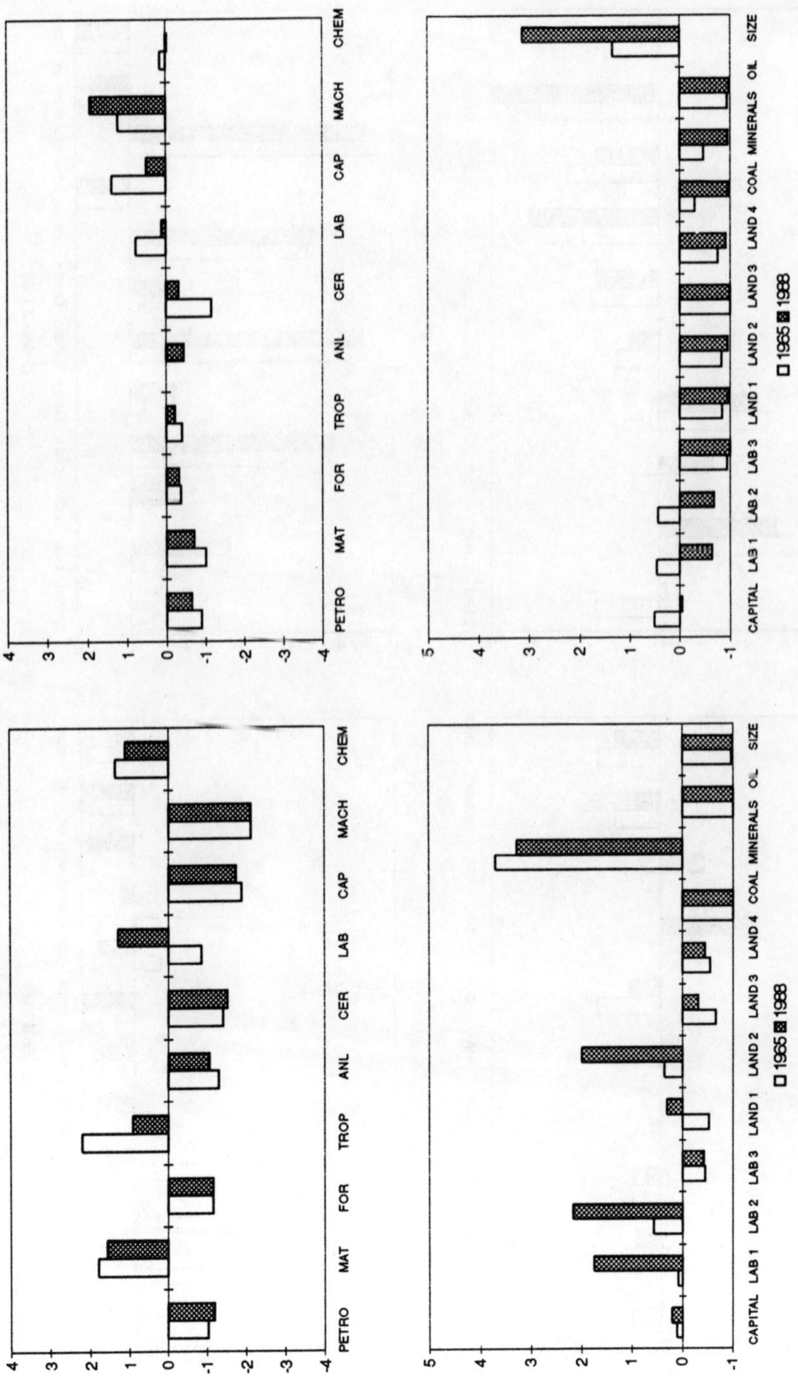
JAMAICA
JAPAN
PETRO MAT FOR TROP ANL CER LAB CAP MACH CHEM
CAPITAL LAB 1 LAB 2 LAB 3 LAND 1 LAND 2 LAND 3 LAND 4 COAL MINERALS OIL SIZE
1965 1988

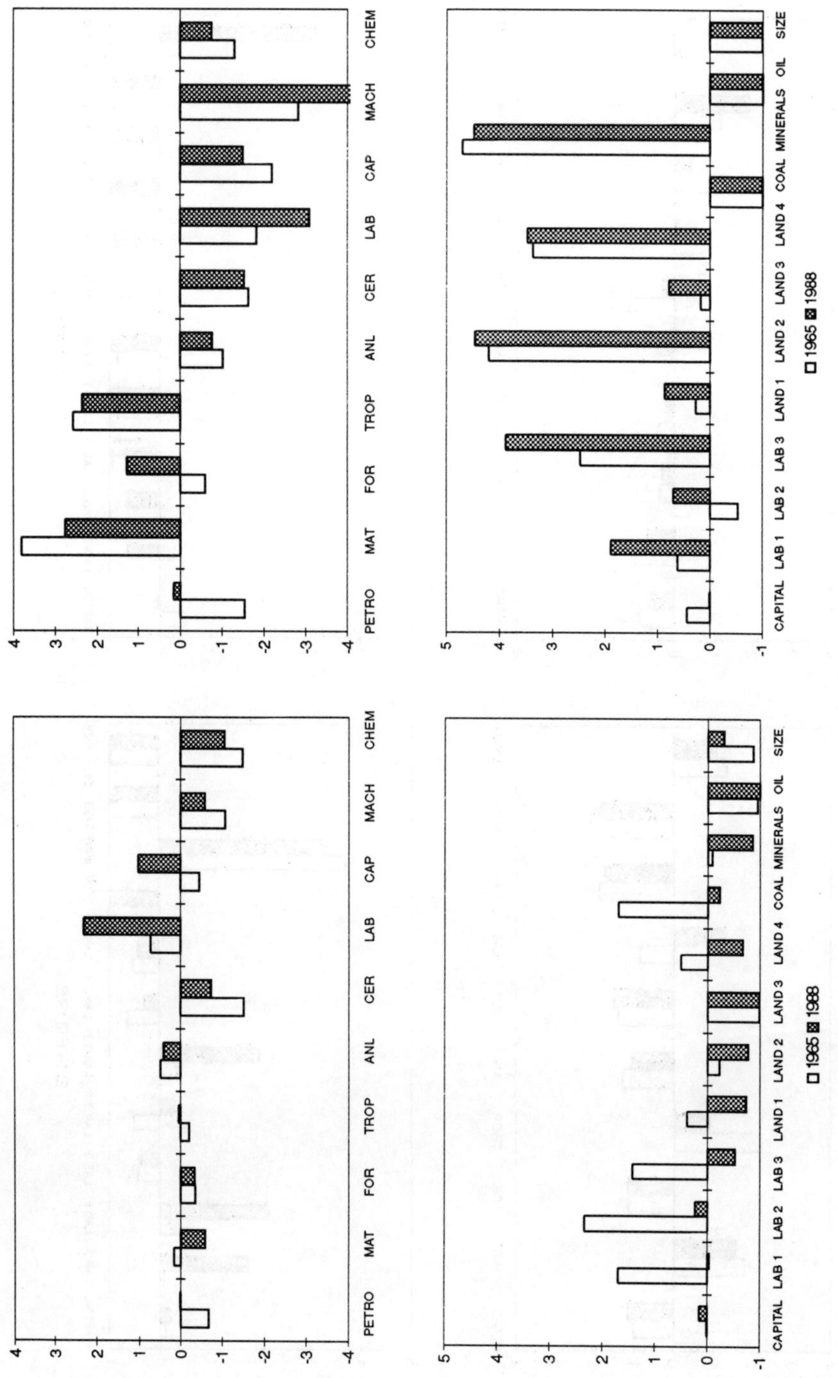
KOREA
LIBERIA
PETRO MAT FOR TROP ANL CER LAB CAP MACH CHEM
4 3 2 1 0 -1 -2 -3 -4
CAPITAL LAB 1 LAB 2 LAB 3 LAND 1 LAND 2 LAND 3 LAND 4 COAL MINERALS OIL SIZE
5 4 3 2 1 0 -1
1965 1988

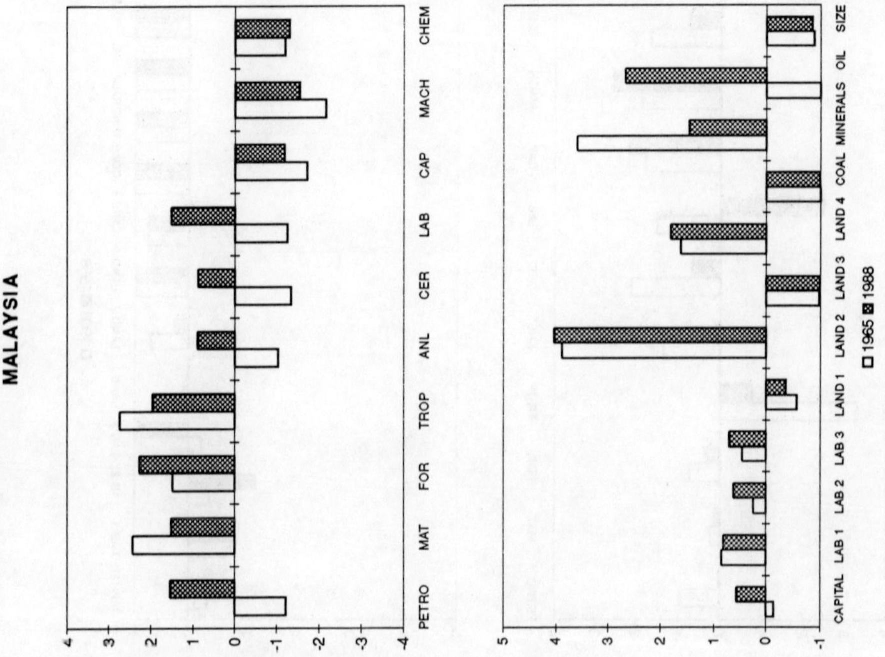
MALAYSIA
PETRO MAT FOR TROP ANL CER LAB CAP MACH CHEM
CAPITAL LAB 1 LAB 2 LAB 3 LAND 1 LAND 2 LAND 3 LAND 4 COAL MINERALS OIL SIZE
1965 1988

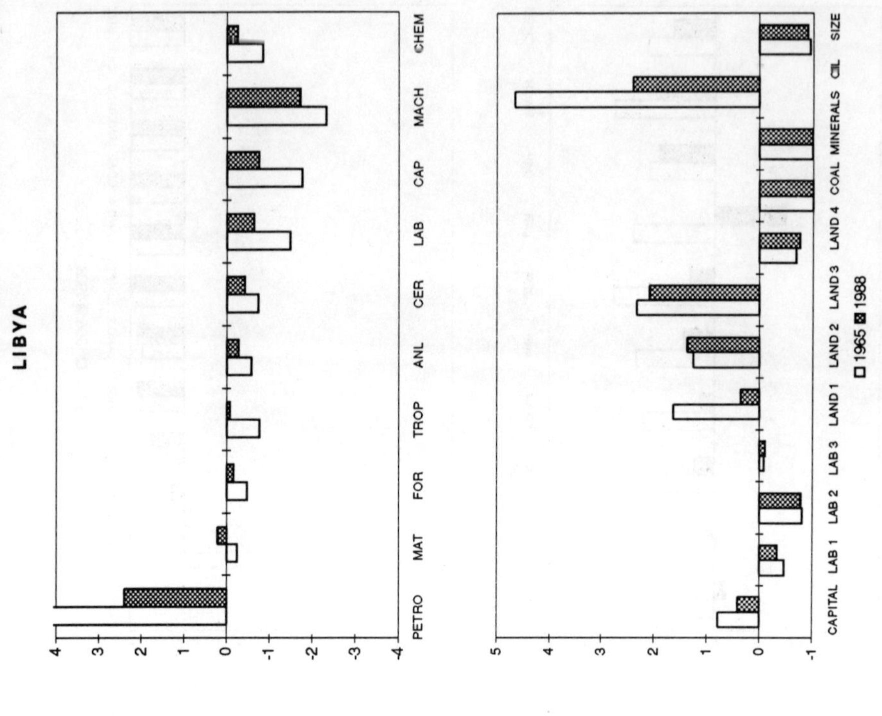
LIBYA
PETRO MAT FOR TROP ANL CER LAB CAP MACH CHEM
CAPITAL LAB 1 LAB 2 LAB 3 LAND 1 LAND 2 LAND 3 LAND 4 COAL MINERALS OIL SIZE
1965 1988

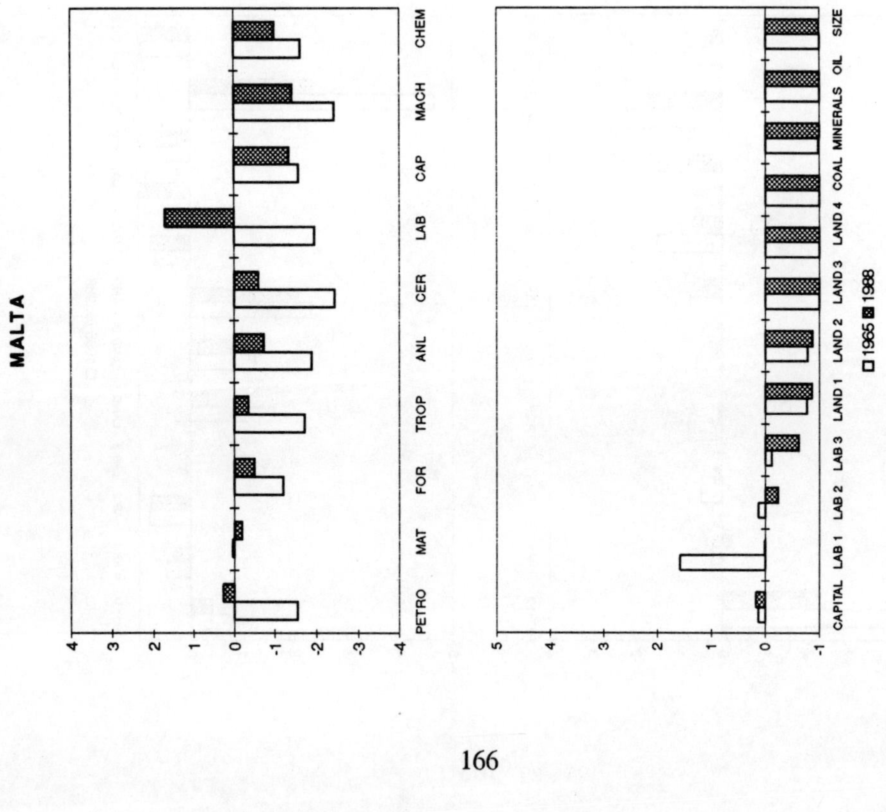
MALTA
PETRO
MAT
FOR
TROP
ANL
CER
LAB
CAP
MACH
CHEM
CAPITAL
LAB 1
LAB 2
LAB 3
LAND 1
LAND 2
LAND 3
LAND 4
COAL
MINERALS
OIL
SIZE
1965
1988

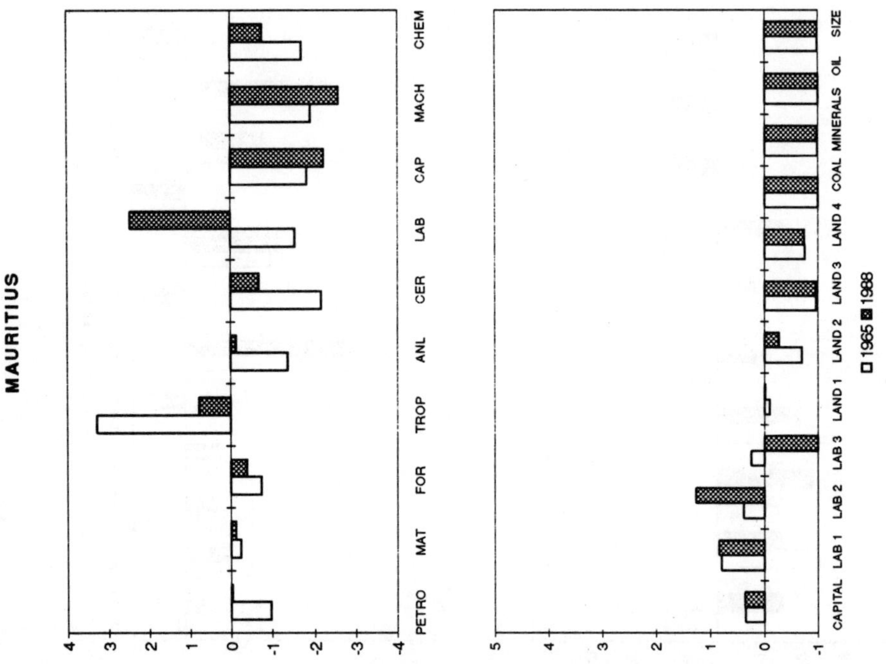
MAURITIUS
PETRO
MAT
FOR
TROP
ANL
CER
LAB
CAP
MACH
CHEM
CAPITAL
LAB 1
LAB 2
LAB 3
LAND 1
LAND 2
LAND 3
LAND 4
COAL
MINERALS
OIL
SIZE
1965
1988

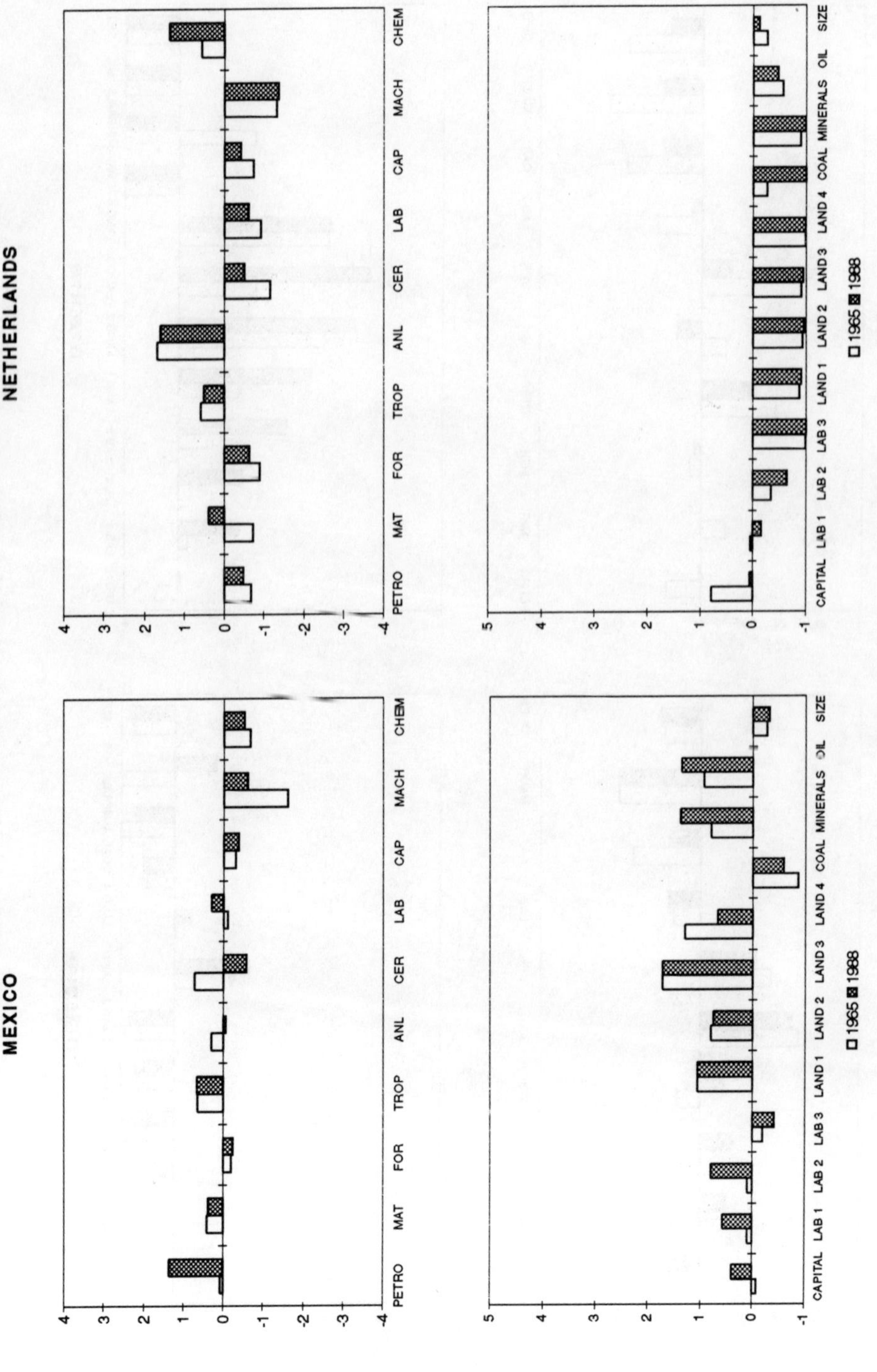
MEXICO
NETHERLANDS
PETRO MAT FOR TROP ANL CER LAB CAP MACH CHEM
CAPITAL LAB 1 LAB 2 LAB 3 LAND 1 LAND 2 LAND 3 LAND 4 COAL MINERALS OIL SIZE
1965
1988

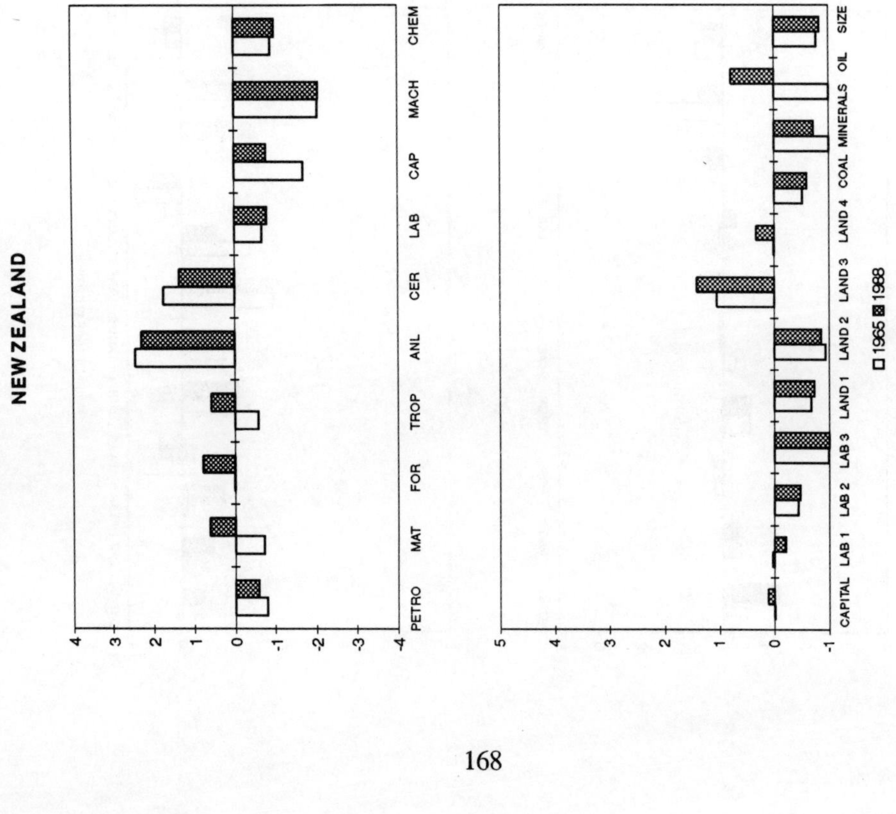
NEW ZEALAND
PETRO MAT FOR TROP ANL CER LAB CAP MACH CHEM
4 3 2 1 0 -1 -2 -3 -4
CAPITAL LAB 1 LAB 2 LAB 3 LAND 1 LAND 2 LAND 3 LAND 4 COAL MINERALS OIL SIZE
5 4 3 2 1 0 -1
1965 1988

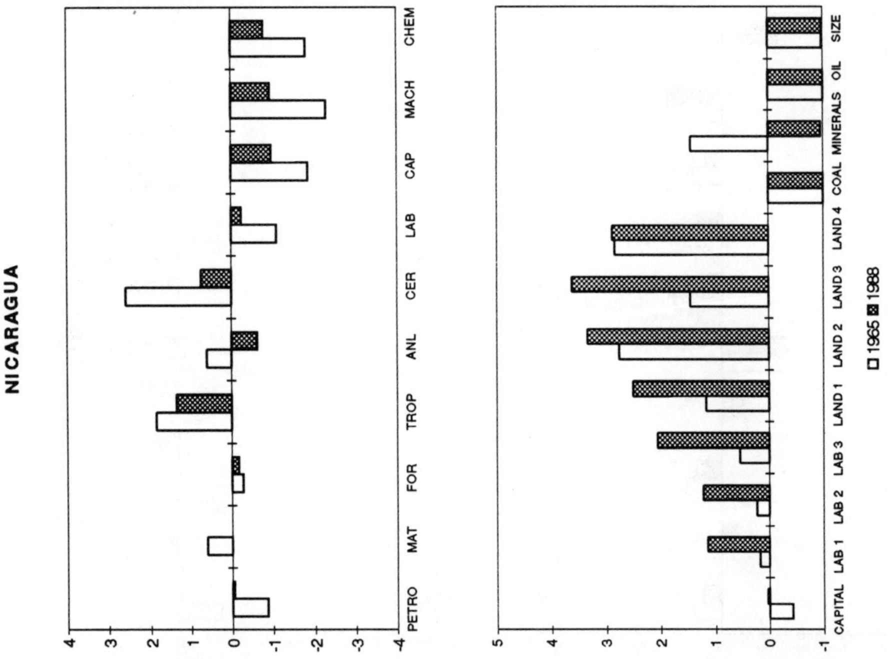
NICARAGUA
PETRO MAT FOR TROP ANL CER LAB CAP MACH CHEM
4 3 2 1 0 -1 -2 -3 -4
CAPITAL LAB 1 LAB 2 LAB 3 LAND 1 LAND 2 LAND 3 LAND 4 COAL MINERALS OIL SIZE
5 4 3 2 1 0 -1
1965 1988

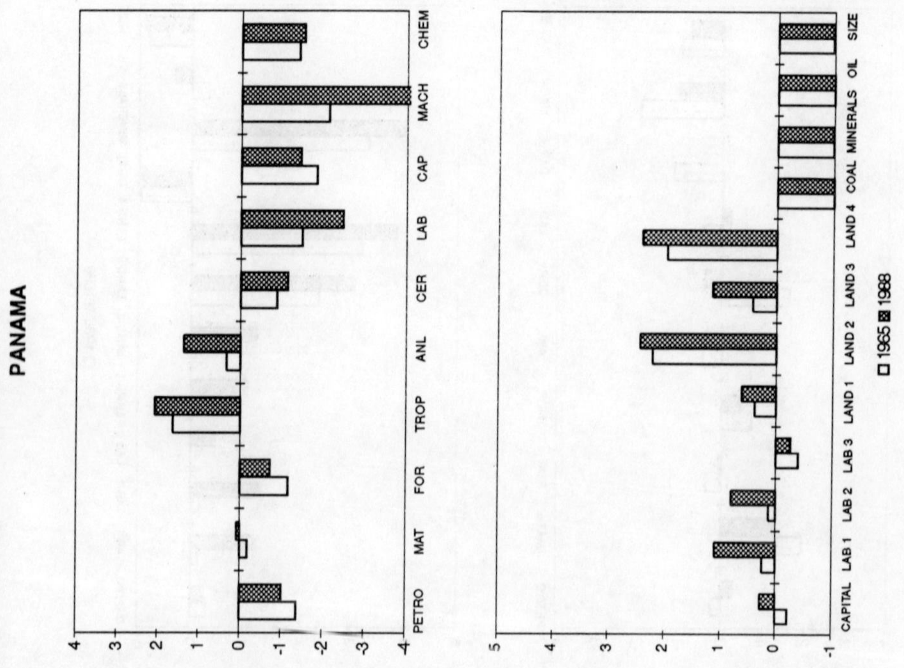
PANAMA
PETRO
MAT
FOR
TROP
ANL
CER
LAB
CAP
MACH
CHEM
CAPITAL
LAB 1
LAB 2
LAB 3
LAND 1
LAND 2
LAND 3
LAND 4
COAL
MINERALS
OIL
SIZE
1965
1988

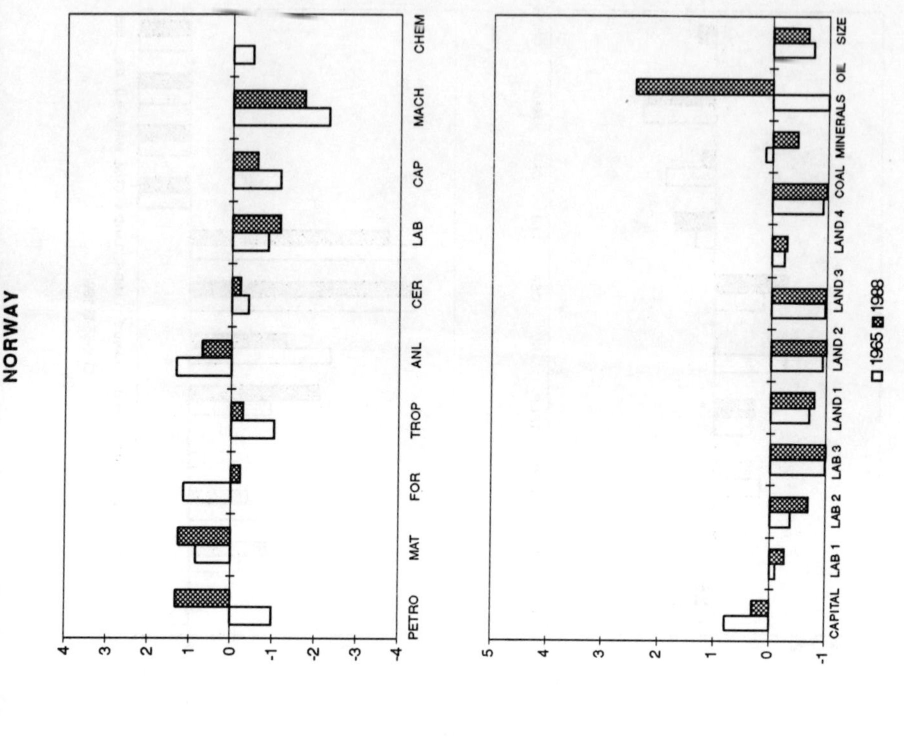
NORWAY
PETRO
MAT
FOR
TROP
ANL
CER
LAB
CAP
MACH
CHEM
CAPITAL
LAB 1
LAB 2
LAB 3
LAND 1
LAND 2
LAND 3
LAND 4
COAL
MINERALS
OIL
SIZE
1965
1988

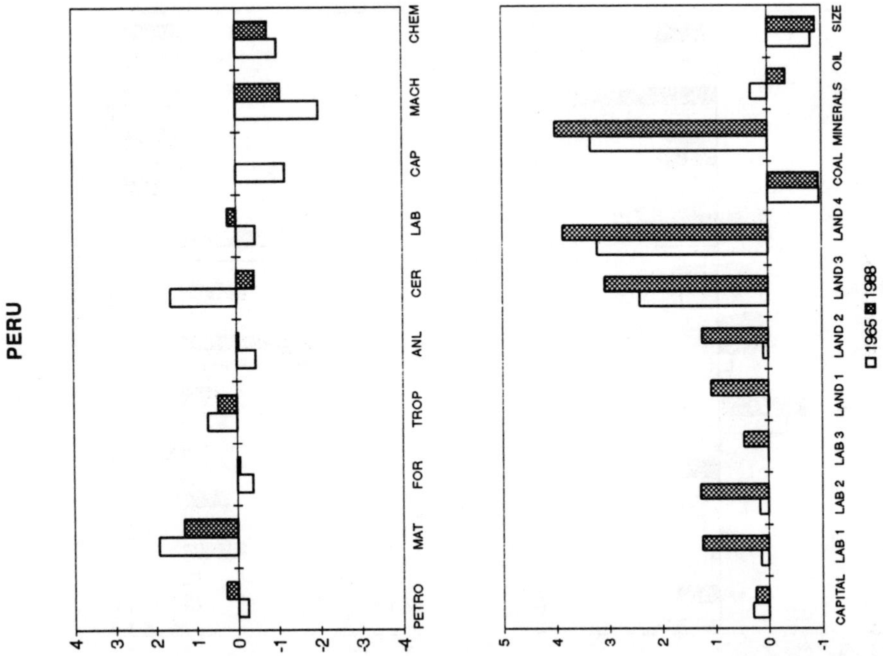
PERU
PETRO
MAT
FOR
TROP
ANL
CER
LAB
CAP
MACH
CHEM
CAPITAL
LAB 1
LAB 2
LAB 3
LAND 1
LAND 2
LAND 3
LAND 4
COAL
MINERALS
OIL
SIZE
1965
1988

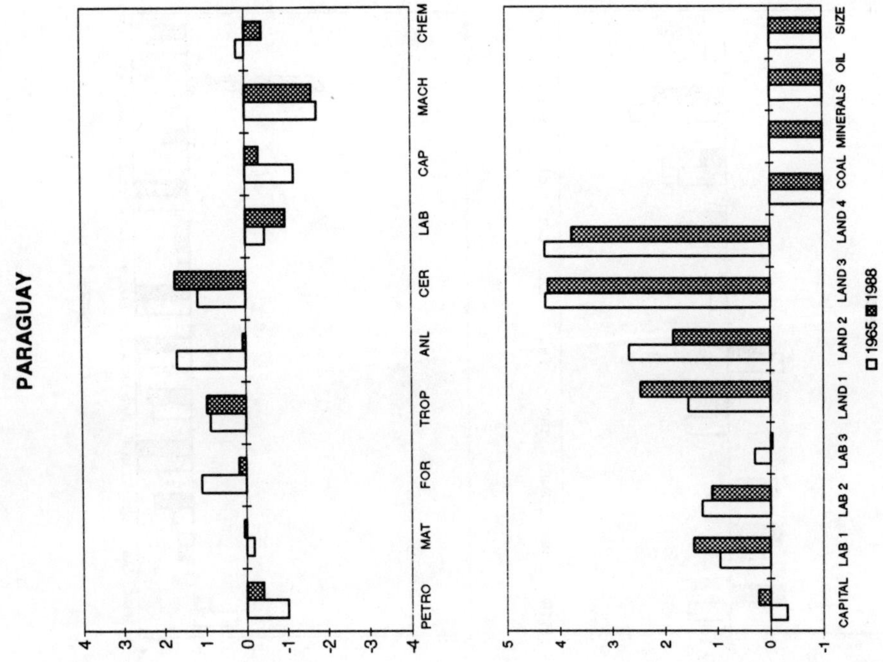
PARAGUAY
PETRO
MAT
FOR
TROP
ANL
CER
LAB
CAP
MACH
CHEM
CAPITAL
LAB 1
LAB 2
LAB 3
LAND 1
LAND 2
LAND 3
LAND 4
COAL
MINERALS
OIL
SIZE
1965
1988

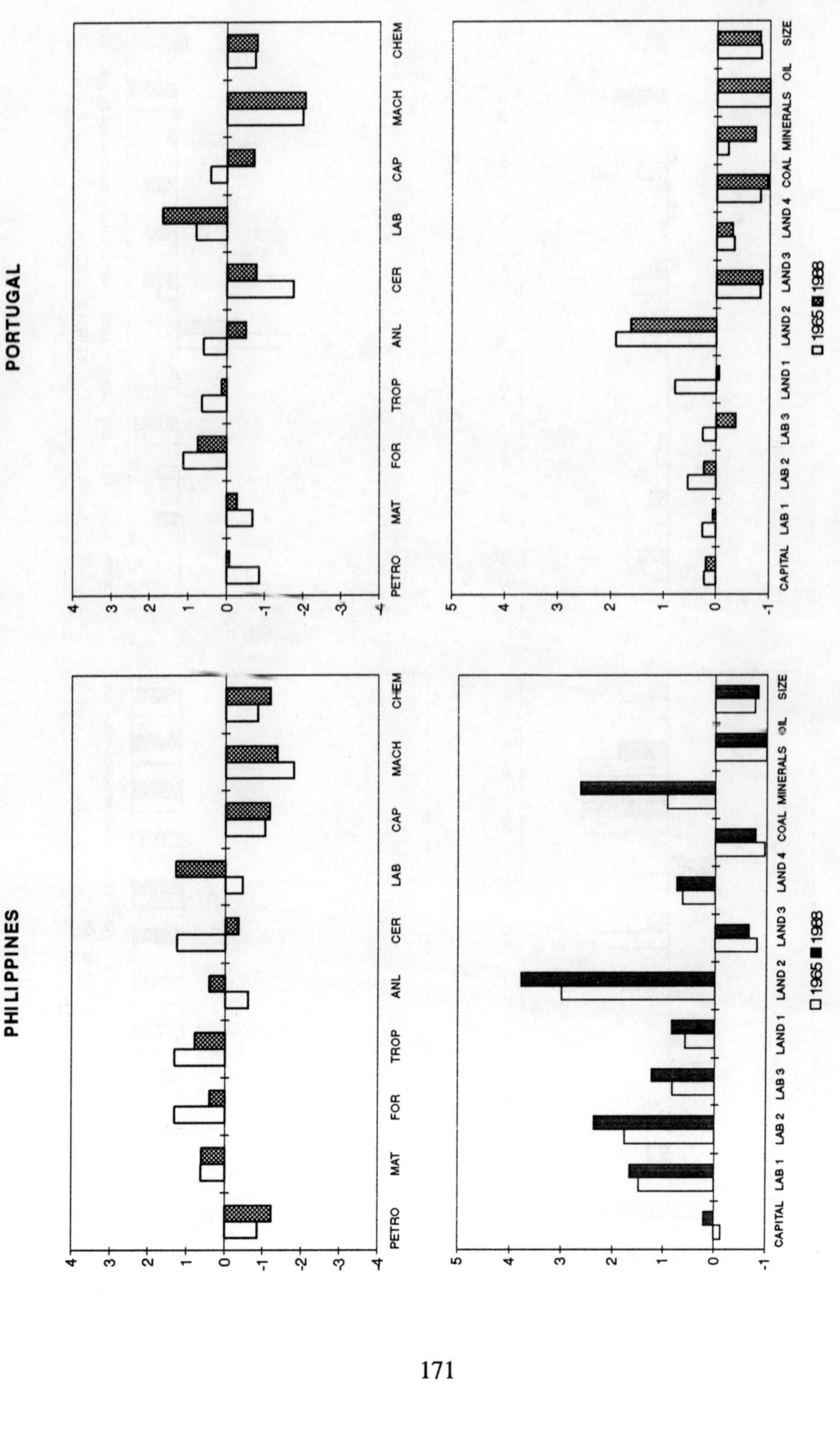
PHILIPPINES
PORTUGAL
PETRO MAT FOR TROP ANL CER LAB CAP MACH CHEM
CAPITAL LAB 1 LAB 2 LAB 3 LAND 1 LAND 2 LAND 3 LAND 4 COAL MINERALS OIL SIZE
1965 1988
4 3 2 1 0 -1 -2 -3 -4
5 4 3 2 1 0 -1

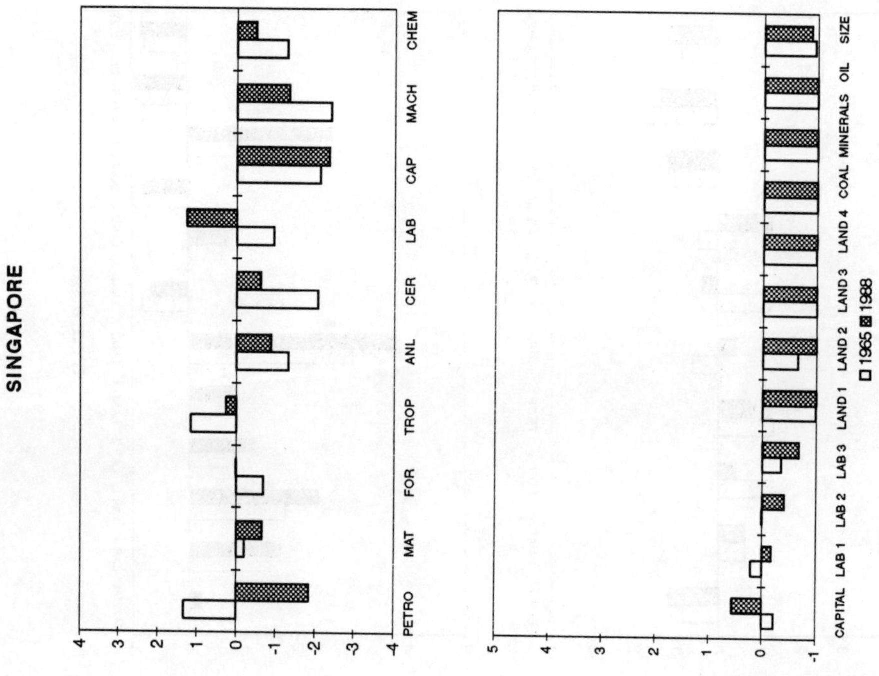
SINGAPORE
4
3
2
1
0
-1
-2
-3
-4
PETRO
MAT
FOR
TROP
ANL
CER
LAB
CAP
MACH
CHEM
5
4
3
2
1
0
-1
CAPITAL
LAB 1
LAB 2
LAB 3
LAND 1
LAND 2
LAND 3
LAND 4
COAL
MINERALS
OIL
SIZE
1965
1988

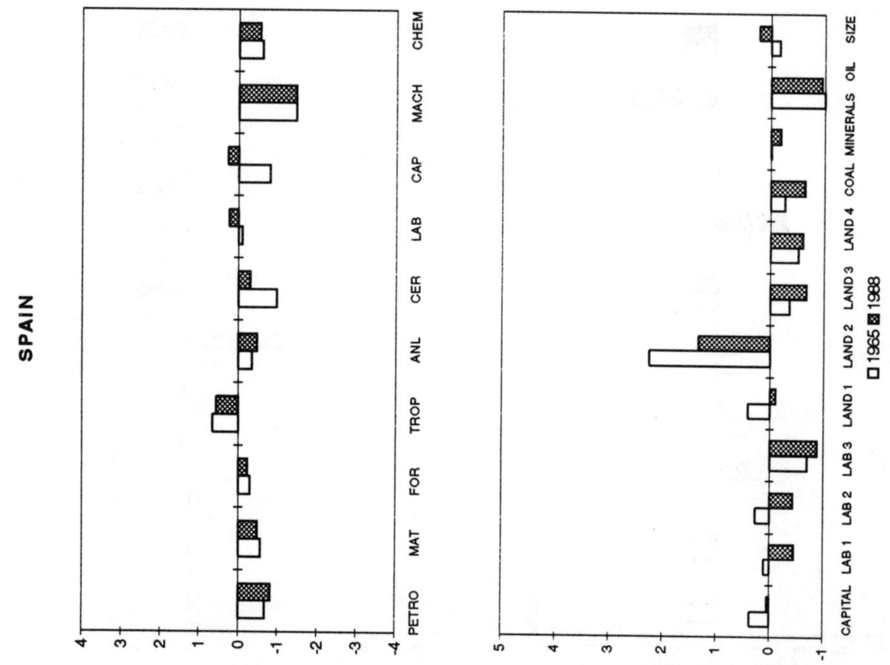
SPAIN
4
3
2
1
0
-1
-2
-3
-4
PETRO
MAT
FOR
TROP
ANL
CER
LAB
CAP
MACH
CHEM
5
4
3
2
1
0
-1
CAPITAL
LAB 1
LAB 2
LAB 3
LAND 1
LAND 2
LAND 3
LAND 4
COAL
MINERALS
OIL
SIZE
1965
1988

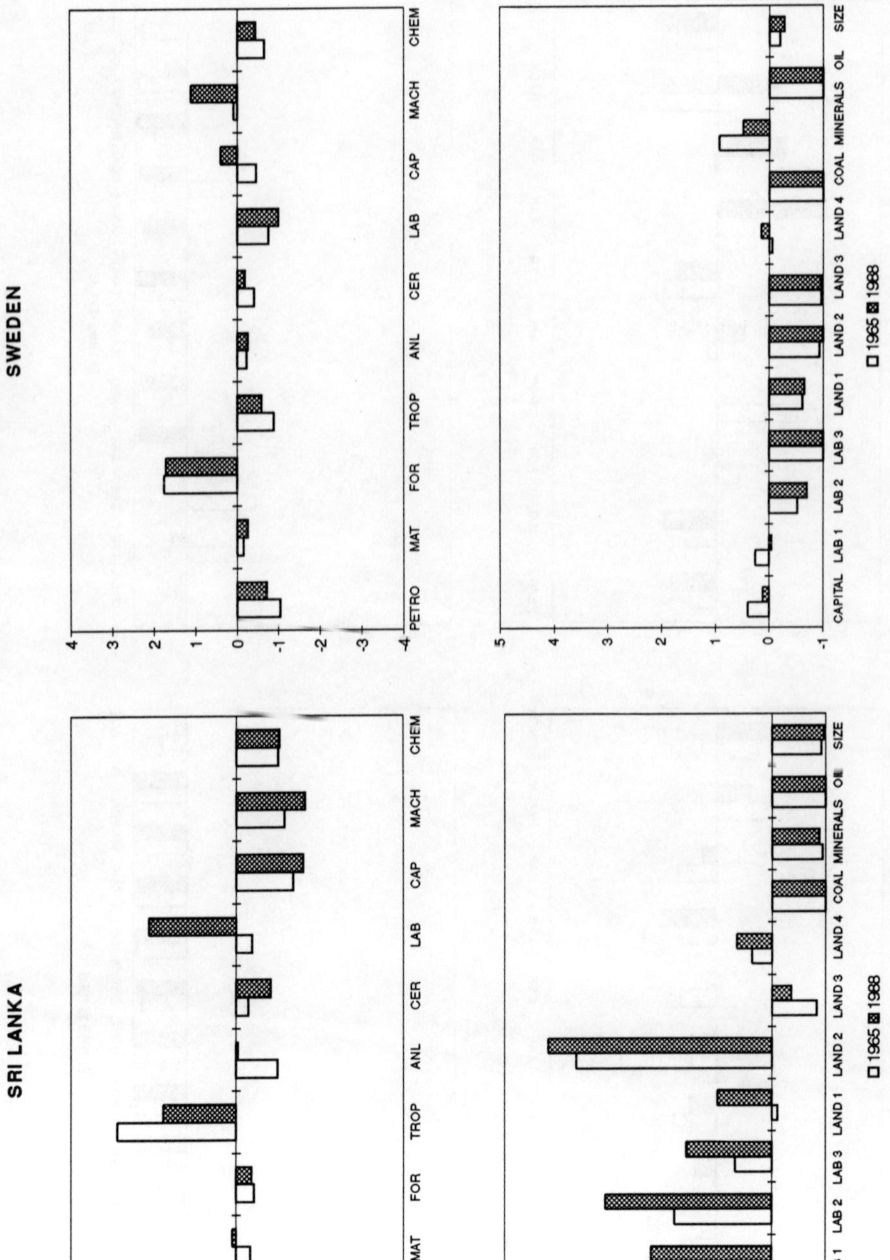
SRI LANKA
SWEDEN
PETRO
MAT
FOR
TROP
ANL
CER
LAB
CAP
MACH
CHEM
CAPITAL
LAB 1
LAB 2
LAB 3
LAND 1
LAND 2
LAND 3
LAND 4
COAL
MINERALS
OIL
SIZE
1965
1988

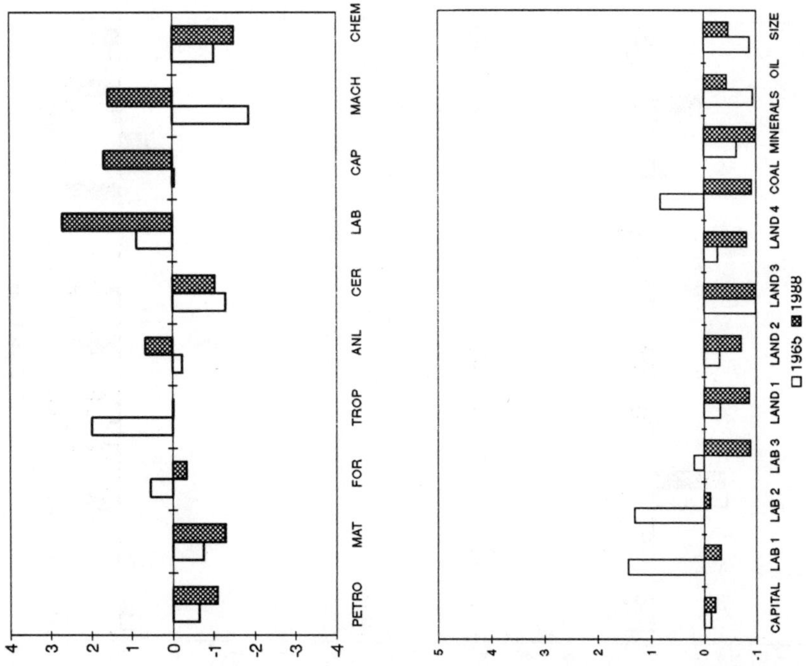
TAIWAN
PETRO MAT FOR TROP ANL CER LAB CAP MACH CHEM
CAPITAL LAB 1 LAB 2 LAB 3 LAND 1 LAND 2 LAND 3 LAND 4 COAL MINERALS OIL SIZE
□ 1965 ▩ 1988

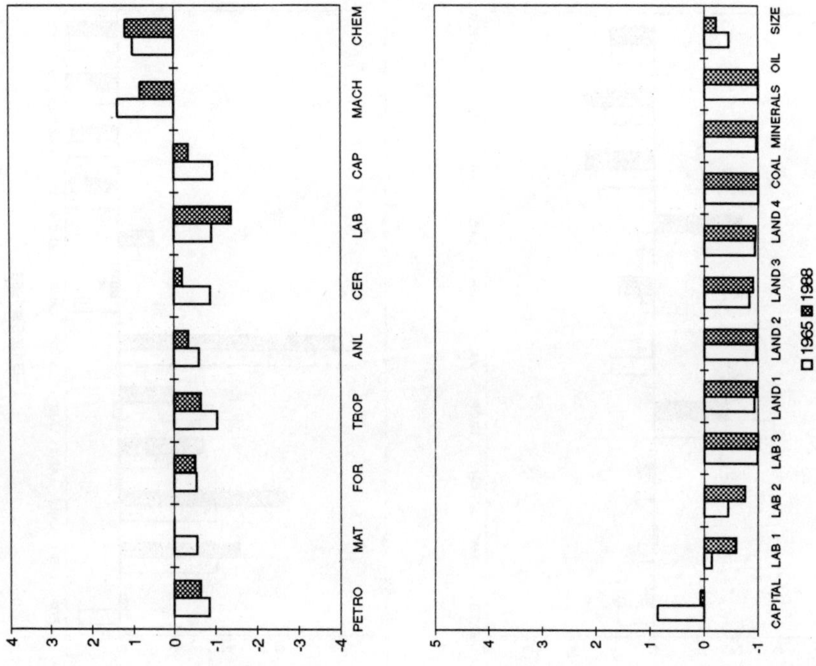
SWITZERLAND
PETRO MAT FOR TROP ANL CER LAB CAP MACH CHEM
CAPITAL LAB 1 LAB 2 LAB 3 LAND 1 LAND 2 LAND 3 LAND 4 COAL MINERALS OIL SIZE
□ 1965 ▩ 1988

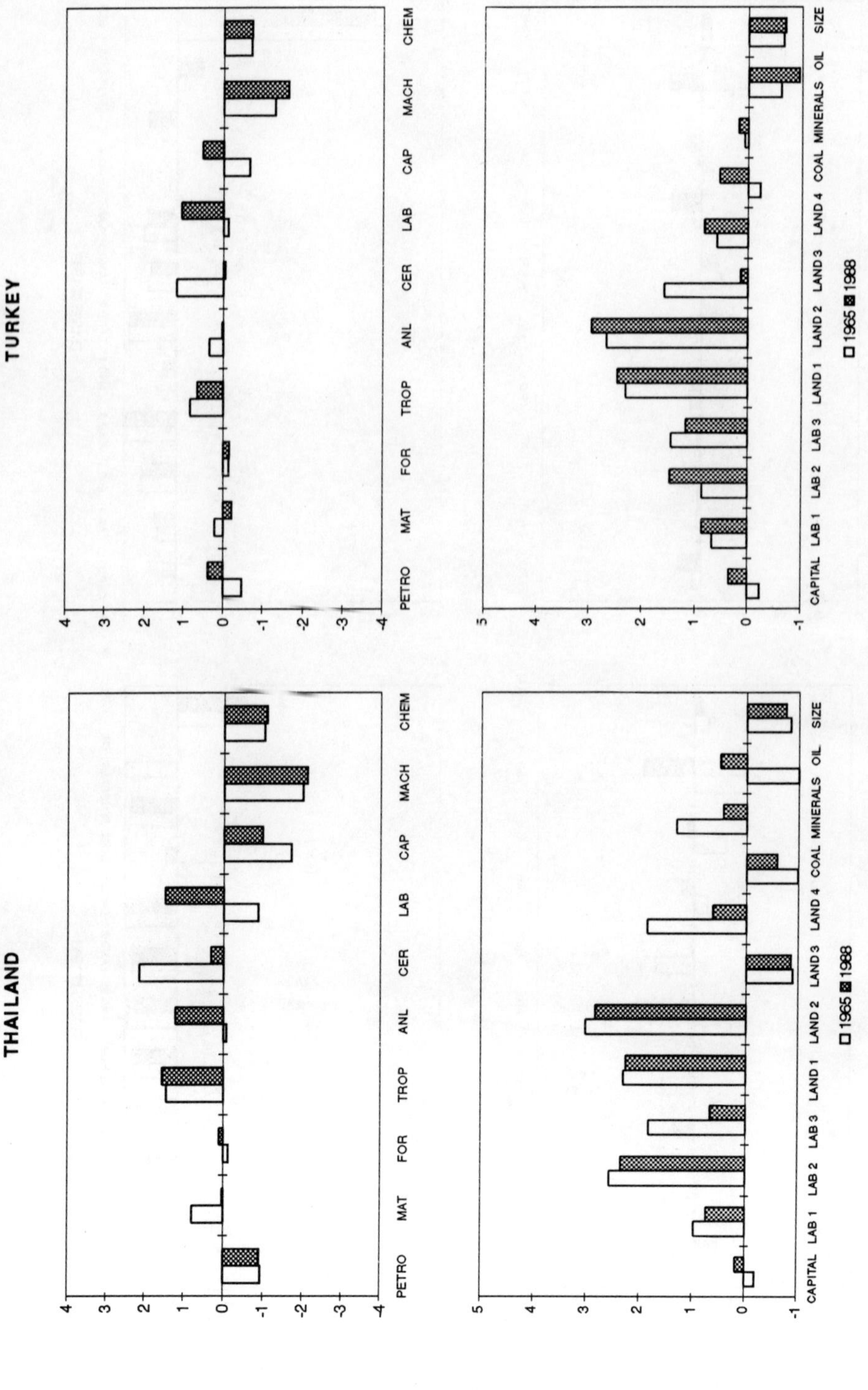
TURKEY
THAILAND
PETRO MAT FOR TROP ANL CER LAB CAP MACH CHEM
CAPITAL LAB 1 LAB 2 LAB 3 LAND 1 LAND 2 LAND 3 LAND 4 COAL MINERALS OIL SIZE
1965 1988
4 3 2 1 0 -1 -2 -3 -4
5 4 3 2 1 0 -1

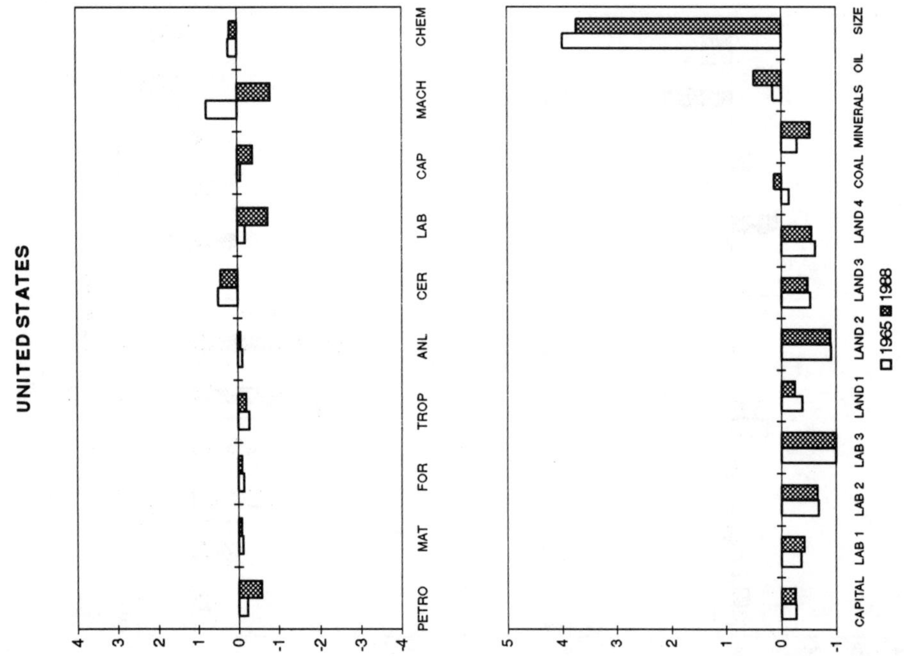
UNITED STATES
PETRO
MAT
FOR
TROP
ANL
CER
LAB
CAP
MACH
CHEM
CAPITAL
LAB 1
LAB 2
LAB 3
LAND 1
LAND 2
LAND 3
LAND 4
COAL
MINERALS
OIL
SIZE
1965
1988

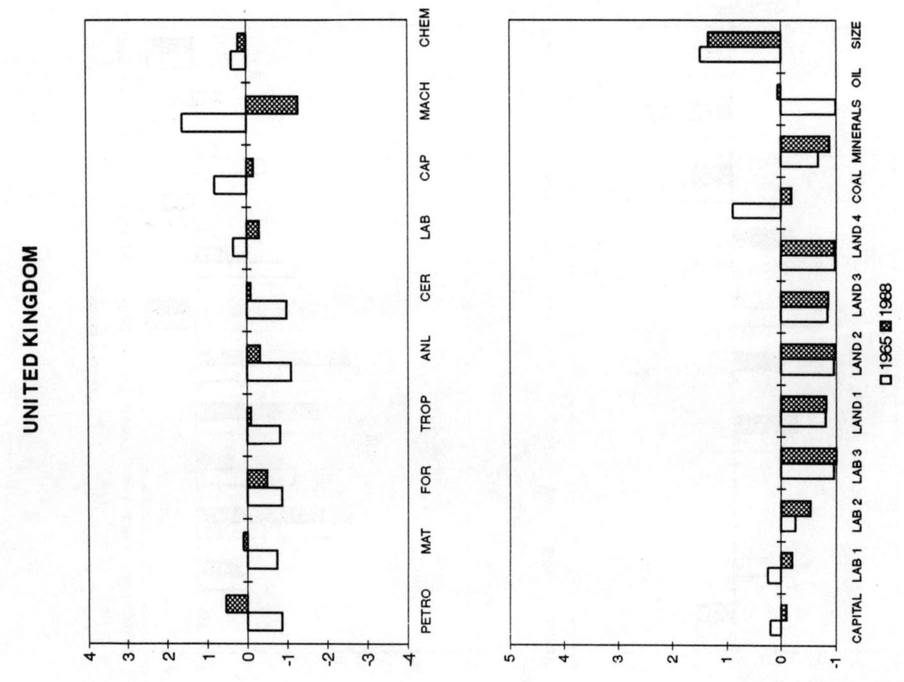
UNITED KINGDOM
PETRO
MAT
FOR
TROP
ANL
CER
LAB
CAP
MACH
CHEM
CAPITAL
LAB 1
LAB 2
LAB 3
LAND 1
LAND 2
LAND 3
LAND 4
COAL
MINERALS
OIL
SIZE
1965
1988

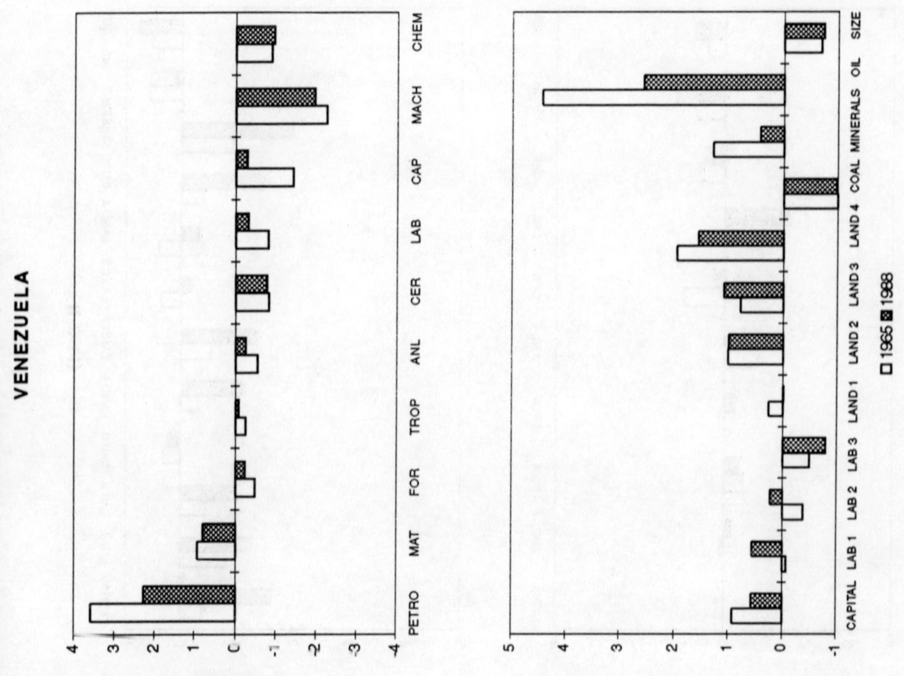
VENEZUELA
PETRO MAT FOR TROP ANL CER LAB CAP MACH CHEM
CAPITAL LAB 1 LAB 2 LAB 3 LAND 1 LAND 2 LAND 3 LAND 4 COAL MINERALS OIL SIZE
1965 1988

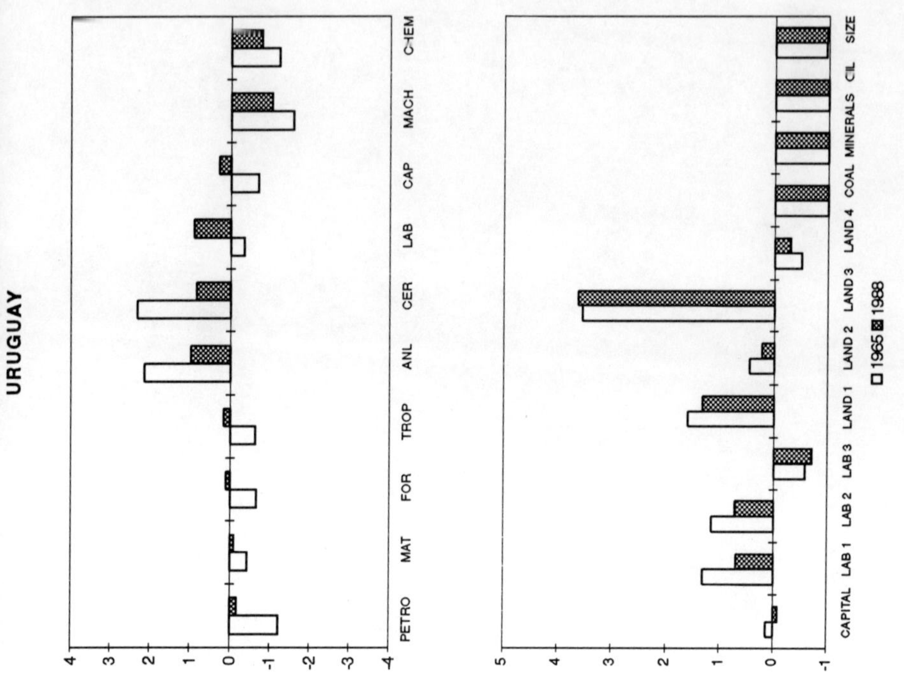
URUGUAY
PETRO MAT FOR TROP ANL CER LAB CAP MACH CHEM
CAPITAL LAB 1 LAB 2 LAB 3 LAND 1 LAND 2 LAND 3 LAND 4 COAL MINERALS OIL SIZE
1965 1988

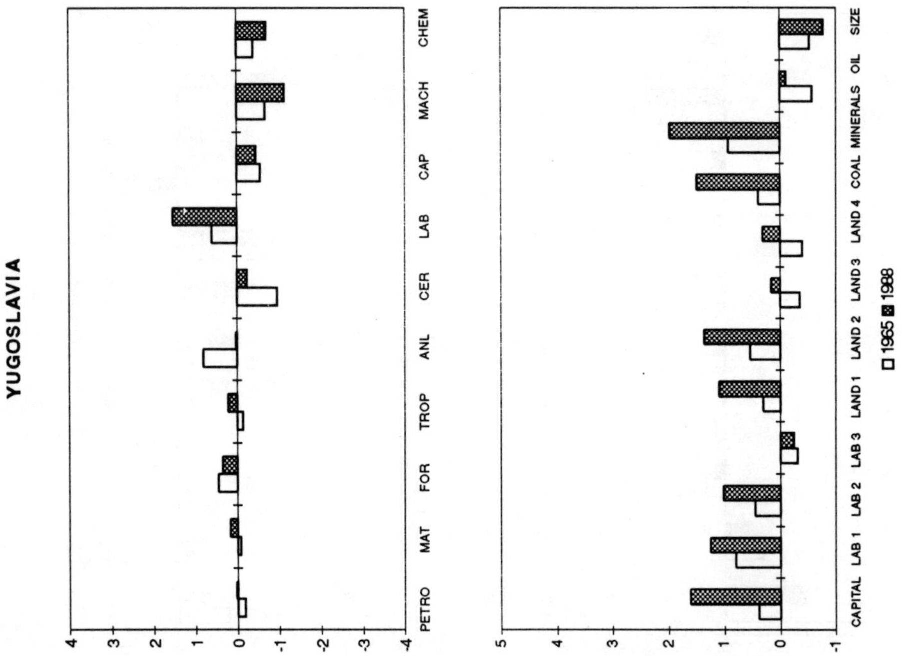
YUGOSLAVIA
4
3
2
1
0
-1
-2
-3
-4
PETRO
MAT
FOR
TROP
ANL
CER
LAB
CAP
MACH
CHEM
5
4
3
2
1
0
-1
CAPITAL
LAB 1
LAB 2
LAB 3
LAND 1
LAND 2
LAND 3
LAND 4
COAL
MINERALS
OIL
SIZE
1965
1988

Notes

Chapter 1

1 Increases may be partly due to the rapid development of intra-industry trade, particularly among the developed countries.

2 In discussing the significance of the trade dependence and resource abundance profiles, Leamer states, 'some may argue that these displays are the most useful part of this book in that they provide a clear picture of the world's trading relations that is not available anywhere else' (Leamer 1984, p. xv).

3 See note 4 in Chapter 3.

Chapter 2

1 There are several excellent surveys covering work in this area — for example, Stern (1975), Deardorff (1982) and Leamer (1984, 1992).

2 The standard assumptions of international trade models as summarised in Leamer's (1980) article are as follows: (a) there are *n* commodities which are freely mobile internationally; (b) there are *n* factors which are perfectly immobile internationally; (c) all individuals have identical homothetic preferences; (d) production functions are the same in all countries and exhibit constant returns to scale; (e) there is perfect competition in the goods and factors markets; and (f) factor prices are equalised across countries.

3 As Casas and Choi (1985) argue: 'Although the actual signs of the indirect net resource flows may not be an accurate indicator of factor abundance, it is possible to infer the latter by computing the hypothetical balanced trade flows of factor services for existing trade data' (p. 612). Then, according to their formula, 'a country with a trade imbalance would have been a net exporter of the services of factor *I* under balanced trade, and the country would therefore be revealed to be abundant in that factor, if the ratio of domestic consumption to endowment of the factor is smaller than the ratio of domestic absorption to income, and vice versa' (p. 613).

4 'These proportions are interpreted as the probability, for a given factor (country), that the ranking of factor contents will match the ranking of factor abundance for a randomly selected pair of countries (factors)' (Bowen *et al.* 1987, footnote 9, p. 797).

5 Bowen *et al.* (1987) collected data on 1966 factor endowments and 1967 trade for 27 countries. The 12 resources are: capital, total labour, professional/technical workers, managerial workers, clerical workers, sales workers, service workers, agricultural workers, production workers, arable land, pastureland, and forestland.

6 However, as pointed out by Kohler (1991), in the sense discussed in his article, 'the focus of the analysis was not so much whether or not this data set support the HOV model, but rather whether or not, or to what extent these tests do or do not exhibit robustness' (p. 165).

7 According to Leamer (1992), an influential research program must include these three layers of intellectual activity, namely a set of issues must first be identified, a conceptual framework or theory then needs to be formulated for addressing the issues and, finally, data that represent the correspondence between the important aspects of the theory and observable events should be collected.

8 Leamer uses the Leontief Paradox as an example. According to Leamer (1980), Leontief's way of comparing capital per man embodied in exports with capital per man embodied in imports is theoretically inappropriate. (See the second section of this chapter for another illustration.)

9 The examination of the 'nonlinear alternatives to the linear maintained hypothesis has uncovered some evidence of nonlinearities in the GNP equation, but the anticipated nonlinearities of the trade equation generally failed to emerge' (Leamer 1984, p. 186). No attempt will be made to address this issue in the current study.

10 For more detailed references to these studies, refer to Chapter 2 of Leamer's book (1984).

11 The factor intensity matrix A in fact contains much more information than would at first appear. For example, because of the complexity of the required qualitative information in higher dimensions, it is much more convenient to condition those trade theorems (the Heckscher–Ohlin, Stolper–Samuelson and Rybczynski theorems all depend on the sign pattern of the inverse of the factor intensity matrix) on complete quantitative knowledge of the factor intensity matrix A. That is, the derivatives of outputs with respect to endowments are collected in the matrix A^{-1}, and the derivatives of factor prices with respect to commodity prices are collected in the matrix A'^{-1}. Measuring A^{-1} is an important empirical task that can be done by regressing outputs on factor supplies or trade on excess factor supplies (Leamer 1984, p. 16).

12 This is mainly because, first, a formal way of dealing with the problem of measurement errors in general is not available and, second, the solution currently available involves Bayesian analysis, which has not yet been widely accepted.

13 Tests of trade theories using econometric approaches encounter another big difficulty in the statistical sense: 'Formal statistical methods of testing hypotheses presuppose the existence of maintained and alternative hypotheses that are precisely defined'. However, 'the present state of economic theory does not allow us to articulate fully and precisely even simple alternative models of trade' (Leamer 1984, p. 45). One attempt was made by Bowen *et al.* (1987) to relax some assumptions in the search for alternatives. 'These authors generalise the HOV model to allow (a) non-homothetic tastes characterised by linear Engel curves, (b) technological differences among countries that affect all technological coefficients proportionately, and (c) various kinds of measurement errors' (Leamer 1992, p. 29). While there are a number of problems with Bowen *et al.*'s (1987) study, including a number of implausible estimates involved in estimating the form of technological differences, Leamer (1992, p. 30) pointed out that its main weakness is that it fails to address the issue clearly.

14 'Because each of the excess factor endowments is a linear function of all factor supplies, $L - YL_w/Y_w = L - (w_L L + w_K K)L_w/Y_w$ and $K - YL_w/Y_w = K - (w_L L + w_K K)K_w/Y_w$,

for almost all distributions of K and L these excess supplies are correlated, and a regression of trade on a subset of the excess supplies yields biased and inconsistent estimates because variables are excluded that are necessarily correlated with the included variables' (Leamer 1984, p. 159).

15 With regard to differences between classical approaches and the Bayesian methodology, the debate between McAleer, Pagan and Volker (1985) and Leamer (1983) is a good example of an uncompromising stand on both sides.

16 For example, as Zellner (1988) argues, 'it is accurate to state that the Bayesian approach encompasses non-Bayesian approaches in the sense that it can produce many important non-Bayesian results as well as other useful results that are difficult to obtain by non-Bayesian methods' (p. 35).

17 As Klepper and Leamer (1984) point out, for the two-variable errors-in-variables (EVM) model, Frisch demonstrates that 'the interval computed from the two regressions corresponding to each variable as left-hand-side variable "consistently bounds" the true regression coefficient' (p. 164).

18 Direct and reverse regressions can best be illustrated using the following formula (see Klepper 1988, footnote 4). Let the regression of x_i on y and the other x_j, $j \neq i$, be denoted as:

$$x_i = a_i y + a_1 x_1 + a_2 x_2 + \ldots + a_{i-1} x_{i-1} + a_{i+1} x_{i+1} + a_{i+2} x_{i+2} + \ldots + a_k x_k + v,$$

where v is a disturbance. Solving out the regression for y as the left-hand-side variable yields:

$$y = -(a_1/a_i)\,x_1 - (a_2/a_i)\,x_2 - \ldots - (a_{i-1}/a_i)\,x_{i-1} + (1/a_i)\,x_i - (a_{i+1}/a_i)\,x_{i+1} - (a_{i+2}/a_i)\,x_{i+2} - \ldots - (a_k/a_i)\,x_k - (1/a_i)\,v.$$

The vector b^i is defined as the vector of coefficients:

$$(-a_1/a_i, -a_2/a_i, \ldots, -a_{i-1}/a_i, 1/a_{i,}, -a_{i+1}/a_i, -a_{i+2}/a_i, \ldots, -a_k/a_i).$$

19 The preceding discussion is applicable to the case of a single equation but, as pointed out by Leamer, 'the evidence can be much stronger if the whole system is analysed because the same hypothetical variables enter each equation' (1984, p. 132). The treatment of under-identified systems of equations with errors in variables was accomplished by Leamer in 1987. The main feature in his study is that in addition to using only the information contained in the first two moments of the data, the other source of information, which is 'a set of observations of other dependent variables that are influenced by the same set of mismeasured explanatory variables' (1987a, p. 894), is used to narrow the bounds. Correspondingly, both diagonal and nondiagonal measurement error covariance matrices are considered in his study. Finally, the data from his work in 1984 are used again for illustrative purposes. This is mainly because the number of explanatory variables exceeds the number of

dependent variables in that data set. Therefore, several smaller systems are discussed.

Chapter 3

1 In using empirical data to develop a correspondence between theory and observable events, 'the tools of formal econometrics may be useful here, but tables and graphs can often be more persuasive' (Leamer 1992, p. 4).

2 The ladders of development reflect quite clearly the changing patterns of world trade and development from the 1960s to the 1980s. However, they have been made only from the perspective of trade structures or composition. Other measures, such as GNP (per capita), economic growth rate and some other social indicators, are needed to give a more comprehensive judgement of the overall performance of different types of countries.

3 Although the correlations between trade and resource endowments reported in this study are high, correlations between trade relative to GNP (per worker) and endowments relative to GNP (per worker) show that, in general, trade in four crops and resource products is better explained than trade in manufactured products. This confirms Leamer's (1984) finding using his data sets.

4 This approach, as Leamer (1984, p. 50) points out, can be said to measure the accuracy of a weakened version of the theory because it does not use data on factor intensities, namely there exists a matrix A such that $AT = E - \alpha E_w$.

Chapter 4

1 Paraguay had net exports of chemicals in 1965, and Jamaica had net exports of chemicals in both 1965 and 1988. The reason was that their chemical exports, aluminium oxide and extract of quebracho respectively, are better classified as raw materials (see Chapter 3), and therefore they are not included in this category.

2 In addition to exports of resource products, Canada, Israel and Norway also had net exports of some agricultural products such as forest products, animal products and cereals; apart from exports of agricultural products, the Netherlands also had net exports of material products.

3 Exports of capital intensive products by China in 1965 did not result in it being placed in subgroup 1; this was because China operated under a centrally planned system at the time.

4 Leamer (1984) tried several different transformations of these data; this transformation was selected because it produced the clearest displays.

5 The first 11 vertical bars in these profiles represent the resource abundance ratios $(E_i/E_{wi})/(Y/Y_w)$, that is, the ratio of resource share to GNP share. The last vertical bar, labelled SIZE, is the country's GNP divided by GNP averaged over all countries in the given year.

6 Leamer (1984) found a similar problem in his data for 1975, and consequently concern has been expressed about the meaning either of the LABOUR 1 category or of resource abundance ratios as indicators of abundance.

7 This phenomenon was also observed in Leamer's data.

8 According to Leamer (1984), this definition is a consequence of the fact that GNP is assumed to be a linear function of the endowments, and the only reason for relatively low labour productivity is relative scarcity of the other resources that form GNP. If GNP is a nonlinear function of the endowments, on average, a comparison of a resource share with the GNP share will not reveal the abundance of the factor compared with other factors.

9 Because the intention is to link these results with the capital/labour ratios reported in the previous chapter, the same country set has been selected for this table.

10 It should be noted, however, that large amounts of GNP in developed countries tend to lower the 'productivity' of these countries' labour forces, since they make the denominator large and eventually lead to low ratios of 'productivity'. It is therefore necessary to be particularly careful in using this measure to compare developing and developed countries.

Chapter 5

* Parts of this chapter are scheduled for publication as a paper in the *Journal of the Japanese and International Economies*, Vol. 9, No. 3 (September 1995).

1 It is interesting to compare this chapter's results with respect to relative factor abundance with those of Chapters 3 and 4, since they illustrate the pattern of relative factor abundance from different angles.

2 The United States was selected primarily because most studies in this area have concentrated their research on the United States.

3 These figures are substantially lower than those reported in Bowen *et al.* (1987), simply because the current study uses a much larger sample size that also includes China.

4 According to Bowen *et al.* (1987), when a country is a net exporter of capital services, this would lead to rejection of the Heckscher–Ohlin theorem by using a sign test if the country's share of world income exceeds its share of world capital. However, what is observed here is that the United States has become a net importer of capital. Therefore, it might be the case that in the United States capital is relatively more abundant than labour, although scarce in the context of the Heckscher–Ohlin model. This point will be discussed further in the next section.

5 See Corollary 2 in Leamer (1980), discussed in Chapter 2.

6 Refer to Corollary 2 in Leamer (1980), discussed in Chapter 2.

7 A proof is provided by Leamer (1980) as follows. Equations (2.1a) and (2.1b) can be rewritten as:

$$K_w = (K_i - K_T)/\alpha_i \quad \text{and}$$
$$L_w = (L_i - L_T)/\alpha_i$$

Thus

$$K_i/K_w = \alpha_i K_i/(K_i - K_T)$$
$$L_i/L_w = \alpha_i L_i/(L_i - L_T)$$

from which equation (2.2) is a consequence.

8 It is of interest to provide updated results using the same set of measures, not only because changes over time that may affect some aspects of the preceding discussion can be revealed, but also because the updated results provide new information about important indicators, such as capital/labour ratios and world shares of capital, labour and GNP, on a cross-country basis.

9 There is no problem in applying this criterion for CASE 3 (see Corollary 3 in Chapter 2). But there is still a problem with CASE 1 since this is the situation Aw (1983) described as a 'sufficiently large' trade surplus. In this situation, according to Aw, $K_i/K_w < L_i/L_w$ if $K_T/L_T > K_i/L_i$ (Chapter 2). However, this condition was rarely met in either 1965 or 1988 (Tables 5.3 and 5.4). This raises a question about the rôle that trade balance plays in determining sign patterns of trade in factor services. The following calculations of changes in capital/labour ratios embodied in net exports with respect to changes in trade balance may provide some clues to this question:

$$\frac{K_T}{L_T} = \frac{K_i - (\frac{Y_i - B_i}{Y_w})K_w}{L_i - (\frac{Y_i - B_i}{Y_w})L_w},$$ where B_i is trade balance and $\alpha_i = \frac{Y_i - B_i}{Y_w}$. Thus

$$\frac{\partial(K_T/L_T)}{\partial B_i} = \frac{[(L_i - \alpha_i L_w)(-K_w)\partial\alpha_i/\partial B_i] - [(K_i - \alpha_i K_w)(-L_w)\partial\alpha_i/\partial B_i]}{[L_i - \alpha_i L_w]^2}$$

$$= (\partial\alpha_i/\partial B_i)\frac{[K_i L_w - \alpha_i K_w L_w - L_i K_w + \alpha_i L_w K_w]}{[L_i - \alpha_i L_w]^2} = \frac{(\partial\alpha_i/\partial B_i)[K_i/K_w - L_i/L_w]K_w L_w}{[L_i - \alpha_i L_w]^2}$$

Therefore $\frac{\partial(K_T/L_T)}{\partial B_i}$ has the same sign as $K_i/K_w - L_i/L_w$. In other words, the use of K_i/K_w and L_i/L_w as a criterion for measuring relative factor abundance may not be affected by trade balance.

10 These three solutions are generally applicable to the situation in both years, but the second and the third ones may be more relevant here since they explain changes that had taken place by the end of the 1980s (see Table 5.4).

11 In a proof of the Heckscher–Ohlin theorem, Leamer (1984, p. 8) demonstrates the role played by consumption share in deriving the net export equation.

12 Leamer (1984, p. 12) provides some evidence for violation of the factor price equalisation theorem by listing agricultural wage (US$/hour) differences among countries. The wage differences show that wages are generally higher in developed countries than in developing countries.

13 This is because country i's income, Y_i, is theoretically equal to summation of multiplication of each factor and its return. In a two-factor (capital K and labour L) world, country i's income can be written as follows: $Y_i = w_L L_i + w_K K_i$, where w_K is return to capital and w_L is return to labour (see equation (2.9)).

14 It is anticipated that natural resource endowments, such as land, coal, minerals and oil, may have some impact on changes in factor abundance ranking.

15 When equation (2.5) is applied here, it is assumed that this equation is accurate. There is no attempt in this book to carry out a formal 'test' of the equation. For a comprehensive test of this sort, refer to Bowen *et al.* (1987).

16 Leamer (1984) uncovered a similar phenomenon. As he pointed out, '[N]ote the abundance for many of these countries of LABOUR 1, a fact that makes one suspicious of the "professional/technical" categorisation' (p. 108). See also the discussion of country group 3 (importers of manufactured commodities) in Chapter 4.

17 These results can only be revealed when land and resource factors are taken into account in addition to those commonly used, namely labour and capital.

18 In fact, it is surprising to find that in 1988 most developed countries had become less capital abundant than the developing countries mentioned here. The three possible solutions provided in this section for a two-factor world are also applicable to this multifactor world.

19 The three-year average number of inversions between the two sign hypotheses SH-II and SH-III is 43 per cent, which is a little lower than the figure of 46.3 per cent reported in Kohler (1991) using data collected by Bowen *et al.* (1987).

Chapter 6

1 Leamer's work (1984) uses data to the mid-1970s.

2 See note 18, Chapter 2.

3 The possibility of underestimating the capital stock number stems from the fact that 'the CAPITAL figure excludes certain forms of human capital that may not be adequately captured by the LABOUR 1/LABOUR 2/LABOUR 3 distinction' (Leamer 1984, p. 145).

4 This calculation was based on cross-country information on agricultural wages (US$/hour) contained in the *Yearbook of Labour Statistics* (International Labour Office 1972). The information can also be found in Leamer (1984, Table 1.1).

5 Although definitions of the four land variables used in this book differ from those used by Leamer (1984), the information provided in his work regarding rents for cropland and pastureland in the United States does help to determine prior means for LAND 1 (arable land) and LAND 3 (permanent meadows and pastures) in the current study. However, it should be pointed out that there may be some overlapping between cropland as defined by Leamer (1984) and LAND 1 and LAND 2 (tropical land) as defined in the current study.

6 The problem of overlapping (see note 5, this chapter) provides the rationale for setting the prior mean for LAND 2 (tropical land) somewhere below that of LAND

1 (arable land). Because of the long production cycle for LAND 4 (forest land), its rent has been set at a relatively low level.

7 Land values tripled from 1958 to 1975 (Leamer 1984, p. 146). Assuming that land values continued to increase at a similar rate, the prior means of these four land variables in 1965 would be about one-half the 1975 value and in 1988 approximately one and a half times the 1975 value.

8 Similar conformity is observed in Leamer (1984) for the MACHINERY equation.

9 Only the CAPITAL coefficient takes on a single sign in Leamer's (1984) calculation of the MACHINERY equation for 1975.

10 Faced with the sensitivity problem, one advantage of applying the Bayesian econometric method is the 'self-correcting feature of Bayesian inferences' (Leamer 1984, p. 178), which allows mistaken priors to be ignored if the data evidence is strong enough. For example, although the prior estimate of the effect of LAND 3 on PETRO is negative, the data indicate clearly that the coefficient is positive (see Tables 6.6, 6.9 and 6.10). Even more convincingly, there is a trend of convergence of Bayes estimates towards the prior expectation from 1965 to 1988 with regard to net export equations.

11 Leamer (1984) attributes these peculiar results to the possibility of nonlinearities. He attempts to uncover evidence of nonlinearities in the GNP equation as well as in the trade equation because 'models that imply nonlinear GNP equations will also imply nonlinear trade equations' (Leamer 1984, p. 180). Although some evidence of nonlinearities in the GNP equation is found in his attempt, 'the anticipated nonlinearities of the trade equation generally failed to emerge' (Leamer 1984, p. 186). No attempt is made in this study to carry out this task.

12 China is not included in the 1965 model estimations because it was a centrally planned economy at the time. Economic reform, which started at the end of the 1970s and resulted in the introduction of a greater numbers of market-driven elements in the economy, provides partial justification for including China in such cross-country analysis by the late 1980s.

13 A large *t*-value is statistically robust since it indicates, as Leamer (1984, p. 153) pointed out, four things: if all the standard assumptions hold, the sign of the coefficient is determined with high confidence by the data; the estimated coefficient is insensitive to the omission of variables; the estimated coefficient is insensitive to the reweighing of observations; and if all the standard assumptions hold, then the data cast doubt on the hypothesis that the coefficient is exactly zero.

Chapter 7

1 See also Anderson's (1987) review of Leamer (1984).

2 Study of intra-industry trade within the framework of the Heckscher–Ohlin theorem represents the attempt to widen the scope of the theoretical framework (see Lloyd 1989 and Tharakan 1989). An attempt can also be made to improve the analytical techniques used in this approach. For example, Klepper's (1988) regressor diagnostics provides information about bounds on the measurement error variances of the

regressors needed to bound any coefficient to a desired interval. The method has the following characteristic: '[R]ather than update a prior distribution for the regression coefficients based on the sample information, the diagnostics are used to provide information about how the sample information would map different priors into posteriors' (Klepper 1988, p. 226).

3 Cross-country analysis of this kind does not provide a direct framework for analysis of an individual country's case. However, the three approaches adopted in this book to uncover sources of comparative advantage and their changing roles over time do provide not only a broad background which can be used to gain an understanding of the general patterns of comparative advantage but also information, for example trade and resource data for each country under study. The combination of the two makes it possible to discuss implications of the main findings of the book for particular groups of economies — the Asia–Pacific economies, for example.

4 Without including China, average annual growth rates from 1965 to 1988 would be 5.7 per cent compared with 5 per cent (world average) for skilled labour (total) and 2.5 per cent compared with 2.8 per cent (world average) for skilled labour as a percentage of total labour. Thus, in per capita terms, the average annual growth rate of these nine Asia–Pacific economies is lower than the world average when China is excluded.

5 Studies on shifts in comparative advantage include, to name a few, Kojima (1964), Johnson (1968), Balassa (1977), Garnaut and Anderson (1980), Anderson and Smith (1981) and Rana (1990). The three propositions raised here are those most commonly put forward in these studies.

6 This is because, as argued by Garnaut and Anderson (1980, p. 387), 'each of the more densely populated countries experienced several years' rapid expansion of industrial output and rising per capita income before experiencing strong upward movement in real wages', and 'prior to this turning point in the economic development of each country, rapid growth in manufacturing output could proceed for some time without loss of competitiveness in the most labour-intensive manufactures'.

7 Increases in a country's export dependence on capital intensive manufactured products and decreases in its import dependence on the same types of products both reflect, from different aspects, that the country is gaining ground in producing these manufactured products.

8 The idea of open regionalism proposed by Drysdale and Garnaut (1993) may be relevant to the harmonious development of a regional economy.

Appendix A

1 Country name abbreviations are used in Chapter 3 when the ladder of development is discussed and in the data set presented in this Appendix.

Appendix B

1 The 62 economies included in this Appendix refer to the 61 economies discussed in the book plus Afghanistan.

2 The better performance of $K(2)$ is judged only by a smaller mean and a smaller standard deviation.

Appendix C

1 These two tables are given in Leamer (1984, p. 277).

Bibliography

Anderson, James E. 1987, 'Review of *Sources of International Comparative Advantage: Theory and Evidence*, by Edward E. Leamer', *Journal of Economic Literature*, Vol. 25, March, pp. 146–7.

Anderson, Kym and Ben Smith 1981, 'Changing economic relations between the Asian ADCs and resource-exporting advanced countries of the Pacific Basin', in Wontack Hong and Lawrence B. Krause (eds), *Trade and Growth of the Advanced Developing Countries in the Pacific Basin*, Seoul: Korea Development Institute.

Aw, B. Y. 1983, 'Trade imbalance and the Leontief Paradox', *Weltwirtschaftliches Archiv*, Vol. 119, pp. 734–8.

Balassa, Bela 1977, 'A "stages" approach to comparative advantage', *World Bank Staff Working Paper*, No. 256, May, World Bank.

Baldwin, Robert E. 1971, 'Determinants of commodity structure of US trade', *American Economic Review*, Vol. 61, No. 1, March, pp. 126–46.

Belsley, D. A., E. Kuh and R. E. Welsch 1980, *Regression Diagnostics*, New York: Wiley.

Bhagwati, Jagdish N. 1972, 'The Heckscher–Ohlin theorem in the multi-commodity case', *Journal of Political Economy*, Vol. 80, pp. 1052–5.

Bowen, Harry P. 1981, 'A multicountry test of the product cycle model', Paper presented to an Econometric Society Annual Meeting, Washington DC, December.

—— 1983, 'Changes in the international distribution of resources and their impact on US comparative advantage', *Review of Economics and Statistics*, Vol. 65, February, pp. 402–14.

Bowen, Harry P., Edward E. Leamer and Leo Sveikauskas 1987, 'Multicountry, multifactor tests of the factor abundance theory', *American Economic Review*, Vol. 77, December, pp. 791–809.

Brecher, R. A. and E. U. Choudhri 1982a, 'The Leontief Paradox, continued', *Journal of Political Economy*, Vol. 90, pp. 820–3.

—— 1982b, 'The factor content of international trade without factor-price equalisation', *Journal of International Economics*, Vol. 12, pp. 277–83.

Casas, F. R. and E. Kwan Choi 1985, 'The Leontief Paradox: continued or resolved?', *Journal of Political Economy*, Vol. 93, pp. 610–15.

Chenery, H. B. 1960, 'Patterns of industrial growth', *American Economic Review*, Vol. 1, September, pp. 624–54.

Chenery, H. B. and Lance Taylor 1968, 'Development patterns: among countries and over time', *Review of Economics and Statistics*, Vol. 1, No. 4, November, pp. 391–416.

Chenery, H. B. and M. Syrquin 1975, *Patterns of Development, 1950–1970*, London: Oxford University Press.

Clifton, David S. and W. P. Marxsen 1984, 'An empirical investigation of the Heckscher–Ohlin theorem', *Canadian Journal of Economics*, Vol. 17, pp. 32–8.

Deardorff, Alan V. 1980, 'The general validity of the law of comparative advantage', *Journal of Political Economy*, Vol. 88, pp. 941–57.

—— 1982, 'The general validity of the Heckscher–Ohlin theorem', *American Economic Review*, Vol. 72, pp. 683–94.

—— 1984, 'Testing trade theories and predicting trade flows', in R. W. Jones and P. B. Kenen (eds) , *Handbook of International Economics*, Amsterdam: North-Holland.

Drysdale, Peter 1988, *International Economic Pluralism: Economic Policy in East Asia and the Pacific*, New York: Columbia University Press/Sydney: Allen and Unwin.

Drysdale, Peter and Ross Garnaut 1993, 'The Pacific: an application of a general theory of economic integration', in C. Fred Bergsten and Marcus Noland (eds),*Pacific Dynamism and the International Economic System*, Washington DC: Institute for International Economics.

Frisch, R. 1934, *Statistical Confluence Analysis by Means of Complete Regression Systems*, Oslo, Norway: University Institute of Economics.

Garnaut, Ross and Kym Anderson 1980, 'ASEAN export specialisation and the evolution of comparative advantage in the Western Pacific region', in R. Garnaut (ed.), *ASEAN in a Changing Pacific and World Economy*, Canberra: Australian National University Press.

Gift, R, and W. P. Marxsen 1984, 'Aggregation and the factor content of trade', *Journal of Political Economy*, Vol. 92, pp. 979–84.

Greene, William H. 1991, *Econometric Analysis*, New York: Macmillan Publishing Company.

Harkness, J. 1978, 'Factor abundance and comparative advantage', *American Economic Review*, Vol. 68, pp. 784–800.

—— 1983, 'The factor-proportions model with many nations, goods and factors: theory and evidence', *Review of Economics and Statistics*, Vol. 65, pp. 298–305.

Harvey, A.C. 1976, 'Estimating regression models with multiplicative heteroscedasticity', *Econometrica*, Vol. 44, pp. 461–5.

Heravi, Iraj 1986, 'The Leontief Paradox, reconsidered: correction', *Journal of Political Economy*, Vol. 94, No. 5, p. 1120.

Hufbauer, G. C. 1970, 'The impact of national characteristics and technology on the commodity composition of trade in manufactured goods', in R. Vernon (ed.), *The Technology Factor in International Trade*, New York: Colombia University Press.

International Labour Office 1972, *Yearbook of Labour Statistics*, Geneva: International Labour Office.

Johnson, Harry G. 1968, *Comparative Cost and Commercial Policy Theory for a Developing World Economy*, Stockholm: Almqvist and Wiksell.

Johnston, J. 1984, *Econometric Methods*, New York: McGraw-Hill.

Klein, Lawrence R. 1988, 'The statistical approach to economics', *Journal of Econometrics*, Vol. 37, pp. 7–26.

Klepper, Steven 1988, 'Regressor diagnostics for the classical errors-in-variables model', *Journal of Econometrics*, Vol. 37, pp. 225–50.

Klepper, Steven and Edward E. Leamer 1984, 'Consistent sets of estimates for regressions with errors in all variables', *Econometrica*, Vol. 52, pp. 163–83.

Kohler, Wilhelm 1991, 'How robust are sign and rank order tests of the Heckscher–Ohlin-Vanek theorem?', *Oxford Economic Papers*, Vol. 43, pp. 158–71.

Kojima, K. 1964, 'The pattern of international trade among advanced countries', *Hitotsubashi Journal of Economics*, Vol. 5, No. 1, June, pp. 16–36.

Leamer, Edward E. 1973, 'Multicollinearity: a Bayesian interpretation', *Review of Economics and Statistics*, Vol. 55, pp. 371–80.

—— 1974, 'The commodity composition of international trade in manufactures: an empirical analysis', *Oxford Economic Papers*, Vol. 26, No. 3, pp. 350–74.

—— 1978, *Specification Searches*, New York: Wiley.

—— 1980, 'The Leontief Paradox, reconsidered', *Journal of Political Economy*, Vol. 88, No. 3, pp. 495–503.

—— 1982, 'Sets of posterior means with bounded variance priors', *Econometrica*, Vol. 50, No. 3, May, pp. 725–36.

—— 1983, 'Let's take the con out of econometrics', *American Economic Review*, Vol. 73, pp. 31–43.

—— 1984, *Sources of International Comparative Advantage: Theory and Evidence*, Cambridge Mass.: MIT Press.

—— 1987a, 'Errors in variables in linear systems', *Econometrica*, Vol. 55, No. 4, July, pp. 893–909.

—— 1987b, 'Paths of development in the three-factor, *n*-good general equilibrium model', *Journal of Political Economy*, Vol. 95, No. 51, pp. 961–99.

—— 1988a, 'The sensitivity of international comparisons of capital stock measures to different "real" exchange rates', *AEA Papers and Proceedings*, Vol. 78, No. 2, May, pp. 479–83.

—— 1988b, 'Cross-section estimation of the effects of trade barriers', in Robert C. Feenstra (ed.), *Empirical Methods for International Trade*, Cambridge, Mass.: MIT Press.

—— 1988c, 'Measures of openness', in Robert E. Baldwin (ed.), *Trade Policy Issues and Empirical Analysis*, Chicago: University of Chicago Press.

—— 1991a, 'A Bayesian perspective on inference from macroeconomic data', *Scandinavian Journal of Economics*, Vol. 93, No. 2, pp. 225–48.

—— 1991b, 'The interplay of theory and data in the study of international trade', in Marc Nerlove (ed.), *Issues in Contemporary Economics, Volume 2, Macroeconomics and Econometrics*, Houndmills, Basingstoke: Macmillan, in association with the International Economic Association.

—— 1992, 'Testing trade theory', *NBER Working Papers Series*, No. 3957, January, National Bureau of Economic Research, Cambridge, Mass..

Leamer, Edward E. and H. P. Bowen 1981, 'Cross-section tests of the Heckscher–Ohlin theorem: comment', *American Economic Review*, Vol. 71, No. 5, December, pp. 1040–3.

Leamer, Edward E. and H. B. Leonard 1983, 'Reporting the fragility of regression estimates', *Review of Economics and Statistics*, Vol. 65, pp. 306–17.

—— 1985, *The User's Manual for SEARCH: A Software Package for Bayesian Inference and Sensitivity Analysis*, SEARCH Version 6, October.

Leontief, Wassily W. 1954, 'Domestic production and foreign trade: the American capital position re-examined', *Econ. Internazionale*, Vol. 7, February, pp. 3–32; Reprinted in Richard E. Caves and Harry G. Johnson (eds), *Readings in International Economics*, 1968, Homewood, Irwin.

—— 1956, 'Factor proportions and the structure of American trade: further theoretical and empirical analysis', *Review of Economics and Statistics*, Vol. 38, pp. 386–407.

Lloyd, P. J. 1989, 'Reflections on intra-industry trade theory and factor proportions', in P. K. M. Tharakan and Jacob Kol (eds), *Intra-Industry Trade: Theory, Evidence and Extensions*, London: Macmillan.

Maskus, K. E. 1985, 'A test of the Heckscher–Ohlin–Vanek theorem: the Leontief commonplace', *Journal of International Economics*, Vol. 19, pp. 201–12.

McAleer, Michael, Adrian R. Pagan and Paul A. Volker 1985, 'What will take the con out of econometrics?', *American Economic Review*, Vol. 75, June, pp. 293–307.

Rana, Pradumna B. 1990, 'Shifting comparative advantage among Asian and Pacific countries', *The International Trade Journal*, Vol. 4, No. 3, pp. 243–58.

Song, Ligang 1993, *Sources of International Comparative Advantage: Further Evidence*, PhD dissertation, the Australian National University.

Stern, Robert M. 1975, 'Testing trade theories', in P. B. Kenen (ed.), *International Trade and Finance: Frontiers for Research*, New York: Cambridge University Press.

Stern, Robert M. and Keith E. Maskus 1981, 'Determinants of the structure of US foreign trade', *Journal of International Economics*, Vol. 11, pp. 207–24.

Summers, Robert and Alan Heston 1984, 'Improved international comparisons of real product and its composition: 1950–1980', *Review of Income and Wealth*, Vol. 30, June, pp. 207–62.

—— 1991, 'The Penn World Table (Mark 5): an expanded set of international comparisons, 1950–1988', *The Quarterly Journal of Economics*, Vol. 106, May, pp. 327–68.

Sveikauskas, L. 1983, 'Science and technology in United States foreign trade', *The Economic Journal*, Vol. 93, pp. 542–54.

Tharakan, P. K. M. 1989, 'Bilateral intra-industry trade between countries with different factor endowment patterns', in P. K. M. Tharakan and Jacob Kol (eds), *Intra-Industry Trade: Theory, Evidence and Extensions*, London: Macmillan.

US Department of Agriculture 1978, *Farm Real Estate Market Developments*, Washington, DC: US Government Printing Office.

Vanek, Jaroslav 1963, *The Natural Resource Content of United States Foreign Trade, 1870–1955*, Cambridge, Mass.: MIT Press.

—— 1968, 'The factor proportions theory: the n-factor case', *Kyklos*, Vol. 21, No. 4, pp. 749–56.

Williams, James R. 1970, 'The resource content in international trade', *Canadian Journal of Economics*, Vol. 3, pp. 111–22.

—— 1977, 'The factor proportions theorem: the case of m commodities and n factors', *Canadian Journal of Economics*, Vol. 10, pp. 282–8.

Zellner, A. 1971, *An Introduction to Bayesian Inference in Econometrics*, New York: Wiley.

—— 1988, 'Bayesian analysis in econometrics', *Journal of Econometrics*, Vol. 37, pp. 27–50.

Index